The End of Knowing

For centuries, knowledge has been thought to be the key to human progress of all kinds and has dominated Western culture. But what if knowing has now become an impediment to further human development? *The End of Knowing* is concerned with the practical consideration of how to reconstruct our world when modernist ideas have been refuted and many social problems appear insoluble. Newman and Holzman suggest provocatively that we should give up knowing in favour of "performed activity." They show how to reject the knowing paradigm in practice and present the many positive implications this has for social and educational policy.

Over the past two decades, a postmodern critique of the modern conception of knowing and its institutionalized practices has emerged. To many, this is a dangerous threat to the tradition of liberal education, strengthened by recent prestigious voices from the physical and natural sciences. *The End of Knowing* challenges even the postmodernists themselves, rejecting the reform of knowing for a totally new performatory form of life. They support their argument with a new reading of Lev Vygotsky and Ludwig Wittgenstein that suggests they were aware of the importance of activity as "pre-postmodernists."

The authors' development community, from which the ideas in *The End of Knowing* have arisen, exists without government or university funding or political affiliation. Their findings offer an alternative to existential despair in confronting a postmodern world without meaning by showing how to make meaning and develop lives through performed activity.

Fred Newman is Director of Training, East Side Institute for Short Term Psychotherapy and Artistic Director, Castillo Theatre, New York. **Lois Holzman** is Director, Center for Developmental Learning at the East Side Institute for Short Term Psychotherapy. Between them they have written nine books and numerous chapters and journal articles.

D0061109

The End of Knowing

A new developmental way of learning

Fred Newman and Lois Holzman

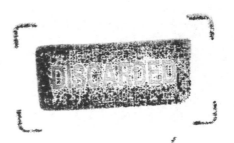

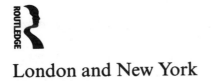

London and New York

First published 1997
by Routledge
11 New Fetter Lane, London EC4P 4EE

Simultaneously published in the USA and Canada
by Routledge
29 West 35th Street, New York, NY 10001

Typeset in Times by Routledge
Printed and bound in Great Britain by Mackays of Chatham PLC,
Chatham, Kent

British Library Cataloguing in Publication Data
A catalogue record for this book is available from the British Library

Library of Congress Cataloguing in Publication Data
Newman, Fred.
The end of knowing/Fred Newman and Lois Holzman.
  October 1996.
  Includes bibliographical references and index.
  1. Knowledge, Theory of–History–20th century. 2. Science–
  Philosophy–History–20th century. 3. Act (Philosophy).
  4. Postmodernism. I. Holzman, Lois. II. Title.
  BD161.N44–1997   96–52856
  001–dc21   CIP

ISBN 0–415–13598–2 (hbk)
ISBN 0–415–13599–0 (pbk)

This book is dedicated to Karl Marx, one of the great modernist thinkers. May he finally rest in peace free from all he knew and from his opportunistic followers, most of whom knew very little but didn't know it.

Contents

viii   *Contents*

Acknowledgments

Our thanks to the hundreds of co-workers, clients, and students involved in our development projects–women and men, adolescents and children–with whom we daily perform our collective lives.

We are particularly grateful to the following people and organizations:

- Our colleagues around the world for ongoing conversation (in person and in print) on matters postmodern–especially Ken Gergen, John Shotter, John Morss, Erica Burman, Ian Parker, and John Jost;
- Our production team–Phyllis Goldberg and Warren Liebesman for invaluable editing and copy editing, Kim Svoboda for typing and retyping constantly evolving drafts, Chris Helm and Karen Steinberg for transcribing The Performance of Philosophy conversations;
- Hugh Polk and the East Side Center/East Side Institute staff for their initial work in analyzing social therapeutic discourse;
- Divisions 10 and 32 of the American Psychological Association for encouragement to present our performatory psychology to a psychological audience;
- Lawrence Erlbaum Associates, Inc., Publishers for agreeing to allow us to reproduce passages that are similar to those found in Chapter 7 of *Schools for Growth*.
- Sage Publications Ltd for permission to reprint material on pages 134–5, from Holzman, "Creating Developmental Learning Environments: A Vygotskian Practice", *School Psychology International*, © Sage 1995.
- Vivien Ward, our editor at Routledge, for her continued support and encouragement.

1 Introduction

When will all these endings stop?

Postmodernism sometimes looks to be one "end" after another (the beginning of the end!): the end of history; the end of truth; the end of philosophy; the end of science; the end of reason; the end of capitalism (if not the transition to socialism). At other times it appears to be a series of potential beginnings: a credo for a truly pluralistic and democratic world in which persons can take on (or perform) ever-changing and diverse roles and actions; a psychology of persons in relationships; liberation from patriarchal dogma, ideology, and metanarrative social coercion; a cultural, constructionist, unscientific approach to human life. However, the recent appearance of a Web site entitled "Everything Postmodern," a regularly updated listing of "po-mo" on the Internet, suggests neither endings nor beginnings. According to the neo-Marxist Frederick Jameson, the term itself, *postmodern*, is too tied to modernism to signal closure and something new (it is, for him, a stage in the development of capitalism (Jameson, 1983, 1984)).

What postmodernism becomes remains to be lived (not seen). *That* it is seems indisputable. After all, the nearly fifty hard scientists, social scientists, and philosophers who participated in a three-day conference in New York City in the Spring of 1995 entitled, "The Flight from Science and Reason," were reacting to *something*. The conference, convened by the New York Academy of Sciences, made front-page headlines in the *New York Times* and other major dailies. As well it should have, in our opinion, for what is at issue is whether or not the 400-year reign of modern science as the exemplar of human knowledge is coming to an end. The conference and its recently published proceedings are part of a much larger serious (if at times foolishly conducted) intellectual debate currently taking place among scientists and non-scientists alike about whether or not science has a future: have we reached the end of science?

Those proceedings, also titled *The Flight from Science and Reason* (Gross *et al.*, 1996), shatter the popular image of research scientists. In responding to the postmodernist "attitude," they have given up objectivity, empirically based findings, and logical argumentation in favor of hyperbole, emotional outbursts, and arguments *ad hominem*. The 600-page volume is little more than a vitriolic "hit-back" on postmodernists and proponents of what the scientists sneeringly refer to as "alternative models." (While some of the authors lump together radical feminists, creationists, social constructionists, phenomenologists, followers of Derrida, homeopaths, and pop psychologists, most of them concentrate on the academics.) Distinguished professors of physics, biology, chemistry, medicine, mathematics, and philosophy of science denounce their postmodern academic colleagues as "hypocrites," "high-jackers," "delusionary," "fraudulent," "willfully ignorant," and "quirky," among other things. Used to the "antiscience" of the right (creationists, for example), these defenders of science and the scientific method are especially outraged at the academic left. As Gross puts it, "a decade or two ago naming oneself a 'progressive' meant aligning oneself with logic, science, and the truth; associating oneself, as it were, with the future, [but] today showing respect for science, or for universalism . . . in a truly with-it college . . . is [to be] a dinosaur" (p. 5). (Two years earlier, Gross co-authored a book entirely on this topic—*Higher Superstition: The Academic Left and its Quarrels with Science*, Gross and Levitt, 1994.)

While Mario Bunge of McGill University's Foundations and Philosophy of Science Unit draws some distinctions between postmodernists and pseudoscientists, he nevertheless regards both as "gangs [that] operate under the protection of academic freedom, and often at the taxpayer's expense" (Bunge, 1996, p. 97). (He also dismisses existentialism as "a jumble of nonsense, falsity, and platitude," p. 97.) The *best* that Wallace Sampson, a professor of medicine, can say about postmodernism is that it is unethical. In the introductory paragraphs of his attack on alternative medicine he links cultural relativism and postmodernism with propaganda, Hitler, and Goebbels (Sampson, 1996, p. 188). Duke University's Martin Lewis, arguing that sociological and technological developments at the end of the twentieth century are "definitive of modernity," pooh-poohs the postmodern thesis as "merely an academic repackaging of the 1960s countercultural belief in the 'dawning of the age of Aquarius' " (Lewis, 1996, p. 221). Nevertheless, Lewis spends twenty pages discussing the destruction wrought by postmodernism on the ecological movement by "the philosophically inclined fringe" (the Greens) who "have undermined the movement from within at the moment of its greatest vulnerability" (p. 223).

In arguing that scientific objectivity and humanistic insight are not at odds, Princeton University's Robin Fox, an anthropologist, produces a classic *non sequitur* that surely (we would hope) embarrassed his more philosophically sophisticated colleagues. Defending the importance of assessing empirical reality against the critical analysis of concepts, he addresses those who engage in "deconstruction as an intellectual activity":

> Of course, you will respond, the existence of empirical reality is what these theories hold to be moot (or at least they question the possibility of our knowing it). To which I can only reply: let me hear you say that when told you need a difficult operation to save your life, or the life of one of

your children. Christian Scientists are at least consistent on this issue; academics who hold these ridiculous theories are simply hypocrites.

(Fox, 1996, p. 342)

With friends like Fox, science hardly needs enemies. Not only is the logic of this statement ludicrous (if you deconstruct concepts, even "surgical" concepts, it follows that you should refuse surgery), not only is Fox's remark *ad hominem*, he also apparently favors consistency over human life; by his own logic, the "consistent" Christian Scientist would, after all, be more likely to die than the "hypocritical" deconstructionist. Whether or not consistency is the hobgoblin of small minds, it seems to be an obsession among some scientists and hardcore empiricist social scientists.

Not coincidentally, Fox argues that his own discipline, anthropology, can be the "shining example" of returning humanism to its original meaning (man, rather than god, as "the measure"); as the "science of mankind," anthropology is perfectly suited to unite humanism and science by applying the rules of science to art, poetry, and other nonscientific human endeavors. With this sleight of hand, Fox (clearly no dialectician) dismisses the heart and soul of the postmodern challenge—that such human endeavors are not subject to the laws of science and that attempting to apply them is distortive, coercive, and elitist.

Fox's mode of argumentation typifies the response of those in the scientific community who are outspokenly alarmed by the postmodern critique of their profession. They self-servingly and arrogantly presume the validity of the very things they claim to be defending, namely science and reason. In doing so, they violate the rules of their own method. So too they abandon logic in favor of the *non sequitur* (as we have already seen) and misapply "the law of the excluded middle." This fundamental law of logic, which modern science inherits from Aristotelian philosophy, states that everything is either an A or not an A ($A \lor \sim A$). Thus, if the postmodernists are challenging rationality, they must be irrational. (A proper use of the law of the excluded middle might be: everyone is either challenging rationality or they are not.) To say that science is a social construct, these exasperated scientists conclude illogically, is to say that it cannot be valid. They should, of course, know better; it is the very category of rationality and the rational–irrational dichotomy that most postmodernists want to do away with (deconstruct).

Moreover, both the "irrationality" and "emotionality" of many of these scientists' accusations are in opposition to their own standards of argumentation and ethics. One wonders how such intelligent *men* (which they are, almost exclusively) can speak so unintelligently, how they can abandon scientific methodology and reason so easily and completely. They seem, in short (pardon the therapeutics), hysterical. Their behavior suggests that they have as much interest in keeping their prestigious jobs and large grants as in advancing science or reasoning. The fight over the flight from science and reason may be as much about money as anything else. Harry Greenberg of the New York Academy of Sciences ends his introduction to the conference proceedings with this warning:

> Such a failure to defend science from its irrational critics can set the stage for a lethal blow when the real budgetary attacks arrive, and they are nearly upon us. Some would say they are here, but I am not so optimistic. If science cannot claim a preeminence for its intellectual virtues or an excellence for its methodologies and sense of design, then it will have great difficulty laying claim to a rational share of the nation's resources for its perpetuation.
>
> (Greenberg, 1996, p. x)

Greenberg's dire prediction is perhaps all the more serious for being tautological: without rationality (that is, science) there would be no basis for claiming a "rational" share of the nation's resources.

In suggesting that opportunism plays a role in these scientists' responses to postmodernism we do not mean to reduce the fight to mere pragmatics (or vulgar economics). Similarly, in pointing out the frequent silliness and hostility of the argumentation, we do not mean to imply that the fight is trivial. Rather, the responses of Gross, Levitt, Lewis, Bunge, Fox, and the others seem to us to be evidence that the issues of the future of science and the possible limits of knowledge are being taken very seriously.

Within a month or two after *The Flight from Science and Reason* was published, there appeared another—very different—dialogue-in-print on the future (or lack thereof) of science. In *The End of Science: Facing the Limits of Knowledge in the Twilight of the Scientific Age* (1996), John Horgan considers whether scientists have discovered everything there is to know and whether science has brought us to the outer edges of knowledge. Having posed this question to dozens of the most prominent researchers in their fields, Horgan (a prize-winning journalist who is a senior writer for *Scientific American*) has written a book that introduces us not only to the latest work by neuroscientists, cognitive scientists, physicists, biologists, and others, but to their assessment of (including their subjective responses to) of the "state of the art" of the modernist pursuit of knowledge and Truth. Juxtaposed with the reactive and, in many cases, reactionary scientists we met in *The Flight from Science and Reason*, Horgan's interviewees help to provide a more complete picture of the process by which the current paradigm shift we are experiencing is taking place.

Here are scientists themselves (and the highly influential, controversial, and relatively recently deceased philosophers of science—Feyerabend, Kuhn, and Popper) seriously questioning whether the scientific age is ending and why. Many, if not the majority, believe that it is. Early on, Horgan tells us about a 1989 symposium that took place at Syracuse University entitled "The End of Science?" The symposium was organized to discuss concerns that the *belief* in science was coming to an end. Yet one of its invited speakers, twenty years earlier, had put forth the thesis that *science itself* was ending. As Horgan tells it, amidst philosophers of science who were challenging "the authority of science," here was

> Gunther Stent, a biologist at the University of California at Berkeley, [who] had for years promulgated a much more dramatic scenario than the one posited by the symposium. Stent had asserted that science itself might be ending, and not because of the skepticism of a few academic sophists. Quite the contrary. Science might be ending because it worked so well.
>
> (Horgan, 1996, p. 9)

Stent's view, as presented in *The Coming of the Golden Age: A View of the End of Progress* (1969) and his conversations with Horgan, are threaded throughout *The End of Science*. The demise of science, Stent contends, is lawful. "Indeed, the dizzy rate at which progress is now proceeding makes it seem very likely that progress must come to a stop soon, perhaps in our lifetime, perhaps in a generation or two" (Stent, 1969, quoted in Horgan, 1996, p. 10). Stent allows that applied science will continue, as will the accumulation of more and more bits of information relative to what we already know. What is ending are the sort of pure science discoveries made by Galileo, Newton, Darwin, and Einstein that so dramatically increased our knowledge of the universe and transformed the life of our species and civilization.

Debates on the future of science are, likewise, debates on the nature of knowledge, truth, and religion. Horgan's dialogue with his readers and those he interviewed quickly turns to "big" questions: Is there such a thing as truth? Is everything knowable? What is the purpose of life? If science is ending, what can we believe in? To some scientists, there are some things—such as the origin of life or the nature of consciousness—that we will never know; they will elude our understanding and forever remain unknowable regardless of what technology we invent, how much money we spend, or how imaginative and brilliant we become. The end of science, for them, is not knowing *everything* but knowing everything that is capable of being known.

The linguist Noam Chomsky provides a particularly apt example: one of the unknowable things is why human beings do science. In conversation with Horgan, Chomsky proposed that the success of science is a chance event; it stems from a coincidental convergence of the truth about the world and the structure of our cognitive space. "It *is* a chance convergence," he continued, "because evolution didn't design us to do this; there's no pressure on differential reproduction that led to the capacity to solve problems in quantum theory. We had it. It's just there for the same reason that most other things are there: for some reason that nobody understands" (quoted in Horgan, 1996, p. 153).

For others, the end of science would mean that we have discovered/uncovered what Horgan calls The Answer ("a theory that quenches our curiosity forever," p. 30). He, among others, is fearful of this possibility:

The ostensible goal of science, philosophy, religion, and all forms of knowledge is to transform the great "Huuh?" of mystical wonder into an even greater "Aha!" of understanding. But after one arrives at The Answer, what then? There is a kind of horror in thinking that our sense of wonder might be extinguished, once and for all time, by our knowledge. What, then, would be the purpose of existence? There would be none.

(Horgan, 1996, p. 266)

Equating science with knowledge, with the search for truth, with the purpose of life, and with what there is to believe in (faith) brings science, ironically, closer and closer to religion. Three centuries ago, modern science defeated religion after an extended and bloody battle with the church, only to be constructed in the twentieth century more and more in the image of religion. In concluding his book, Horgan asks (and in so doing, he is speaking for several of the scientists with whom he spoke): "And now that science—true, pure, empirical science—has ended, what else is there to believe in?" (p. 266). Some of them, especially the scientific theologians, say the answer is God.

In selectively reviewing these two books, *The End of Science* and *The Flight from Science and Reason*, we hope to have conveyed some of the drama and historical significance of the debate and controversy over modern science. To our way of thinking, it signals the potential for monumental change in human life. One of our favorite statements by one of our favorite intellectual influences, Lev Vygotsky, helps complete our thought. In arguing that revolution, not evolution, is characteristic of history, Vygotsky noted that "A revolution solves only those tasks which have been raised by history: this proposition holds true equally for revolution in general and for aspects of social and cultural life during a revolution" (Vygotsky, quoted in Levitin, 1982, frontispiece).

We also hope to have conveyed some of what we found helpful about these books. In different ways, they expose both the seduction and the dead end (as opposed to "the limits") of knowledge. For neither those scientists fighting for their lives nor those musing about the purpose of life engage the historical viability or validity of *knowing* itself. On the one hand, they accuse those who challenge the insistence of science that it has a privileged relationship to reality and human progress, that it is the *only* kind of knowledge, of being heretics and worse. On the other hand, they argue over whether there is anything more to discover about the universe, the brain, the mind, or the origin of species and debate whether we have reached the limits of knowledge. But decrying those who challenge the One Way to Know or suggesting that there might not be anything more to know is a far cry from suggesting that we *no longer need to know* and, moreover, that our continued employment of knowing (cognition, epistemology) when it has outlived its usefulness is potentially destructive of human life and development. We believe that the circumstances of history demand more than an examination of science and scientific knowing. Rather, what is required is an investigation of knowing itself that entails not only how human beings have done knowing over the centuries but the presuppositions of the "epistemic meta-narrative"—the story/myth that human life and growth *require* a way of knowing the world. It is this *epistemic posture* (considered by many to be as natural as our upright stance) more than any particular epistemological position that fascinates and disturbs us. This book is part of our call for *the end of knowing* as the revolutionary, humane, and developmental move our species needs to make at this moment in history.

ENGAGING REALITY

Unlike some postmodernists, we have no real quarrel with the claim of science to preeminence or with its methodologies and sense of design. The scientific and technological discoveries and inventions of chemists, physicists, biologists, neuroscientists, astronomers, and other natural and physical scientists are, to us, indisputable. In the postmodern and post-postmodern future, science might well remain preeminent. It is the all-pervasiveness (the "religious-ification") of science, in our view, that poses the serious threat to humanity. The so-called social or human sciences, in particular, have been seriously misshapen—perhaps irrevocably—by the hegemony of the modern scientific and epistemological paradigm. As we, among others, have written about extensively, for the greater part of this century most natural and physical scientists stood by quietly while psychology (along with other disciplines) created itself in science's image and convinced enough people that it was capable of making bona fide knowledge claims about human life and relationships (Danziger, 1994; Gergen, 1994; Newman and Holzman, 1996). No doubt the failure of the hard scientists to issue any serious critique contributed to the success of the social science scam.

Now, however, many of these same hard scientists and hardcore modernists are "exposing" the "pseudoscientific" nature of the postmodernized social sciences (Gross and Levitt, 1994; Gross *et al.*, 1996), declaring that the method, categories, and criteria of science are the only possible ones, that to understand *is* to be scientific, and that everything can and must be understood relative to a scientific (that is, their) framework. The authoritarianism of science's defense of itself has been, understandably, a major impetus for and target of continuing postmodern critiques of science.

Yet we think science is too easy a target (not to mention the wrong one). More difficult is the task of taking on directly the epistemological authoritarianism that underlies and informs the authoritarianism of science. It seems to us that modern science has been able to get away with declaring itself the one true path to reality (understanding the world, finding the Truth) because its proponents, critics, and just about everyone else presuppose that there must be a path, that the world must somehow be known and understood. The nearly complete domination of philosophy by epistemology that occurred during this century (which we shall discuss in Chapter

2) has had the effect of muting the critically important distinction between having a conceptual framework (a way of knowing, a path, a view, a theory) for engaging the world or reality and actively engaging the world or reality. The result is the typically unstated assumption that human engagement is made possible by worldviews, theoretical constructs, and abstractions. The postmodern challenge to modern epistemology includes deconstructing its presupposition of "a knowing mind confronting a material world" (Gergen, 1994, p. xx). But is the postmodern rejection of the epistemic posture complete?

We think not. More often than not, what postmodernists propose are alternative kinds of knowing minds and alternative ways of knowing. The terms coined by the influential American psychologist Jerome Bruner are useful here. He describes the turn away from a "paradigmatic posture" in which knowing and understanding are posited on general laws, categories, and inductive and deductive truths, toward a "narrative posture" in which knowing and understanding are not explanatory but interpretive (Bruner, 1993). Thus, meaning is said by the postmodernists to reside in our conversations, in our discourse, in the language we create and use, rather than "out there" in the objects our language supposedly denotes or "in our minds." We live and make sense of the world, then, not by coming to know something that is already there, but through the socially constructed narratives we continuously create. This view—that human "world-structuring" is linguistic rather than cognitive—dominates much of postmodern social constructionism. Yet this seemingly non-epistemological construct still presupposes that we *must* structure the world. It still implies that our lives as lived *must* be mediated by some sort of knowing.

For those of us who wish to find a way of eliminating the dualism that separates human beings and the material world, the problem with any type of mediation theory is that it reintroduces the dualism on another level. If reality is what we construct through our stories, words, narratives, and discourse, then there must be something our stories and words are *about* (Newman and Holzman, 1996, p. 8). If everything must mean *something*, and what it means derives from how language is *used* (a current popular view), then there must be something relative to which we are making meaning when we use language.

The narrative posture of postmodernism does not, in our opinion, succeed in liberating us from the knowing mind. Many postmodernists take meaning-making to be an interpretive act. How we know is not through reasoning or explaining, they say, but through socially constructed interpretations—clearly an important step away from the patriarchal absolutism of modernism but not yet a complete break with cognitive models. We return to John Horgan's conversations about the end of science to illustrate how insidious the cognitive bias is.

Among the social scientists Horgan interviewed was the anthropologist Clifford Geertz, for whom anthropology is an interpretive science akin to literature and literary criticism: it is "imaginative writing about real people in real places at real times" (Geertz, 1988, p. 141). Summarizing "Thick description: Toward an interpretive theory of culture" (Geertz, 1973), Horgan tells us that in this classic essay Geertz is insisting that the anthropologist "must interpret phenomena, must try to guess what they *mean*," and that "a culture consists of a virtually infinite number of . . . messages, or signs, and the anthropologist's task is to interpret them. Ideally, the anthropologist's interpretation of a culture should be *as complex and richly imagined as the culture itself*" (Horgan, 1996, p. 154, emphasis added).

Some (including us) might well question why this should be the case. More to the point, however, is how it *could* be the case. Consider the assumptions that must be made in order even to consider the possibility: How can the culture "itself" be "complex and richly imagined?" A culture cannot imagine itself; surely, Geertz must mean that the people of the culture are doing the imagining. If so, then being a member of a culture implies having to have a view of it—for example, as complex or not, as richly or poorly imagined. It implies the mentalistic acts of abstracting and generalizing and structuring. It implies that essential to the social-cultural activity of people creating culture together is their interpreting of their activity. Ironically, Geertz winds up imposing the anthropologist's view on the "real people in real places at real times"—the natives, like the anthropologist, must be interpreting, for there is nothing else relative to which the anthropologist's interpretation of the culture can be judged except the natives' interpretation of their culture. That interpretive anthropology employs a cognitive paradigm goes without saying, and does not concern us here. Our point is that we see here the authoritarianism in the cognitive model of human relating where it is not intended.

We are, of course, not denying that human beings structure the world, create theoretical constructs, conceptual frameworks, or engage in abstraction (such as interpretation and explanation). Nor do we think that these capacities are in themselves problematic. We are suggesting, however, that we human beings do these things far less than philosophers, scientists, and social scientists have led us to believe. Moreover, this all-pervasive cognitive bias has brought our species dangerously close to developmental paralysis. Another of our favorite intellectual influences, the philosopher Ludwig Wittgenstein, has said, "You can fight, hope, and even believe without believing scientifically" (Wittgenstein, 1980a, B69). Building upon his anti-foundationalism and taking liberties with his provocation, we offer this paraphrase: "You can fight, hope, and even believe without knowing." We do not assume that there must always be something other than human activity, that is, something about it or something it is about. Of course, we do not *know* this to be the case!

STOP MAKING SENSE

Contemporary analysts of human life are, in our opinion, overly concerned with the human capacity to make sense of the world. Marxists, feminists, critical theorists, and various postmodernists hold (however unwittingly) to a cognitive model of engaging reality. It is to some of them that we now turn.

In *Postmodern Theory: Critical Interrogations* (1991), Steven Best and Douglas Kellner assess the contributions and limitations of postmodern theory almost exclusively via an examination of the ideas and intellectual histories of contemporary French postmodernists including Baudrillard, Derrida, Foucault, and Lyotard. Best and Kellner provide impressive summaries of the work of these intellectuals, but their primary goal is evaluative: their concern is the relevance of postmodern theory to critical social theory and radical politics. From their vantage point, postmodern theory (whether of the Derridean, Lyotardian, or feminist variety) repeatedly falls short for its consistently "undertheorized" social criticism. In their view, Lyotard, for example, fails "to produce critical perspectives on modernity as a socioeconomic phenomenon"; in his best-known work, *The Postmodern Condition* (1984), he "limits himself" to a critique of modern epistemology rather than addressing "modernity as historical process" (Best and Kellner, 1991, p. 165). In turning away from social analysis and critique toward philosophy, these American authors say, Lyotard thereby becomes "abstract and distanced from the social realities and problems of the present age" (p. 165).

And yet, what if the problems of the present age (we do not wish to commit ourselves to reality, social or otherwise) are—as we have already suggested—located significantly in modern epistemology (or, in what amounts to the same thing, in the populist primacy of knowing)? What if "modernity as historical process" is so bound up with the social-cultural-historical construction of epistemology (the epistemological bias) that it is not unreasonable to say, as Lyotard does, that modernity *is* reason? Best and Kellner (unlike Marx, we would argue) apparently consider epistemology to be distinct from the socioeconomic phenomenon of modernity. The postmodern focus on knowledge, they say, is one characteristic of this intellectual movement that renders it "politically disabling" (p. 296). Instead, they insist that macro-level perspectives and analyses, and political and economic theory of the sort postmodernists are prone to reject are essential to radical political agenda. They thus fault the postmodernists for not being radical enough.

We agree with Best and Kellner that postmodern critiques are insufficiently radical. However, we have very different reasons for thinking so. Moreover, the direction we urge taking is quite the opposite of what they recommend. To Best and Kellner, postmodern theory is to be faulted for overidentifying modernity with modern epistemology; to us the postmodernists have not taken their epistemological critique nearly far enough. As we see it, the target of the postmodern critique only appears to be episte-mology—that is, knowing as the dominant mode of understanding. For when postmodernists call for or generate alternative epistemologies (such as a social epistemology or a feminist epistemology) that reject modernism's most flagrant presuppositions—truth, the self, objectivity— they are, in effect, perpetuating rather than challenging the constraining and conservatizing nature of *any* epistemic view of the world. We argue in this book that in order for postmodernism to become world historic (revo-lutionary) it must make a direct attack "against epistemology" (to borrow Adorno's title, 1982, if not his approach). A revolutionary shift beyond modernism entails moving beyond epistemology (frames of mind, points of view) altogether.

What could lie "beyond" epistemology? How can we be calling for "the end of knowing?" How could we possibly make sense of where we (as a species or a civilization or a person) are in the absence of some epistemolog-ical framework? How could we know what to do (or, for that matter, what we are doing) without depending on some knowledge criteria? And how could we do anything without knowing if or what we are doing? Is our suggestion that human life can be lived without a "frame of mind" merely a product of our (the authors') "New York frame of mind?" We appreciate such questions—indeed, they occurred (obviously) to us! Yet given that our enterprise is to abandon the epistemological, we are not sure what to do with them other than pointing out that these queries only "make sense" within the *sense-making framework* of an epistemological paradigm. Again, we find Best and Kellner's critique of postmodern theory helpful in making our point. Their modernist commitment to epistemology, to theory and abstrac-tion, to a point of view, to understanding as sense-making, is clear, as in the following passage:

> Most postmodern theories can make little sense of the dramatic events of the era, while its claims concerning the end of history, society, the masses, and so on are laughable in the face of the resurgence of historical drama and upheaval. Indeed, it is ironic that during this period of exciting historical and political development certain postmodern theorists are prohibiting precisely the sort of theory needed to make sense of current historical events. It is also ironic that in this era of worldwide struggles for democracy postmodern intellectuals are trying to dissolve the key concepts of the democratic revolution.
>
> (Best and Kellner, 1991, pp. 296–7)

Best and Kellner's insistence that "current historical drama" can be and must be made sense of is, on our reading, strikingly ahistorical. It presumes a universal, abstract, and essentialist history "out there" (dualistically divided from its makers and sense-makers), always capable of being cogni-tively understood if only we apply the right theory. Theory, for them, is how we relate to the world. It is an instrumental tool. Without theory, they warn, we are lost, without anchor, disoriented, "condemned to live among the fragments" of contemporary life (p. 301).

Social democratic advocates of "radical political change," Best and Kellner offer Marxism and critical theory as candidates for engaging social reality. Not surprisingly, they fault postmodernists for rejecting these tools of analysis. Structurally, their argument parallels those of the defenders of science against the postmodern challenge. In place of the scientific paradigm, they relate to Marxism uncritically as "the" way to engage reality. In doing so, their intellectual commitment to the first principle of modern epistemology—that we cannot move (live our lives) without conceptual frameworks, worldviews, and theories—is as uncritically conservative as Gross, Levitt, and the others. And in spite of their far greater familiarity with postmodern writings, Best and Kellner are equally dismissive (even if they are more polite) of the methodological challenge posed by them. Here is an example of their critique:

> It is our view that postmodern theorists like Foucault, Baudrillard, and Lyotard, have made a serious theoretical and political mistake in severing their work from the Marxian critique of political economy and capitalism precisely at a point when the logic of capital accumulation has been playing an increasingly important role in structuring the new stage of society which can be conceptualized as a new economic and technical restructuring of capitalist society. Indeed, we would argue that Marxian categories are of central importance precisely in analyzing the phenomena focused on by postmodern social theory: the consumer society, the media, information, computers, and so on.
>
> (Best and Kellner, 1991, p. 300)

The best of postmodernism, in our opinion, explicitly rejects categorization and theorizing as human endeavors that are increasingly irrelevant to our times. Best and Kellner seem oblivious to this important methodological challenge in their assumption that Marxian categories and critique are more relevant than ever. As they reiterate and expand their position a page later, we see again how they dismiss postmodern attempts to reject instrumentalist totalizing theory and grand metanarratives:

> Yet against Lyotard and others who reject macrotheory, systemic analysis, or grand historical narratives, we would argue that precisely now we need such comprehensive theories to attempt to capture the new totalizations being undertaken by capitalism ... one needs new critical theories to conceptualize, describe, and interpret macro social processes, just as one needs political theories able to articulate common or general interests that cut across divisions of sex, race, and class. . . . Cognitive mapping is therefore necessary to provide theoretical and political orientation as we move into a new, dangerous, and exciting social and political terrain.
>
> (Best and Kellner, 1991, p. 301)

Here the *non-revolutionary* nature of their political position—the need for theory to articulate common interests and cognitive mapping to orient us as we move—is clear. But where is the revolutionary Marx? Particularly in his early writings, Marx railed against the dualism of theory and practice, with its relegation of practice to the application of theory, and the idealism of notions such as contemplation and mental criticism (and, we would add, "orientation" and "cognitive mapping"). Best and Kellner fail to appreciate Marx as both intellectual and political revolutionary (and that the two were inseparable). Marx did, after all, tell us that "The philosophers have only *interpreted* the world, in various ways; the point is to *change* it" (Marx, 1973, p. 123). Furthermore, he did not leave untouched the question of how to change it: "Not criticism but revolution is the driving force of history" (Marx and Engels, 1973, p. 59). Yet Best and Kellner opt for interpretation and criticism, seeking to resurrect abstract Marxian categories for the purpose of making sense of this moment in history rather than to make history.

Best and Kellner are not alone in failing to appreciate Marx's revolutionary challenge to epistemology (which was, we would admit, never thorough or consistent). In particular, Marxists and postmodernists alike often miss Marx's attempt to escape from the epistemic posture in favor of a new ontology. If revolution is the driving force of history, to Marx the driving force of revolution is *revolutionary activity*. At its best, Marx's dialectical historical materialism was radically monistic, as expressed, for example, in the following: "The coincidence of the changing of circumstances and of human activity or self-changing can be conceived and rationally understood only as *revolutionary practice*" (Third Thesis on Feuerbach, Marx, 1973, p. 121). In our opinion, Marx's greatest and most overlooked discovery was the human capacity for "revolutionary, practical-critical activity" (as set forth in the First Thesis on Feuerbach, Marx, 1973, p. 121).

Our argument for the end of knowing is neither nihilistic nor pessimistic. We urge the abandonment of the instrumentalist, non-revolutionary search for new postmodern epistemologies because, for us, the "tasks raised by history" are ontological rather than epistemological. We believe that a shift in ontology—*from cognition to activity*—is itself the practical-critical revolutionary activity required to live and move and grow "among the fragments." It is Marx as non-instrumental, revolutionary methodologist that we seek to complete.

We are greatly aided in this task by Lev Vygotsky (his follower) and Ludwig Wittgenstein (nobody's follower). Both breathe new life into Marx's conception of revolutionary activity. Both the early Soviet psychologist/methodologist and the iconoclastic Austrian-born philosopher, whose writings many regard as the most influential of the twentieth century, challenged the epistemological paradigm of their respective fields. (Vygotsky had the additional burden of a revisionist Marxism rapidly becoming cognized—that is, epistemologized—

and dogmatized.) Activity took center stage in their sometimes seemingly abstract but always exceedingly practical work. We believe that Vygotsky gave psychological specification to *revolutionary, practical-critical activity*: human learning and development, Vygotsky discovered, *are* such revolutionary activities (rather than behaviors following laws of conditioning or innate traits following laws of evolution). He further recognized that the investigation of activity necessitated the creation of a new psychology—one can no more study activity with tools invented to study behavior than one can study the brain with a magnifying glass—and his life's work was devoted to what he called the "search for method" (Vygotsky, 1978, p. 65).

Wittgenstein, in his later writings, exposed and hoped to free us from the pathology embedded in our language. He sought to help us see language as activity, as a "form of life," something thousands of years of metaphysical thinking about thinking and about language have made very difficult, so that we could get on with things, so we could move "from here to there" (Shotter and Newman, 1995). Interpretations, explanations, and other methods of appraisal (what philosophy and psychology are) only serve to confuse and obfuscate, especially with regard to subjectivity and the language of so-called mental states (such as feelings, perceptions, thoughts, and beliefs). More an "anti-philosopher" than a philosopher proper, Wittgenstein abandoned philosophy and devised language-games (philosophizing without Philosophy; see Newman, 1996; Newman and Holzman, 1996) which "make the problem vanish" (Wittgenstein, 1961).

As we have touched upon in our remarks thus far, many contemporary thinkers, including postmodernists, do not share our view that Marx, Vygotsky, and Wittgenstein were sensitive to the need to go beyond epistemology and, furthermore, that each partially succeeded in creating/discovering a new non-epistemic ontology—activity. Yet we have found these three inventive methodologists invaluable in our work in precisely this way. The varied psychotherapeutic, educational, and cultural projects we and our colleagues have developed that have given rise to this and our other writings have as well informed our reading of Marx, Vygotsky, and Wittgenstein. In our ongoing search for a practice of method, the three of them have been brought together in some unique ways.

ACADEMICS IN AN ANTI-INSTITUTION

How we have brought them together is inseparable from *where* (socio-historically speaking) we have done so. The work we have been doing for nearly thirty years is an attempt to create independent institutions and organizations (taken together, they comprise what we now call a *development community*) that are inclusive, radically democratic, and potentially developmental. As we saw it from the beginning and still do, financial independence is a necessary condition for creating environments not overdetermined by the conservatizing constraints of traditional societal institutions, environments in which the traditional knowledge-seeking and knowledge-producing paradigm (complete with concepts such as proof, hypothesis testing, objectivity, results, and evaluation) and its accompanying institutional arrangements (such as boundaries, categories, definitions, rules and regulations) are not built in. Our early projects—free schools, communes, health clinics, and therapy collectives—were among the thousands of radical political-educational-therapeutic alternatives that sprang up all over the US during the 1960s, only to fold or become co-opted into the mainstream in the increasingly conservative environment of the late 1970s.

That we survived and continued to grow had everything to do with the fact that our work was not affiliated with any university and not funded by corporate donations, foundation grants, or government subsidies. Running an afterschool program to help young people develop alternatives to violence, for example, is one activity when its history includes having received a government or foundation grant (or when the work is done under the pressure to "publish or perish" and for the purpose of getting tenure); it is quite another activity when its history includes no such contractual relationships (direct or indirect) with the state. Building a psychotherapeutic practice that "serves" poor people, to take another example, is one activity when its existence depends on government funding and legislative mandates and thus requires the use of the *DSM-IV* (even its least offensive diagnosis); it is a different activity when it does not label (by the numbers or otherwise), and when poor and middle-class people are in therapy together by virtue of people with more money choosing to subsidize the participation of people with less money because they believe it is psychologically helpful and/or politically important.

Independence did not, of course, guarantee that what we would create would be qualitatively different. It only opened up the *possibility* for a new kind of institution, specifically, an *anti-institution* (Holzman and Newman, 1979). The *practice* of independence is the organizing activity of reaching out to people from all class and ethnic backgrounds, in all neighborhoods and walks of life, and giving them the opportunity to support work of this kind if they believe it to be of value. To the extent that we have not replicated traditional institutional arrangements it is a consequence of our practice of method, an explicitly participatory activity that

> entails the continuous, self-conscious deconstruction of the hierarchical arrangements of learning, teaching and knowing . . . confronting biases, definitions and judgments in an ongoing way . . . [and] self-criticism from the perspective of the positive continuation of the developmental environment, not merely from the negative perspective of responding to imposed, societal values and norms.
>
> (Holzman, 1995b, p. 24)

Intellectual interests and academic training were neither the impetus nor theoretical guide for our ongoing work. To the extent that we choose to identify motivational forces, ours were political, ethical, and, above all, practical rather than intellectual. Our commitment was not simply to negate existing structures, systems, or ideas but to build something (an environment, a community) free of the assumptions of existing systems, most particularly the assumption that all human life and growth necessarily require systemization (appraisal abstracted from activity) (Newman, 1996; Newman and Holzman, 1996). It was this overwhelmingly complicated and seemingly impossible task that, we felt, was a necessary precondition for creating/discovering something of value for all people. Nevertheless, the building of this development community has as an important component a rich intellectual history. Creating an environment in which this history could be transformed and continue to develop is a significant factor in our ongoing engagement with the leading intellectual movements of our day.

Both of us (and those of our co-workers—a small minority even in the early days—who had academic backgrounds) come from traditions that were challenging modern epistemology. At the time (the 1960s), of course, the issues were not phrased in such neat postmodern terms. In Newman's field, philosophy, the issues had to do with the nature and status of scientific knowledge and explanatory, descriptive, and interpretive paradigms. In Holzman's field, developmental psychology and psycholinguistics, the issues had to do with ecologically valid methods of data collection and analysis.

Newman studied at Stanford University when it was a center of a "happening" philosophy in the US—philosophy of mind, philosophy of science, and philosophy of language. These years of "the Wittgensteinian revolution" (Newman, 1996; Newman and Holzman, 1996) were a time when Philosophy itself (philosophy as a system of thought) was being challenged. The philosophical roots of postmodern deconstruction—which would become, over the next three decades, the basis for a serious challenge to psychology, the other social sciences and, in turn, science itself—were taking hold. Of particular interest to Newman was the problem of historical explanation, a topic then being explored by Hempel (1965) and, in reaction to him, Davidson (1980), Dray (1957), and Scriven (1959). Newman's *Explanation by Description* (1968) was an effort to further distinguish historical explanation from the causal-deductive paradigm of explanation that was applied to physical phenomena. Historical explanations are not answers to causal questions but to "what happened?" questions; in fact, they are not explanations at all, but descriptions. Newman, at the time unacquainted with either Marx's conception of practical-critical activity or Soviet activity theory, was fascinated by the relationship between doing philosophy and what comes out of the doing; he was already coming to believe that the activity itself must be included as a relevant factor in what one discovers or creates through the activity.

This conviction (coupled with a generally skeptical attitude toward the overrated value of knowing in our culture) informed how Newman taught

philosophy in the few years before he left academia for community organizing and radical politics. Focused more on the activity of doing
philosophy, on creating philosophical dialogues (not yet Wittgensteinian
language-games) than on teaching the Great Works, his classes were
oriented to doing philosophy rather than to knowing Philosophy. He was
helping his students participate in creating a learning community—what we
now refer to, in Vygotskian language, as *developmental learning* or the
activity of *learning-leading-development*. Off the campus, one of the first
learning activities of our development community (then a radical commune)
was a study of symbolic logic that simultaneously engaged the "mental
blocks" students encountered in attempting to study it.

Over the next ten years, Newman and his co-workers were involved in
political organizing and radical psychology. He developed a self-consciously
political psychotherapy practice and center, and schooled himself in Marx,
other Marxist theorists, and left political movements nationally and interna-
tionally. During this period, Newman produced a body of political writings
that attempted to reinvigorate the methodology of Marx rather than repeat
what, to him, was the dogmatism of much of contemporary Marxist
thought. The central problem Newman engaged, which he took to be
methodological, was how to create a left movement in the US that was fused
with the class *and* mainstream located. From the earliest writings (for
example, an article entitled "Witchdoctory: The method of proletarian
misleadership," 1983, first published in 1975), Newman argued that revolutionary practice was anti-epistemological and necessitated the elimination of
interpretation. Here and elsewhere, he was primarily concerned with the
relationship of the activity of organization to the institutions of society, and
critiqued the left's cognitively overdetermined practice, particularly its
adherence to Marxist categorization (abstraction). The US working class,
for example—*as activity*—had to be brought into existence through the
building of its institutions. (Many of these writings were brought together in
a 1983 issue of *Practice: The Journal of Politics, Economics, Psychology,
Sociology and Culture*.)

Holzman was trained in and shaped by intellectual traditions that
challenged existing paradigms in psychological research. In the early
1970s, she was involved in studies of children's early language that
looked outside developmental psychology proper for tools with which to
create a new research methodology. With Lois Bloom (one of the first
researchers to pioneer longitudinal, observational methods for studying
language and cognitive development in very young children) as her
mentor, Holzman was a member of a research team at Teachers College,
Columbia University which produced a series of investigations that—in
postmodern terms—related to language as socially constructed and situated, its acquisition by children as constructed-in-action, and its analysis
as essentially an interpretive rather than an explanatory scientific enterprise (Bloom *et al.*, 1974; Bloom, Lightbown, and Hood, 1975; Bloom,

Hood, and Miller, 1975; Bloom *et al.*, 1976; Holzman published as Hood from 1974 until 1983). Her dissertation research on how children between two and three years of age use causal language and are said to express causal relations touched on the issue of explanation. While the focus of the study was empirical, it contains a methodological critique not only of the dominant experimental paradigm but also Piaget's "clinical method" for the way they both impose adult (investigator, "etic" as opposed to "emic") categories on data and draw unwarranted conclusions about children's thinking from what children say (Hood, 1977; Hood and Bloom, 1979).

Holzman subsequently joined a research team at Rockefeller University's Laboratory of Comparative Human Cognition which, under the direction of Michael Cole, set out to develop alternatives to the positivist and mentalistic paradigm of cognitive (and, by extension, educational) psychology. Cole was in the beginning stages of developing what has now become cultural psychology—a method of scientific inquiry that relates to cognition, learning, schooling, literacy, and language as cultural phenomena. Earlier in his career, Cole studied in Moscow with the Soviet neuropsychologist Alexander Luria, a student and follower of Vygotsky. Luria had introduced Cole to Vygotsky's work (Cole, 1979), and Cole in turn introduced it to his colleagues at the Laboratory and to American psychology. (Jerome Bruner, who wrote the oft-cited introduction to the first English language publication of Vygotsky's *Thought and Language* in 1962, actually did the introducing. But it was Cole's efforts in the 1970s—including the publication of the journal *Soviet Psychology* and of *Mind in Society*, 1978, a short collection of Vygotsky's writings Cole edited with John-Steiner, Scribner, and Souberman—that brought Vygotsky and the possibilities of a new approach to cognition and language to the attention of American psychologists.)

Concerned with social inequality, the members of the Laboratory hoped to discover some things that could help transform class, race, and gender bias in schooling practices. They were convinced that the dominant psychological paradigm—its view of what a person is, and what learning and development are—plays a significant role in who becomes a successful learner and who does not. The early work of the Cole lab culminated in the monograph *Ecological Niche-picking: Ecological Invalidity as an Axiom of Experimental Cognitive Psychology* (Cole *et al.*, 1978)[1] in which it was argued that the psychological laboratory was more than a physical space; it was a methodology that systematically excluded critical features of human life and growth. Cole, Hood, and McDermott devised ethnographic analyses (conceptually shaped by Vygotsky's claim that learning and development are social-cultural activities) of children's social interactions in and out of school. They presented a psychology of "person–environment interface" as a positive alternative to the dominant mentalistic, individuated *ecologically invalid* psychology. (See also Hood *et al.*, 1980; McDermott *et al.*, 1978; McDermott and Hood, 1982.)

We (the authors) began to work together in 1976. The major focus of our collaboration was creating a psychology in the service of a progressive political vision. With a handful of others in the mental health professions and social sciences, we founded the New York Institute for Social Therapy and Research in 1978 as a therapeutic, training, education, and research center with several locations in the New York metropolitan area. We self-published several documents articulating the methodological foundations of our work. *Practical-critical Activities* (Newman, 1977) put forth, in a polemical blend of Marxist and analytic philosophy discourse, the premises and practices of a new organization of revolutionary politics and revolutionary psychology. Drawing connections between the crisis in science and in the economy, Newman implicated paradigmism as the no longer effective method of reconciling contradiction, charging that contemporary psychotherapy was a secular religion functioning as a mass institution designed to reconcile the population to a zero-growth economy. Locating "freedom as *mental* rather than *historical* and struggle as *personal* rather than *collective* and *classwide*," he wrote, therapy "advocates the position (implicitly or explicitly) that the next stage of human growth must be mental" (Newman, 1977, p. 97). He argued instead for "science without paradigms," concluding with a brief discussion of "non-reconciliative therapy" (what would, over the next twenty years, develop into the cultural-performatory approach of social therapy).

The Practice of Method: An Introduction to the Foundations of Social Therapy (Holzman and Newman, 1979) took up where *Practical-critical Activities* left off. The title derives from the common characterization of Marxism as "the method of practice" (or "praxis"). "Practice of method" was an attempt to capture what (as we understood it) we were doing, as informed by our understanding of Marx's non-dualistic, historical conception of method—in which the "premises" are people "in their actual, empirically perceptible process of development under definite conditions" (Marx and Engels, 1973, pp. 47–8). We distinguished between the revolutionary activity of practicing method and the method of practice, which is a particular method that is applied to some piece of social reality. Our effort was to go beyond the point-of-viewism of the method of practice and to escape the dualism inherent in *applying method*. This distinction is explored more fully in *Lev Vygotsky: Revolutionary Scientist* (Newman and Holzman, 1993).

In *The Practice of Method*, we attempted to show how the traditional Western conceptions of understanding, explaining, and meaning are over-determining of emotional language and emotional experience. Our analysis of the role historically played by psychological science—along with psychotherapy—in constructing our conceptions of development, emotions, normality, and pathology made its first appearance in this manuscript, where both Vygotsky's and Wittgenstein's views on meaning and the emergence of language were discussed. While not yet fully appreciating how methodologically radical was Vygotsky's claim that creating a new psychology requires method as "simultaneously the tool and the result of the study" (Vygotsky, 1978, p. 65), we did see its practical-critical relevance to Marx's dialectical historical materialism:

> For Marx, *determinism is a social fact* (social facts are not determined) and therefore we must show how "tools and results" are themselves a product of tools and results; we must show how *determinism is historical, not how history is determined.*
>
> (Holzman and Newman, 1979, p. 65)

During the 1980s our activity-theoretic view of the relationship between speaking and thinking was being formulated. In a series of articles, we argued that Vygotsky was best understood as a Marxist, revolutionary methodologist who offered a powerful alternative to conceptions—such as mediation, intersubjectivity, and pragmatics—being put forth as social-cultural alternatives to a representationalist conception of language (Holzman, 1985; Holzman and Newman, 1985, 1987; Hood *et al.*, 1982).

Our current understanding of language as activity (the performance of conversation) derives from our practice. The years of practicing social therapy, training lay and professional clinicians in the approach, and creating developmental, conversational environments in educational settings with children and adults have been one of the most gratifying experiences of building community. It has also been one of the most intellectually exciting and creative. It is the area where the two most important influences in our respective intellectual histories—Ludwig Wittgenstein and Lev Vygotsky—reappear and help create something beyond what either they or we could have done "on our own." (See "Beyond the Pale" in Chapter 5.) *Lev Vygotsky: Revolutionary Scientist* (Newman and Holzman, 1993) is primarily a theoretical discussion of Vygotsky's contribution to creating the kind of revolutionary science activity needed to reinitiate human development. Rather than a review of Vygotsky's ideas, it is our reading of Vygotsky as an affirmation of the philosophical and political power of the fundamental socialness of human beings. Our most recent work, *Unscientific Psychology: A Cultural-performatory Approach to Understanding Human Life* (Newman and Holzman, 1996) expands that discussion, locating both Wittgenstein and Vygotsky as "prepostmodernists" who serve to bridge the gap between the stifling scientific psychology of modernism and the possibilities presented in its current postmodernization. In characterizing a "Wittgensteinian-Vygotskian synthesis" we locate our practice and theoretical understanding both within and beyond current intellectual movements, notably social constructionism and activity theory. *Schools for Growth: Radical Alternatives to Current Educational Models* (Holzman, 1997) refocuses the Vygotskian–Wittgensteinian cultural-performatory approach to human life on schooling, learning, and development.

Our concern is to practice method, to create new forms of life, to build environments that are at once the context for revolutionary activity and revolutionary activity itself. To the extent that sense-making is at all relevant to this task, it is activistic rather than epistemological. It is not, nor does it depend upon, a knowing of any kind but is created through (and simultaneous with) practicing method rather than being an appraisal generated from hypotheses prior to, or interpretations after, practice. We thus write conflictedly, wary of the abstraction and systemization that is inevitable in the act of writing. Our goal is not to explain or inform but to provoke.

2   The epistemological bias

Philosophical thoughts about *things* and *relationships* frequently begin when we are quite young. Witness the Greeks! At an early age some people notice that two things are significantly *the same* (identical) only if they aren't. For if two things are *really* only one thing, then the identity claim (A=A) is trivial (in a way that "7+5=12," "The morning star is the evening star," or even "Shakespeare is the author of *Hamlet*" aren't). Identity and its various paradoxes, problems, and dilemmas are ancient puzzles. Why, then, does so much of postmodern thought appear to make so much of it? Are there new paradoxes, problems, or "dilemmas of identity" rooted in certain specific features of contemporary life (for example, what Gergen, 1991, calls "the saturation of self" by mass communication)? Or have psychologists and other postmodernists only recently become sufficiently philosophically sophisticated to notice? Is postmodernism (especially of the psychological variety) merely soft-headed philosophy of social science? Are we witnessing a full blown, revolutionary paradigm shift, or is the postmodern brouhaha nothing more than the social sciences and humanities understandably and desperately fighting back against the victory of modern (hard) science in the battle for epistemic hegemony?

Similarly, the paradoxicality of truth (or, more dramatically, Truth) is as much a feature of modernism as truth itself. The self-referential paradoxes (can something—or anything—be true of itself?) have been apparent, at least to some, not for minutes but millennia. Why, then, the sometimes self-righteous postmodern shout to abandon truth altogether? Is it all a passing fancy, or the extraordinary discovery of a fatal flaw in the modern worldview? Does the problem of identity (*self*) to which philosophically oriented psychologists in general and postmodern psychologists in particular address themselves have anything to do with identity (*sameness of things*)? Why are so many (relatively speaking) in the human sciences taking these matters so seriously (relatively speaking)?

The scientific revolution which was surely the midwife to modernism was itself philosophically (ontologically) grounded in the recognition that motion and not stillness is the fundamental state of the physical universe. In turn, this metaparadigmatic ontic shift led relatively rapidly to new ways of looking at various segments and sub-segments of physical, chemical, and biological reality (see, for example, Butterfield, 1962). Indeed, so powerful was this metashift that reality itself (at least its substance, if not its Aristotelian particularized form) was redefined in terms of it: Aristotelian teleology gave way to Newtonian causality over a brief 100-year period starting with Galileo. The technological advances associated with the birth of science (and vice versa) and the industrial advances that made them all-powerful and omnipresent (particularly in the more wealthy sections of the globe) assured for modernism a hegemonic status as a worldview.

Postmodernism, at first glance, seems more exclusively critical, philosophically speaking, than does modernism. There often appears no positive philosophical (ontological) shift analogous to the earlier modern one from stillness to motion; hence the unoriginal name "post-modernism." Indeed, for some postmodernists (and perhaps many or most) this is an essential feature and virtue of postmodernism: it is fundamentally or essentially anti-paradigmatic. Paradigm shifts and conceptual frameworks of all kinds are exactly what we do not want, says the postmodernist. There *is* no way of seeing the world which is ultimately a better or best (most accurate or truthful) way; the religiosified belief that there must be is what is wrong with modernism.

In this way much of postmodernism leaves itself open to the (modernist) charge of relativism. If there is no true way, the critics of postmodernism argue, then there is no way to determine what is objectively true. Social constructionism, for example, leaves us (they say) without a way of discriminating between alternative constructions (large or small). Often the modern–postmodern debate reduces to a kind of academic name calling, with modernists (or, at least, critics of "relativistic" postmodernism) charging that postmodernism fails as a possible (or actual) paradigm shift and postmodernists responding that in fact postmodernism is a perspective based on the failure of paradigmism. Ironically (and interestingly), three particular modernists (at least temporally speaking) are increasingly appealed to by both sides (all sides) in this debate; they are Marx, Vygotsky, and Wittgenstein. These radical critics, three *enfants terribles* of mainstream modernism, have emerged as godfathers to many postmodern thinkers. The social constructionist Kenneth Gergen, influenced to varying degrees by the three godfathers, is one of postmodernism's several fathers; he is, perhaps, its primary Anglo-American father. In *The Saturated Self: Dilemmas of Identity in Contemporary Life* (1991), Gergen writes:

> The postmodern condition more generally is marked by a plurality of voices vying for the right to reality—to be accepted as legitimate expressions of the true and the good. As the voices expand in power and presence, all that seemed proper, right-minded, and well understood is subverted. In the postmodern world we become increasingly aware that the objects about which we speak are not so much "in the world" as they

are products of perspective. Thus, processes such as emotion and reason cease to be real and significant essences of persons; rather, in the light of pluralism we perceive them to be impostors, the outcome of our ways of conceptualizing them. Under postmodern conditions, persons exist in a state of continuous construction and reconstruction; it is a world where anything goes that can be negotiated. Each reality of self gives way to reflexive questioning, irony, and ultimately the playful probing of yet another reality. The center fails to hold.

(Gergen, 1991, p. 7)

Gergen has given careful intellectual expression (and, thereby, much respectability) to postmodernism and, in particular, social constructionism. He has functioned as a well-constructed bridge between the philosophical critics of science, psychology, and traditional epistemology and psychologists themselves. Applying philosophical/psychological postmodernism to concrete institutionalized human practices (for example, psychotherapy, politics, and communication), he has established the relevance of various postmodern insights to life as lived in contemporary society. In *The Saturated Self* (1991) and elsewhere he offers a social-psychological analysis of the transforming conditions of contemporary culture that have produced a postmodern world. He plays a progressive role within and impacts on institutions and organizations of psychology, such as the American Psychological Association. Gergen's writings and lectures, therefore, serve not only to articulate his own social constructionist views on postmodern matters, but as a kind of summing up of the movement. As such he is twice over vulnerable to his critics (those who disagree with him and those who disagree with how he has, implicitly or explicitly, characterized them). All in all, Gergen has emerged as a locus of study for postmodernists of all stripes.[1] For these reasons, in this and subsequent chapters we will often turn to his work.

ONTOLOGY VS. EPISTEMOLOGY

As already noted, modernism (and its historical, institutional catalyst, modern science) evolved from a fundamentally *ontological* shift: the shift from stillness to motion as the natural state of the physical world. This profound transformation of the ontological paradigm prefigured the emergence of a new age of epistemology (often called modern philosophy)—300 years of thinking about thinking (and other related mentalistic topics) which culminated in this century in philosophy's self-liquidation as a thing in itself and its becoming, to use modern (logical) positivist language, "a handmaid to science." Over this period of time (but most especially in this century) modern philosophy (epistemology) and its beneficiary and benefactor, modern science, came to "live by taking in each other's wash" (to use J. L. Austin's eloquent and all-purpose phrase, Austin, 1962). All other branches of philosophy (such as metaphysics, ontology, and ethics) were essentially orphaned by epistemology even as epistemology (modern philosophy) turned into metascience (philosophy of science and logic) or methodology.

Ironically, the transformation of philosophy into epistemology—designed to give philosophy a bona fide subject matter, that is, modern science—led to philosophy ending up with no subject matter at all. For positivist epistemology and methodology created criteria of significance which, by uniquely identifying the meaningful with the scientific, thereby ensured that philosophy (epistemology) itself could not pass the test. Hence, philosophy atrophied and died; first by identifying itself exclusively with epistemology and then by overidentifying (equating) epistemology with modern science and its method (Adorno, 1982; Feyerabend, 1978; Newman and Holzman, 1996; Rorty, 1979, 1982). Philosophy, like the rest of the world, became so enamored of modern science that it forfeited its traditional role as metatheory. The millennium, in the form of modern science, had come. Philosophy hailed the Savior—and went out of business. Little wonder then that Anglo-American postmodernists (mainly non-philosophers—specifically, psychologists) concerned with the limits of science—in particular, social science and cognitive science—would have nowhere to turn (philosophy was now in the museum of antiquity). Neither is it surprising that they would turn (insofar as they turned at all) to epistemologized philosophy—philosophy's "final form"—as the academic fossil of greatest relevance.

If this overly broad picture is deemed completely inaccurate for European or Continental traditions in philosophy and psychology, it is surely suggestive of the contemporary Anglo-American tradition. The point here is that when postmodern psychologists (especially of the Anglo-American variety) turned to philosophy to get help in framing questions (if not finding answers) about the foundational efficacy of the social sciences, it was an already moribund and overly epistemologized philosophy to which they turned. The philosophical paradigm itself had for hundreds of years been effectively epistemologized; ontology, in particular, had been virtually abandoned as metaphysical and meaningless. Hence, the kind of *ontological* shift (from stillness to motion) which had triggered the modern age was, for the most part, unthinkable to many of the early postmodernists just coming to philosophy of science for guidance.

It is only with their relatively recent discovery of Wittgenstein's work (a fierce critique of epistemologized philosophy) that the postmodernists within psychology revealed the extent to which they had been overdetermined by the paradigm of modern philosophy (epistemology). For the postmodern interpretations of Wittgenstein seem to us to miss the very purpose, point, and historical setting of Wittgenstein's anti-epistemological, anti-cognitive, *therapeutic* endeavor. Interestingly, Wittgenstein is misunderstood by postmodern psychologists in much the same way that Vygotsky's anti-psychological, revolutionary, cultural perspective and

Marx's anti-interpretational, dialectical perspectives are misunderstood by the neo-Vygotskian and neo-Marxist revisionists.[2] As we noted in Chapter 1, what these three radical critical modern philosophers/psychologists share is a recognition (more accurately, a disposition to revolutionary activity that gives rise to one) that an ontological practical-critical transformation is demanded to challenge the methodological hegemony of modern epistemology. By insisting (implicitly, if not explicitly) that its proper concern is to challenge modern individuated *ways of knowing*, postmodernism (particularly of the psychological variety) thereby gives *itself* over to epistemology. Wittgenstein, Marx, and Vygotsky share a fundamental commitment to a revolutionary ontic shift (not an epistemic alteration) from interpretive cognition to activity (most particularly, *revolutionary activity*) as the dominant unit of human intercourse. It is this revolutionary feature of Wittgenstein, Marx, and Vygotsky which is typically (intentionally or unintentionally) overlooked by postmodern psychologists.

THE PARADIGM OF PARADIGMISM

Perhaps the complex point (piece of postmodern history or performance) we are trying to clarify can best (read: cognitively) be made by briefly examining paradigmism. In contemporary (highly epistemologized) philosophy of science, paradigmism is first "discovered" ("invented," "narrated") by the late philosopher/historian of science Thomas Kuhn. In his now classic work, *The Structure of Scientific Revolutions* (1962), he socio-historically defines science in terms of the rise and fall of paradigms, the varied models or conceptual frameworks which provide the working scientist (at whatever level) with a "way of looking at" varied empirical observations, which makes them coherent and, thereby, theoretically useable—in the sense that a way of looking at the facts (the observations) is suggestive of other things to look at, which leads to further verification or falsification, and/or new discoveries.

Conceptual frameworks, paradigms, or *ways of looking at* things are a critical epistemological/cognitive component of observation itself, as modernists from Kant to Kuhn to cognitive scientists have argued, in our opinion, correctly. Ways of looking (paradigms) have a complex history; they rise and fall. Ironically, they are subject to "falsification" and revolutionary rejection by observations—observations which they themselves (the ways of looking) go a long way to determining (defining). This is a well-known logically paradoxical situation typically resolved, from a practical-philosophical point of view, pragmatically. Quine's epistemological pragmatism obviously influenced Kuhn's view on the history of science. In his seminal and still relevant essay, "Two dogmas of empiricism" (1963), Quine sums up the matter this way:

As an empiricist I continue to think of the conceptual scheme of science as a tool, ultimately, for predicting future experience in the light of past experience. Physical objects are conceptually imported into the situation as convenient intermediaries—not by definition in terms of experience, but simply as irreducible posits comparable, epistemologically, to the gods of Homer. For my part I do, *qua* lay physicist, believe in physical objects and not in Homer's gods; and I consider it a scientific error to believe otherwise. But in point of epistemological footing the physical objects and the gods differ only in degree and not in kind. Both sorts of entities enter our conception only as cultural posits. The myth of physical objects is epistemologically superior to most in that it has proved more efficacious than other myths as a device for working a manageable structure into the flux of experience.

(Quine, 1963, p. 44)

Quine's well-known pragmatic resolution, often recast over the years, has most recently been updated by postmodern, post-cognitivist social psychologists. For example, Gergen (1994) writes:

There is little reason to believe that we literally experience[3] or "see the world" through a system of categories . . . there is no viable explanation for how the cognitive *a priori* could be established. However, we gain substantially if we consider the world-structuring process as linguistic rather than cognitive. It is through an *a priori* commitment to particular forms of language (genres, conventions, speech codes and so on) that we place boundaries around what we take to be "the real." . . . In Goodman's terms, it is *description* not *cognition* that constructs the factual world.

(Gergen, 1994, p. 37)

This recasting of cognitivism and paradigmism into language form builds on almost half a century of work in linguistics, philosophy of science, philosophy of language, and, perhaps most importantly, the language of philosophy; in its twentieth-century death throes contemporary epistemologized philosophy, in effect, "turned into" the study of language.

What, then, is language? If cognitivism reintroduces the traditional paradoxes of mentalism (as Gergen himself goes on to show, 1994), do we have a clear enough understanding of language to prevent the reemergence of those nasty dilemmas and paradoxes? Decades of language study by a wide variety of researchers suggest that no agreed upon answer to this question is at hand. In our opinion, a "proper" postmodern reading of Wittgenstein, Vygotsky, and Marx is critical to furthering this enterprise. However, such a reading is unlikely—if not impossible—if we postmodernists are unprepared to reject our epistemologized modern (and postmodern) world ("reality") and find (discover) an ontologically new "way of being"—not a "way of seeing"—for human intercourse (and meta-intercourse). It is epistemology itself, it seems to us, not simply mistaken epistemological views, that must be rejected in favor of *activity*—not activity *viewed epistemologically*; indeed, not activity *viewed* at all. The postmodernists, particularly the Anglo-American psychologists/philosophers, often seem unprepared or unwilling to make this revolutionary activistic shift.

Ironically, such revolutionary faintheartedness on the part of many post-modernists is philosophically inconsistent even with the grandfather and official metaparadigm-maker, Kuhn. For surely the falsification (deconstructive elimination) of such fundamental epistemological concepts as individuated self-identity and truth would signify that we are in a revolutionary phase of the historical revolutionary/evolutionary dialectic of science and/or philosophy and, thereby, would require a rejection of epistemology (as paradigm) altogether in favor of (or, at least, in preparation for) a new paradigm or, alternatively, something to replace paradigmism. By and large, this has not happened. Postmodernism, in general, seems strangely unwilling to go beyond itself. It implicitly (and, in many cases, explicitly) denies development (including its own development!), a direct consequence of its failure to "overthrow" epistemology.

Richard Rorty's postmodern populist pragmatism and Gergen's thoughtful social constructionism (in some ways two extremes) each illustrate this denial. In his introductory essay to *Consequences of Pragmatism* (1982), Rorty says:

> Pragmatists think that the history of attempts to isolate the True or the Good, or to define the word "true" or "good," supports their suspicion that there is no interesting work to be done in this area. It might, of course, have turned out otherwise. People have, oddly enough, found something interesting to say about the essence of Force and the definition of "number." They might have found something interesting to say about the essence of Truth. But in fact they haven't. The history of attempts to do so, and of criticisms of such attempts, is roughly coextensive with the history of that literary genre we call "philosophy"—a genre founded by Plato. So pragmatists see the Platonic tradition as having outlived its usefulness. This does not mean that they have a new, non-Platonic set of answers to Platonic questions to offer, but rather that they do not think we should ask those questions anymore. When they suggest that we not ask questions about the nature of Truth and Goodness, they do not invoke a theory about the nature of reality or knowledge or man which says that "there is no such thing" as Truth or Goodness. Nor do they have a "relativistic" or "subjectivist" theory of Truth or Goodness. They would simply like to change the subject.
>
> (Rorty, 1982, p. xiv)

Simply change the subject! A good idea, in our opinion, but what exactly does it mean? First, what is the subject? For example, is it Truth or truth? Or the "literary genre," Philosophy (or philosophy), which birthed it? And does changing *it* mean holding on to *it* while radically (or not so radically) transforming *it*? Or does it mean getting rid of *it*? The idiom "changing the subject," in ordinary discourse, often means (is used) to move on to something else. But *what* else? And does what we move on to bear any non-trivial relationship to what we "gave up" on? Rorty does not consider such matters. By the time we finish reading the essays in *Consequences of Pragmatism*, we discover that Rorty has justified the resurrection of Philosophy (philosophy) on—what else?—pragmatic grounds: Philosophy (with a capital "P") or philosophy (with a small "p") is whatever professional philosophers do *at work* (Rorty, 1982, pp. 211–30).

Rorty's "revolution" (he is, he says, a "leftist"; Rorty, 1996b) is ultimately limited to "stamping out" a handful of capital letters in "key" words, among them "Expert" and "Philosophy." But the "cash value" in a real, philosophical, pragmatic, William Jamesean sense is unchanged. Philosophy, says Rorty, is "just what we philosophy professors do" (Rorty, 1982, p. 221). While Marx, Wittgenstein, and Vygotsky are, it seems to us, more than fully prepared to destroy (scientifically or otherwise) bourgeois ideology, philosophy, and psychology respectively, Rorty offers to lead a revolution in spelling conventions. Is that the conservative essence of postmodernism, or at least the pragmatic version of it? We are not advocating the taking up of arms here. We are, however, demanding scientific revolution in Kuhn's sense and beyond it. Our revolution must be directed against epistemology and its progeny, so-called scientific method. We must abandon even the pseudo-Marxist critical theoretic method of practice in favor of the post-postmodern *practice of method* (Holzman and Newman, 1979).

Gergen is by no means a vulgar pragmatist; nevertheless, in our view, he is still too much under the influence of pragmatism and epistemology to see (and do) what we are urging is necessary for postmodernism to become revolutionary. A case in point is the valuable exegesis on cognitivism he delivers in the recent *Realities and Relationships* (1994):

> The preceding arguments amplify the concerns of previous chapters in extending the range of impediments to a cognitive account of human knowledge. As they suggest, the cognitive orientation not only removes from scientific interest the vast share of human concerns, it is also unable to explain either the origin of its structures or the means by which cognition affects action. As I have suggested in earlier chapters, the major difficulties with the cognitive orientation in psychology derive from the more general problems inhering in a dualistic metaphysics. . . . When a real world is to be reflected by a mental world and the only means of determining the match is via the mental world, then the real world will always remain opaque and the relationship between the two inexplicable.
>
> Yet, as we have seen, there is another revolution taking place within the intellectual world, one that not only allows these hoary problems to be abandoned, but invites new forms of inquiry. It is a revolution that extends across the disciplines and which replaces the dualist epistemology

of a knowing mind confronting a material world with a *social episte-mology*. The locus of knowledge is no longer taken to be the individual mind but rather patterns of social relatedness.

(Gergen, 1994, pp. 128–9)

Gergen's "revolution" (really a reform) clearly is not directed *against* Epistemology (or Rorty's preferred "epistemology"), but against dualism and dualist epistemology. But what are "patterns of social relatedness"? Logically prior to that question, and of greater significance, is the following: to what frame of reference, paradigm, or linguistic convention should we appeal in determining what "patterns of social relatedness" mean? Presumably "patterns of social relatedness" are not postmodern or social constructionist candidates either for *sense data* or *thing-in-itself* status. To be sure, Gergen seems quite aware that he must maintain an epistemology in order for "patterns of social relatedness" to make any sense at all; hence "social epistemology." But is Gergen merely giving us a new vocabulary as opposed to Rorty's new grammatical style? Why not just call it "social dualism?" Obviously because the term "social dualism" is too blatant a paradox. But then "social epistemology" is hardly less so.

Science is, as a matter of social-cultural historical record, dualist. Arguably, it is even "social dualist!" Modern epistemology, the "handmaid" of science, is likewise dualist. The unwillingness to *revolutionize* (polemicize against) epistemology—to attempt merely to reform it by adding the adjective "social"—can therefore not eliminate the paradoxes of mentalism and cognitivism (no matter how much we "linguistify" matters). Nor can it provide us with the social ontological shift (the revolutionary activity) necessary either to create a new paradigm or to move *beyond* paradigmism (after all, still another epistemologized concept) altogether. In the final *analysis,* Gergen (like so many other postmodernists) is simply looking for another *way of seeing* things, another analysis but not another activity. In this way, postmodernists are characteristically entrapped in the epistemological machine.[4]

Gergen's "second revolution"—the "good" revolution—is not, of course, a revolutionary activity, still less a revolution, at all.[5] It is simply another way of seeing *things*—the things in question being not *substantively* individuated but rather "patterns of social relatedness." Notice that we said "substantively individuated" and not "formally individuated." The polemic of most postmodern psychologists is against individuated minds and/or identities but not against *identification* (sameness) itself. Hence, particular patterns of social relatedness are, presumably, identical or identifiable with (or not identical or identifiable with) others. The logic and epistemology of particularity and individuated identification are not fully challenged by most postmodernists because epistemology is never fully challenged. The social constructionists (and other postmodernists) are still searching for a view—a point of view. The move from cognition to description, like the move from individuated mind to social relatedness (including patterns thereof), does not free us from the paradoxes of dualism that are modern epistemology. For as long as *knowing*, as a complex alienated cultural organization of a varied set of institutionalized human activities, is hegemonic, *dualism* remains dominant. There is no way of knowing which is non-dualistic, so far as we can tell. No doubt Gergen's offer of *détente* with other non-constructionist social psychologists is well intended. But the preconditions for such a *détente* must include a readiness on the part of all (the social psychological community and beyond) to give up knowing, even if they do not assent to the method of social constructionism.

BUT CAN WE REALLY GET BEYOND MODERNISM (THAT IS, KNOWING)?

Can we really give up knowing? And, you may reasonably (and philosophically) ask, "How would we know?" This may appear to be still another quasi-self-referential paradox. But it isn't. For there is an answer—a non-paradoxical answer—to the question, "How would we know?" We wouldn't. Yet the force of modern *epistemologism* is so great that many find it almost inconceivable to accept such an answer. If something is, mustn't it be at least possible to know that it is? This, of course, is the voice of epistemologized modernism speaking. It is the typical dualistic reduction of ontology to epistemology—the insistence of science and modernism that everything (worthy or not worthy of a name or a description) must be knowable. But if a challenge to that claim is successful, it will not be *known*, we think. It will "merely" be performed.

Still the question "Can we give up knowing?" remains. This question *can* be answered, even if we do not know the answer. But in answering (or, at a minimum, exploring) it, we recommend doing so in a way which gives up our deep-rooted modernist need to know that we have done so. Such an exploration entails abandoning not simply the troublesome substantive conceptual elements of epistemology (mind, self, truth, and company) but epistemology itself as a form of life. Consequently, we must analytically eliminate the substantive myths of modernism (among them the individuated mind, the individuated self, and individuated cognitions) only as we deconstructively/reconstructively (socially activistically) eliminate the mythic ancient (Aristotelian) *forms* of modernism (explaining, describing, interpreting, identifying, and knowing). The perfectly reasonable question, however, remains: *Can we do this?* Can we stop knowing?

At this point in the discussion, the normative and the descriptive virtually merge. *Can* we stop knowing and *should* we stop knowing seem almost inseparable in a still modern environment which identifies (implicitly if not explicitly) knowing (or knowledge) with both the Good and the Real. Such is our Platonic heritage, silly and sad even dressed up in modern scientific (and even postmodern) garb. Isn't giving up or stopping knowing a violently reactionary act? What, some may ask, would become of all that is known were we to give up knowing? Wouldn't postmodernism, if "enacted," lead us back into the dark ages? Isn't enlightenment an absolute, positive species value?

Let us point out that if we were to "give up" knowing it would not involve "giving up" all that is known. Indeed, the coming into dominance of knowing (modern science and enlightenment, epistemology and its related values) did not (for better or for worse) entail the elimination of "not knowing" (religion and/or ideology). Obviously, the Church inquisitors and fathers who insisted on Galileo's recantation thought quite reasonably that it might. They were mistaken. They underestimated the power of religion (and the malleability of the bourgeoisie). Knowing has a long tradition of living side by side with not knowing.[6] Hence there is good reason to believe that post-postmodern secularist not knowing (performing) could live side by side with what is known. The bridges built by modern science and technology (with the help of workers!) will not fall if postmodernism is "enacted;" neither will the books and memories of practices used in building such bridges. Bridges will continue to be built in the post-postmodern age much as faith found a place in the age of doubt.

It is not the success of science or dualistic epistemology that is being challenged; it is the tautological equation of knowledge and progress. Surely the "evidence" for that claim has become questionable here in the twentieth century. For while extraordinary socio-technological advances have been plentiful, species development has been, in the opinion of many, conspicuously missing. Most have "analyzed" these matters in terms of the conceptual shortcomings in the "idea of progress" or in the "idea of development." But to us it is the *practice* of knowing which must be questioned and, ultimately, "overthrown."

Yet notwithstanding the bleak realities of the twentieth century— despite the persistence of straight-out fascism and other forms of reaction worldwide, despite the failure of modern science and technology to produce even a glimmer of the expected utopia or even, more locally, simply a great (or, indeed, even a better) society—it remains the prevailing view that knowledge, and therefore science, and thus knowing, form the road to a better world. Obviously, there are forces on the fast expanding ideological right who believe otherwise. But traditional modern ideological liberalism (in academia as in politics) appears increasingly to define itself in knee-jerk reaction to the radical right. Thus it typically overidentifies with modern science even, ironically, as science itself moves more and more to the right. Indeed, as we shall explore in Chapter 4, one of the more important reasons for abandoning the left–center–right social-political paradigm and its deadly liberal offshoot, identity politics, is that it is a fundamentally (epistemologically) dualistic and reactive model; left, center, and right simply do not provide the necessary categories of discernment (of any kind) in contemporary, complex, pluralistic, post-modern, world historical society.

Many in the liberal (or pseudo-liberal) establishment (including the "very old left") defend science, knowledge, and knowing and, indeed, function specifically to halt the dread disease of postmodernism in favor of a kind of new-age pragmatism. In warning of the dangers to the tradition of American liberal education lurking in postmodernism, Louis Menand, a professor of humanities at the City University of New York, comments:

> The threats these two elements—the new emphasis [of the postmodernists] on the fundamentally political character of education and scholarship, and anti-essentialism—pose to the future of liberal arts education are not primarily philosophical. The problem is, to put it crudely, a marketing one. Public universities are heavily subsidized. Private universities are very expensive. If we say universities are places in which academics possess knowledge about the world—indeed, in many respects, possess a monopoly on knowledge about the world—and they will impart this knowledge to you for a fee, which you may pay in taxes or tuition, then you can decide that the knowledge is worth acquiring and pay to support the knowers. But if we say universities are places in which academics, each according to his or her political bent, come up with competing interpretations of texts, none of which can claim to be true in any ultimate sense, and people can go to hear these academics argue with one another about the interpretations and learn how to argue about them, too, I think people will wonder what they are paying for.
>
> (Menand, 1995, p. 143)

In his final paragraph, Menand brings his neo-liberal pragmatism to its crude conclusion:

> It has taken a long time for academic postmodernists to see that the ultimate target of their criticism of traditional forms of knowledge is the institution in which they work, and that postmodernist thinking does not merely redefine that institution philosophically, but also undermines its very structure. Seeing this much, contemporary academics ought to see as well how serendipitously this undermining meets the interests of those who are not friends of liberal arts education and scholarship, particularly when the latter are subsidized by public money. Administrators financially answerable to state legislatures would love to melt down the disciplines, since that would allow them to deploy faculty more efficiently, and the claim that disciplinarity represents a factitious organization of knowledge is as good an excuse as any. Further, there are many people who would love, on political as well as financial grounds, to dispense with the protection of academic freedom. For these people, too, the argument that disinterestedness is a false standard serves their purposes very nicely. My analysis may sound like an expression of nostalgia for the old justifications for academic study. It is not. It is only a note of warning about the uses to which some of the new justifications can be put.
>
> (Menand, 1995, p. 144)

So, says Menand, if philosophy and liberal education in general are what philosophers and liberal educators (respectively) do at work, then to question the validity of their intellectual project in so fundamental a way as postmodernism does is to question the legitimacy of that work and, thereby, to render oneself useable by the forces of reaction.

Such is the unscientific inquisition-style attack of "old guard" liberalism against what grand inquisitors Gross, Levitt, and Lewis label "The Academic Left," as we saw in Chapter 1 (Gross and Levitt, 1994; Gross *et al.*, 1996). Of course, Menand is right. Postmodernists with academic positions, if they are honest, run the risk of "biting the hand that feeds them." So, indeed, do medical biologists who might be hot on the trail of an inexpensive cure for cancer. Should we urge them to stop? Presumably, Menand might be inclined to say yes. Of course, he might argue that a cure for cancer still leaves work for medical biologists, while the postmodern critique undermines the humanities and social sciences altogether. And what if medical biology found a cure for all disease? Human labeling, it has been argued, is a serious modern disease; some would even say, or suggest, that modern psychology itself is a disease.[7] We think the proper name for the relevant disease is epistemology. Postmodernism is, or can be, a "cure" for all these "diseases." Menand and other neo-liberal pragmatists are correct in recognizing that the social implications of postmodernism are profound. If knowing itself is fully or even partially invalid, then the current institutionalized structure and practice of knowing-related activities (including the college and university system, as well as the rest of our educational system) should be thoroughly deconstructed and reorganized.

The academic postmodernists are under severe pragmatic pressure to "not go all the way." Not surprisingly, they have complied. It is not a bad rule of thumb to look to your severest critics to discover the most extreme implications of your positions. In this respect Menand is useful. Postmodernism is not simply "the academic left," a term used disparagingly by "postmodern red-baiters" who sound—to those of us who have been around long enough—remarkably like "sold out old leftists" of another age, snarling the words "new left." Postmodernism is not "left" at all. Neither is it center or right. Postmodernism is, rather, scientifically revolutionary in its potential. But to realize that potential it must become wholeheartedly (revolutionarily) opposed to epistemology; it must be ready, willing and able to abandon knowing itself. Once again, the question arises: can that be done? The role of the postmodern theoreticians, it seems to us, is to give up *point-of-viewism* (including especially their own) altogether in favor of a new activity which is not to be known but to be engaged in. The postmodern revolution will not be known at all; indeed, it will be unknowable (neither true nor false); it will, instead, be *performed*.

To accomplish their particular task (to perform their role), the postmodern theoreticians will need to move at once but not alone beyond petty pragmatism and beyond deadly, moribund epistemology. To do so they must be ready to take on not simply individuated (self) identity, but identity (formal identity) itself. For as pernicious as self may be, it is *sameness* that has always served as the stickiest ideological glue of modernism, epistemology, and knowing. We will not know if this can be or has been done. Still, there are important steps to be (perhaps they have already been) taken.

IT'S ALL THE SAMENESS TO US[8]

An orthodox modern analytical philosophical formulation[9] of the classical Greek (Plato's) definition of knowing might look something like this:

   x knows y if and only if

1   x believes y
2   x has good reason to believe y
3   y is true.

Countless critical and not so critical philosophical words have been written over the millennia about each and every aspect of this definition/explication. What is believing? What kind of a thing believes— what is x in (1)? What kind of a thing is believed—what is y in (1)? What are good reasons? Indeed, what are reasons? What kind of a thing "has" reasons—what is x in (2)? What kind of a thing has "good reasons to be believed"—what is y in (2)? What is truth? What kind of a thing is true— what is y in (3)? And so on.

   Yet it is somehow the very ("thingified") form of this explication which many postmodernists have found at once most troublesome and, in certain ways, inscrutable. The form itself appears to assert that knowing is a *relationship* between a knower (x) and something which is known (y). But while knowing, on this traditional account, *is a relationship*, relationship is rooted in dualism, a worldview of endless and varied particulars (individuals) which are interconnected in complex ways by particular abstractions called relationships. The strict ontological monism of the early Greek thinkers (and the need to recognize both Parmenidean *permanence* and Heraclitean *transitoriness*) was resolved by Plato and his student/critic Aristotle with a dualism which integrates both. For while the *knower* (the subject) might always be mistaken (a victim of illusion, as Heraclitus thought), the *known* (the object of knowledge) must be true (an unchanging totality, as Parmenides thought).

   The substantive (ontological), although in many cases trivial, investigations of Earth's basic material by the so-called pre-Socratics from Thales (water) to Democritus (atoms) are reconciled *epistemologically* by Plato and Aristotle. While the theories of these two philosophical giants are complex, two words can be used to express the basic conceptual idea behind them: epistemological dualism. Thus understood, epistemological dualism is itself a conceptual paradigm whose function was (as it still is) to account for intrinsically flawed *knowers* (human beings) somehow having access to perfect ideas, that is, *Truth*. The Platonic explication of *knowing* gives full expression in both its content and its form to the paradigm of epistemological dualism. It is this dualism which quite reasonably most agitates and irritates the postmodernists.

But while the individuated knower, *x*, and the abstraction Truth (or true proposition or accurate description or fact), *y*, are troublesome enough in themselves, it is the ancient philosophical notion of *relatedness* (relationship, relationality) which to us is at the root of the dualistic dilemma and at the heart of the epistemological paradox. Relationships (in both the ancient and modern dualistic sense) and relationality, it seems to us, are as much members of the family of concepts which constitute dualism as *individuated* self and *abstract* truth.

Perhaps even more than self and truth, relationality is fundamental to the Greek–modern dualistic conceptual solution. Subjects and predicates live symbiotically. And it is the way they live which must be uprooted, lest they return in ever new paradoxical forms. Thus what is most problematic in the simple declarative "The book is red" is neither books (or a particular book) nor redness, but "is." For what is "is," conceptually, other than a technique for "relating" the "unrelatable?" While the "is" of *predication* and the "is" of *identity* are traditionally distinguished for analytical purposes, the two "to be's" are, no doubt, themselves closely related. The point here is not that the sentence "The book is red" is obscure in its conventional usage, but that the standard explications of such sentences (or utterances) introduce dualistic conceptions which, taken together with the conceptual underpinnings of other perfectly comprehensible sentences (their usage in themselves) of a given language (say English), permeate the culture in the form of a worldview. Such a worldview comes to inform, to varying degrees and in subtle but significant ways, our understanding of the meaning of the linguistic discourse of a language community taken as a whole. Thus, while the understanding of each sentence or utterance (its usage), taken in itself, might not appear to present any serious problems, the underlying conceptions (sometimes correctly explicated by philosophers, psychologists, and linguists) can produce, over time, a systematic distortion of great cultural significance.

Vygotsky's writings about speaking as *completing* thinking (rather than expressing it) are most helpful here.

> The structure of speech is not a simple mirror image of the structure of thought. It cannot, therefore, be placed on thought like clothes off a rack. Speech does not merely serve as the expression of developed thought. Thought is restructured as it is transformed into speech. It is not expressed but completed in the word. Therefore, precisely because of the contrasting directions of movement, the development of the internal and external aspects of speech form a true unity.
>
> (Vygotsky, 1987, p. 251)

Moving to language, pure and simple, does not eliminate cognition (although it might eliminate cognitions). If Vygotsky is correct (and we believe he is), thinking and speaking (a language) form a unity. The subtle presuppositions discussed above enter the unity thinking/speaking at the thinking end, if you will, but given the unity, they permeate the whole (that is, including the speaking). This is the case even if the speaking of a particular sentence in a given context at a given moment is, in itself, utterly clear *in its usage*.

We are suggesting that the ancient Greek conception of relation (albeit in modern, perhaps even postmodern guise) lives on as a *formal* dualistic posit (thingification) even in the work of many postmodernists who have thoroughly rejected self, truth, and . . . dualism! In effect, they have tried to separate "dualism" from "epistemological." But *epistemological dualism* (including its inseparability from relationality and identity) is, it seems to us, indivisible.

What, then, is a relation or a relationship or relationality, or even "patterns of social relatedness?" And what is its/their relationship to identity and/or sameness? A relation (or a relationship or a "relatedness") is a conceptual tool used, effectively, to divide an indivisible manifold (in our case, the world in all its unified complexity) into an infinitude of particular relational connections to (descriptions of) either other particulars (for example, *Sarah's bicycle is to the immediate right of Joe's bicycle*) or abstractions, such as a class (for example, *Sarah's bicycle is red*).

The division of the indivisible process world into varied relational characterizations has, undoubtedly, been the necessary conceptual, structural (logical/syntactical) accompaniment to knowledge of (knowing) the (physical) world. Modern science (the epitome of knowing in Western culture) can be understood as a critical refinement of this relational form of knowing, made possible by observation and mathematicalization, and the development of technology, commerce, and industry necessary for its pragmatic success. Modernism (including modern science) never challenges this basic relational model of knowing, since it is its logical/methodological subtext.

The relationally divided world, in turn, rests on (more accurately, is inseparable from) the fundamental conception of identity or sameness. Neither a Parmenidean, monistically viewed world nor a constantly in flux Heraclitean world requires the notion of identity or sameness, for in the former there is only one thing (everything) and in the latter things are insufficiently stable ever to be identified *as things*. No. Sameness and identity are not required unless and until there are discernible (and varied) *things*, that is, until the world (actually its description) is epistemologically relationalized and particularized. Moreover, once the world is relationalized and particularized, sameness is absolutely necessary to "bring back together" a "now logically and linguistically divided" world. Things and relations "live by taking in each other's wash."

Relationally structured thought and language are, as has often been pointed out, best understood in terms of mapping. A map is an effectively divided "picture" of an indivisible piece of worldly space. If the map and the space were the same there would be no value in the map, and/or the space would be rather small. The danger is that the relationships holding among elements of the map (primarily attributional and identificational relationships) will become confused with the elements of the space which the map is supposed to represent. Children frequently think that Albany is an inch and a half away from New York City because, on the New York State map, the word "Albany" is an inch and a half away from the words "New York City." Many adults think that the west is always to their left because it appears that way on the map when it is held right side up.

The endless and complex relationships developed for the "thought and language" map(s) of our culture are not infrequently confused with the world (the "reality") which they purport to represent. Indeed, it could be argued that "reality" is itself nothing more than a metamap term used to distinguish the map from what it ostensibly maps. The world is not "reality"—it is all that the world is. The most fundamental of possible map-to-mapped confusions centers on the twin conceptions of *relation* and *particularization*. For in the world there are no *things*. Nor are there *relations* between them. So far as we can tell, there are not even "patterns of social relatedness." Things, relations, and "patterns of social relatedness" are not in the world; they are required to *know* things about the world. They are mapping terms, epistemological vocabulary words. This is not, of course, to deny the *materiality* (or, as we prefer to call it, the *historicality*) of the world. It is, rather, to insist on the unbridgeable gap between mapped and map and, in doing so, to question the efficacy of mapping for any given area—or kind of understanding—of the world. Knowledge of nature has, no doubt, been profoundly advanced by scientific mapping. The understanding of human subjectivity, we would argue, has not. But then there is no reason why it should have been.

It is the recognition of mapping as simply a particular form of understanding—knowing—which postmodernism, we think, must further advance. There is nothing sacred about the knowing form of understanding. Quine (1963) speaks of "the myth of physical objects [being] epistemologically superior to most." But what of the myth of epistemology itself? And what of the myths—relations, particulars, sameness, and identity among them—which formally comprise epistemology? Social epistemology, relationality, and/or "patterns of social relatedness" are contradictions in terms. They are, as we understand them, a way of abandoning traditional scientific psychology while holding on to traditional knowing (epistemology).

It is only through ridding ourselves of knowing that we can rid ourselves of self (identity) and truth, for the "natural" abode of self and truth in Western culture is in the sentence form "*x* knows *y*." Only when knowing is rejected will self and truth lose their social communicative function. Efforts to preserve knowing and eliminate self and truth will produce (and have produced) alternatives to self and truth (for example, narratives and descriptions), which leave us with the same paradoxicality with which we began, since it is knowing (and relationality) that generate and sustain the contradictions of epistemological dualism. And it is the "is" of both identification and predication which is at the linguistic core of our relationally overdetermined conceptual framework. Again, what makes "The book is red" (or "The morning star is the evening star") conceptually troublesome is the relationality of the "is"—not the difficulty in figuring out what it is to which "the book" or "red" *corresponds*. For while the words "book" and "red" are easily recognized as mapping terms, "is" is frequently treated as a term which "travels back and forth" between the map and the mapped. Some would argue that "is" is ontological in its very essence; "common sense" tells us that whether it means "to be," "to be a property of," or "to be the same as," or—from a set theoretic vantage point, "to be a member of,"—"is" is not the name or description of something, but the existential *state of everything*. So, for example, in the notation of predicate logic, existence is indicated not by a variable, predicate, or even a constant, but by an extra-formulaic existential quantifier $[(\exists\ x)\ \_\_\ x\ \_\_]$ (to be read "There exists something such that . . . ". But "is" is no more *of the world* than "tyrannosaurus rex." It is no less a mapping term than "Buenos Aires." It lives, together with *selves* and *truths* and *relationship*, in the map, not the mapped. "Is" is a most critical element of *epistemological dualism*.

A revolutionary shift beyond modernism, in our view, must move beyond relationality; beyond sameness and/or predication, beyond "is-ness," beyond materialism, idealism, and the foolish anachronistic debates between idealists and materialists, relativists and anti-relativists, *ad infinitum*, and, perhaps most fundamentally, beyond epistemology altogether—beyond knowing. In our opinion, there is far too much at stake (practically speaking, nothing less than continued human development) for postmodernists to abandon bad scientific psychology only to reinvent bad epistemologically overdetermined philosophy.

THE CHARGE OF RELATIVISM

Perhaps the most important observation about relativism is that it is relative, that is, it is a term which makes sense only relative to some notion of truth, accuracy, correctness, or the like. Perhaps the second most important observation is that this first observation is not so frequently made. Why? We think it is because even those who seek to "give up" truth wish to hold on to some form of knowing which, in turn, demands some form of truth. However, any polemic against truth which does not also abandon knowing is, for us, subject to critique. In making clearer what we mean, it will be useful, we hope, to consider a contemporary case study of a polemic against such a polemic and, thereby, to understand better both the virtues and the failings of such polemics and metapolemics.

Accordingly, we consider in some detail here the charge of relativism leveled against social constructionism by Jost and Hardin (1996). In "The practical turn in psychology: Marx and Wittgenstein as social materialists" (written as a commentary on Ian Parker's 1996 critique of Wittgenstein), Jost and Hardin attempt to "rescue" Wittgenstein from classification as a "social constructionist" and, thereby, as a relativist. In our opinion, however, they thereby seriously misrepresent Wittgenstein (and Marx) as "pro-truth" and "pro-epistemology." Their dialogue—a reasonable example (case study) of contemporary critical, postmodern, and/or Marxist psychologists discussing (debating) philosophical issues—helps us to take still another look (in context) at the "godfathers" Marx, Vygotsky, and Wittgenstein, and their joint effort to create an anti-epistemic, activity-theoretic mode of understanding. To complete (in Vygotsky's sense) this discussion, we will examine (we hope in an appropriately non-epistemic way) the look of an activity-based, performatory approach to understanding, in particular, human subjectivity and, therefore, human understanding itself by focusing on our own developmental social therapy research.

Early on, Jost and Hardin say the following:

> Although few if any commentators have come right out and claimed that Wittgenstein *is* a "social constructionist," many have implied very close connections between Wittgenstein and social constructionism.... Gergen ..., for example, writes that "social constructionism is a congenial companion to Wittgenstein's ... conception of meaning as a derivative of social use" ..., an assumption that is made also by Parker. If social constructionism is considered to be a theory of the person as a product of ongoing social relations ..., then perhaps Marx and Wittgenstein may be regarded as social constructionists in this sense.
>
> More often than not, however, the term "social constructionism" is used to describe an epistemological position that is relativistic and skeptical about the possibility of objective knowledge (e.g., Gergen, 1994).
>
> (Jost and Hardin, 1996, pp. 388–9)

And a few lines later:

> We believe that the term "social materialist" is a better characterization of the views of Marx and Wittgenstein, because they do not make the epistemological assumption that social reality more than physical reality is a mere "construction" of the human mind ..., an assumption that may be identified as idealist in the sense outlined above .... For Marx and Wittgenstein *the social is as real as anything*; it is the primary substance of human life, the principal foundation of ideas and action. This is different from saying that social factors are reducible to economic conditions alone, as Harré ... takes the "socio-materialist" position to imply. Rather,

we are arguing that according to Marx and Wittgenstein social life *is* one of the most important material bases of human experience.

(Jost and Hardin, 1996, p. 389, emphasis added)

Jost and Hardin go on to criticize Parker for calling Wittgenstein a relativist; they consider Parker's critique to be due to "a common misreading among psychologists who draw on Wittgensteinian themes . . . to buttress relativistic claims" (p. 387). For example, they fault Gergen for using Wittgenstein to support the claim that "any given action may be subject to multiple interpretations, no one of which is objectively superior" (p. 388). Jost and Hardin then seek to show how much of an anti-relativist Wittgenstein really is by pointing to his comment that "it is possible to 'compare our system of knowledge' to someone else's and to conclude that 'theirs is evidently the poorer one by far" (p. 388).

What we find most interesting in all of this is what Gergen, Parker, and Jost and Hardin share with each other but not, in our opinion, with Wittgenstein and Marx (or with Vygotsky). For in different ways the former all insist on the epistemological framework; they are locked in the epistemological machine, committed to knowing. In the name of Marx (for one), Jost and Hardin take offense at Gergen's "relativistic" remark: "Any given action may be subject to multiple interpretations, no one of which is objectively superior." Yet it was Karl Marx who insisted that the point is not to interpret the world, but to change it! It is interpretation itself, not the multiplicity of interpretations, which we think Marx would find objectionable. Jost and Hardin must be saying something like: Insofar as Marx does see the point of interpretation, he regards some as better and some as worse. (They offer an analogous argument on behalf of Wittgenstein.) But isn't this something like saying: Insofar as an atheist believes in God, he prefers the Judeo-Christian one? Jost and Hardin are right, in our opinion, to point out Gergen's possible misreading of Wittgenstein (in particular, the so-called meaning–use equation), but if Jost and Hardin can subtextually use the "insofar as" argument to support Marx, then why can't social constructionists like Gergen use the "insofar as" argument to support themselves? Marx's comment on interpretation and change, after all, was no idle observation but, in our opinion, the essence of his life's work— politically and intellectually.

No doubt Gergen could argue that sentences of the form "*x* is a better explanation than *y*" or "*x* is a more accurate description of *e* than *y*" are not true by virtue of something called a correspondence with something called reality (or a portion thereof), but are as much socially constructed as any other piece of language. As such, Gergen might continue, these two sentences are more acceptable than others, such as "*y* is a better explanation than *x*," where sentences including the phrase "more acceptable than" are themselves more or less acceptable but still remain comprehensible only as social constructions, not as truth or acceptability in the classical modern sense. After all, it is the modern sense of truth that social constructionists are challenging. The social may well be " . . . as real as anything." But surely Gergen would (or could) insist that this is the very issue; that is, how real is anything?

In a letter to us (part of a collegial correspondence), Jost writes:

> It seems to me that the burden is on people who seek to deconstruct "truth" to spell out exactly what criteria for "better descriptions," etc. exist, if they are committed to avoiding relativism. In the end, I am unwilling to grant that there are no criteria for assessing accuracy with regard to versions of reality (though I admit that the issue may be diffi-cult and controversial at times).
>
> To say that some descriptions of reality are more accurate than others is not so different from what previous generations meant by "truth." I guess this is "truth" with a small "t" avoiding metaphysical and religious aspects. It's a de-mystified version of truth. I think that science, along with history, reason, art, and other things, can help us in our pursuit of more accurate and better visions of social reality.
>
> (Jost, 1996, personal communication)

But Marx, Wittgenstein, and Vygotsky are concerned with much more than a Rorty-ish changing of capital letters to small letters. Indeed, they are all interested in posing a revolutionary challenge to conceptual frameworks and, thereby, to knowing itself as conceptually and modernistically under-stood. It is worth noting that in the excerpt from Wittgenstein to which Jost and Hardin appeal it is not particular truths but "systems of knowledge" that Wittgenstein says can be adjudged better or worse. Moreover, even such judgments are subject to Quinean pragmatic and/or Gergenesque social constructionist deconstruction; there is, in the case of "systems of knowl-edge" (as opposed to isolated single truths), less likely to be another system (a metasystem) to which one appeals in judging them "true" or "false."

What we see as common to Marx and Wittgenstein is not so much that they agree on the answers to the questions and issues Jost and Hardin raise (such as what is real), but that they are not particularly interested in these issues because they reject the very categories in which they are posed. "The social is as real as anything," while a commitment to activity (as we use the term) is not a commitment to objectivity and/or truth. Both Marx and Wittgenstein attempt to go beyond truth-referential, identity-based episte-mology, beyond knowing, to something more activity-based.

The strategic similarities of Marx and Wittgenstein can be seen in the following two statements:

> This method of approach is not devoid of premises. It starts out from the real premises and does not abandon them for a moment. Its premises are men, not in any fantastic isolation and rigidity, but in their actual, empiri-cally perceptible process of development under definite conditions. As

soon as this active life-process is described, history ceases to be a collection of dead facts as it is with the empiricists (themselves still abstract), or an imagined activity of imagined subjects, as with the idealists.

(Marx and Engels, 1973, pp. 47–8)

But how many kinds of sentences are there? Say assertion, question, and command?—There are countless kinds: countless different kinds of use of what we call "symbols," "words," "sentences." And this multiplicity is not something fixed, given once and for all; but new types of language, new language-games, as we may say, come into existence, and others become obsolete and get forgotten. (We can get a rough picture of this from the changes in mathematics.) Here the term "language-game" is meant to bring into prominence the fact that the speaking of language is part of an activity, or of a form of life.

(Wittgenstein, *PI,* 1953, p. 11)

For Marx (who, in our opinion, must always be taken literally), the premises are not propositional truths (nor, therefore, are the conclusions) but the activity of the human laborer; for Wittgenstein it is the activity of human speaking which must be exposed, not the truth or even the usage, in order to demystify essentialistic, foundationalistic, truth-dominated epistemology and metaphysics. Marx's conception of revolutionary activity is what connects him and Wittgenstein (and Vygotsky). Social constructionism in particular and postmodernism in general do well to reject truth, objectivity, correspondence, relationality—epistemology—altogether, while ontologically "adding" activity (as in relational activity) to the meaning of social.

But perhaps it is ultimately Vygotsky, the psychologist godfather, who is most helpful on these matters. It is in his experimentally supported characterizations of the "relationship" (actually a unity, a non-relationship) between thought and word (thinking and speaking) that we come to see, perhaps, the origins of epistemological dualism. We find Vygotsky's thinking on the matter consistent with Wittgenstein's more speculative (therapeutic) study of language games as exposing activity and forms of life as well as with Marx's more traditionally philosophical commitment to anti-interpretive revolutionary activity. Vygotsky's "discovery" of the zone of proximal development (zpd) grows concretely out of his anti-expressionist understanding of thinking and speaking. He says:

The relationship of thought to word is not a thing but a process, a movement from thought to word and from word to thought. . . . Thought is not expressed but completed in the word. We can, therefore, speak of the establishment (i.e., the unity of being and nonbeing) of thought in the word. Any thought strives to unify, to establish a relationship between one thing and another. Any thought has movement. It unfolds.

(Vygotsky, 1987, p. 250)

And in an oft-quoted (and, we believe, oft-misunderstood) characterization:

Every function in the child's cultural development appears twice: first on the social level and later, on the individual level; first between people (interpsychological), and then inside the child (intrapsychological). This applies equally to all voluntary attention, to logical memory, and to the formation of concepts. All the higher mental functions originate as actual relations between people.

(Vygotsky, 1987, p. 57)

Such an anti-expressionist, completist theory of thinking/speaking makes clear (to us, at least) that epistemological dualism is not a discovery of the "true" relationship between knower and known but a systematic misrepresentation of the actuality of human development (and learning). For the unity of thinking/speaking and the "two planedness" of inter-subjective and intra-subjective do not require (indeed, do not allow) relational unification. Dualism is not "how the world is" but a profound mischaracterization (however ingenious) of how we learn (how the world is) and develop. This Platonic epistemological misunderstanding, further transformed and "thingified" ("brought down to earth") by Aristotelian logic, is what became the methodological basis (subtext) for modern science (and, through modern science, for modernism in general).

To be sure, it was a most valuable (and remarkable) error. For it facilitated the "objective" relational study of nature with its accompanying technological discoveries and inventions, and thereby of human progress, almost beyond belief. Still, it derived from a thoroughgoing misunderstanding of human learning/development itself. No surprise, then, that when this mistaken metaview of human subjectivity (epistemological dualism or knowing) is applied to the study of subjectivity itself (so-called scientific psychology), modernism is thereby thoroughly exposed. For it is the non-relational unity of human development—thinking/speaking as process and activity—that produces relationality; it is not relationality as an ontic (and, in Plato's case, cosmological) fact that produces our understanding of understanding and other subjective features of the universe. This is neither an affirmation of idealism nor a denial of materialism. It is, rather, an anti-epistemological, revolutionary practice of method. Marx puts the matter this way:

The question whether objective truth can be attributed to human thinking is not a question of theory but is a practical question. Man must prove the truth, i.e., the reality and power, the this-sided-ness of his thinking in practice. The dispute over the reality or non-reality of thinking that is isolated from practice is a purely scholastic question.

(Marx, 1973, p. 121)

But for Marx a practical question is a practical-critical question, a question of revolutionary activity.[10] And this is not Marx denying his "materialism" (nineteenth-century language for a nineteenth-century thinker); it is Marx affirming his dialectical method. Even if we still remain interested in labeling, Marx was not a materialist who happened to be dialectical; he was a dialectical materialist.

So, too, was Vygotsky. His discovery of the zone of proximal development offers us much more than a better understanding of epistemological dualism; it provides us with a general framework for going beyond modern knowing altogether to a postmodern activity-theoretic form of understanding. Most neo-Vygotskyians reject this kind of understanding of understanding and/or of the zpd as a paradigmatic revolutionary breakthrough largely because they have no interest in "giving up" knowing (see, for example, Lave and Wenger, 1991; Moll, 1990; Newman *et al.*, 1989; Rogoff, 1990; Wertsch, 1991). Thus the reformist neo-Vygotskians, like the reformist neo-Marxists and neo-Wittgensteinians, seek to "epistomologize" and, thereby, to de-revolutionize the three godfathers.

To us, however, Vygotsky's discovery of the zpd is nothing less than Galilean in its significance. It is the discovery of a new ontological unit (actually a revolutionary unity) specific to and necessary for understanding—not knowing—human life activity (Newman and Holzman, 1993, 1996). Over almost a quarter of a century of Vygotskian-based social therapeutic group work with thousands of people, the two of us with the rest of our development community have explored the value and nature of an anti-epistemological approach. The activity of the social therapy group does not consist in expressing what is going on "in one's head" (or anyone else's head, for that matter), but in completing in conversation the unity that is thinking (feeling)/speaking. Such completion is open to all in the group (not simply the thinker/feeler who "begins" the process). The unit of non-epistemic "study" (it is not study in the modern scientific sense at all) is not the deeper private significance of anyone's inner self but an activity-theoretic understanding—the collective creation (the activity) of ever-changing conversations, or forms of life. Freed from the constraints of epistemological knowing of a mythological inner life, the social therapeutic approach allows us to continuously create new social unities (new forms of life) which serve to make the "presenting problem" (in the language of orthodox clinical psychology) "vanish" (in Wittgenstein's language). For the inner "problem," thus activistically understood, does not cry out for an epistemic "solution." The endless subtextual epistemological mental presuppositions (self, unconscious motives, drives, inner mental life, depth, and the rest) give way (vanish with the "problem") in the creative context of conversation.

To assist people in such creative conversation we appeal to a common enough human capacity that, for most of us, has atrophied after the first few years of childhood: the ability to perform. Vygotsky's completionist tool-and-result methodology (as opposed to a traditional, causal, instrumentalist tool-for-result approach) allows him to recognize the critical importance of imitation in human development and, thereby, of learning which leads development—to him, the only kind of learning worthy of the name (Vygotsky, 1978, 1987). Imitation (which Vygotsky takes pains to distinguish from mere mimicry) is that quite extraordinary capacity of our species to be (to perform as) other ("a head taller," as he said) than who we are. To be other than who we are is, arguably, the essence (not of the human being who, for us, has no essence) but of the human social activity. (We discuss the developmental significance of performance and our practice of method more extensively in Chapter 5.) And, of course, it violates every rule of the epistemological, logical, and traditional methodological paradigm.

Bishop Butler's observation, "Everything is what it is and not another thing" has guided modern thinking, including modern thinking about thinking, since the fifteenth century when he made it. But it is that very kind of thinking, that profound epistemological error (actually the error that is epistemology), to which Vygotsky and his modern revolutionary partners, Marx and Wittgenstein, stand firmly opposed. Postmodernism will not, to our way of performing (not of thinking), be "post" anything until this is understood (not known) completively.

3 Radically reforming modern epistemology

Since the earliest days (the late 1960s) of what we have come to refer to as our developing development community, we have been sensitive to the difference, in practice, between reform and revolution. Furthermore, we have been mindful that our decision to engage in revolutionary practice brings with it an obligation to look very seriously at any and all sincere reform efforts, since reform is obviously the preferred (as the more humanly conservative and therefore least disruptive and destructive) route to qualitative social change. We are talking here of our political practice and posture. While, of course, we are not and do not seek to be exempt from societal pressures and pulls toward (and from) such conservatism—for example, to rescue psychology from its crisis rather than to do it in—our research base (its location and activity) is specifically designed (tool-and-result-ishly) to support a revolutionary posture in a way that state-sanctioned institutional bases do not.

As we have noted in Chapter 1 and elsewhere (Holzman, 1986, 1995b, 1996; Holzman and Newman, 1979; Newman, 1977; Newman and Holzman, 1996), the environment in which social critique is conducted is not merely a context in which the work gets done nor an adjunct to it, but is integral to its meaning, that is, its meaning-making. Our "research laboratory" (our meaning-making community) is a continuously evolving, self-conscious activity of creating an environment that is not overdetermined by epistemology and the varied institutional arrangements that perpetuate it.

That there are many people who are attempting radically to reform modern epistemology—to rid it of its most obvious methodological flaws, its subtle and not so subtle constraints on human creativity and invention, and its insidious elitism and process of marginalization—seems completely reasonable to us, even desirable. However, it is not what we are doing nor what we have done—unless you insist a priori that what we have done can only be *known* from an institutionalized, epistemologized point of view. You are probably right. But still, why would you insist upon it?

Our study of and involvement with reformist social critique has been, over twenty years, undertaken from (as) this revolutionary practice. Exploiting (practicing) the dialectic between the continuous creation of (developing) the development community and our engagement with more traditionally located social critics has been invaluable to us in sharpening our formulations and expanding our work both quantitatively and qualitatively. (We hope it has been of some use to our "reformist" colleagues.) This book is a report from our laboratory. In this chapter we continue to build our case against epistemology—for the end of knowing and the rediscovery of development—through the work of examining what we take to be the contributions and the limitations of some of the most significant attempts to critique modern epistemology and create something beyond it.

Once again, Gergen helps us begin. In establishing the context for his argument that social constructionism has the potential to deal with the "crisis in representation" in a reconstructive and not merely deconstructive manner, he provides a useful classification of critical intellectual movements that challenge a representationalist view of language and, by extension, objective knowledge (Gergen, 1994). He divides the various poststructuralist, postempiricist, and postmodern schools of thought into ideological critiques, literary-rhetorical critiques, and social critiques, which differ from one another in what they choose to emphasize as the primary source of truth claims and in what they take language to be. Thus, the ideological (such as the critical theory of the Frankfurt School, other Marxist critique, and much feminist theory) reveal the ideological biases and moral and political purposes of seemingly objective accounts of the world (truth claims). The literary-rhetorical (poststructuralists and deconstructionists) focus on the discursive history of truth claims, for it is from this history that they gain their significance. Language is seen as primarily persuasive (performative rather than denotative) and metaphorical. The social critique stems from attempts to reveal the social origins of scientific thought (including the works of Mannheim, Weber, Kuhn's *The Structure of Scientific Revolutions* (1962), and Berger and Luckmann's *The Social Construction of Reality* (1966); contemporary terms for this kind of analysis are science studies and the sociology of scientific knowledge. Truth claims are said to derive from social process; scientific knowledge is determined by complex social interests and interactions; science is fundamentally social (or, more accurately, societal).[1]

Although the distinctions among these traditions are less clear-cut than the scheme implies, it is fair to say that proponents of each spend much of their time pointing out their own virtues and each other's shortcomings, all according to the criterion of which is a better critique of modern epistemology. We are sympathetic to Gergen's worry that, as these traditions are "parasitic on prevailing assertions of truth," if truth-bearing scholars ever "tire of playing the fool and set off for the intellectual high ground of critique, no high ground will remain—all will be flat" (Gergen, 1994, p. 45). His own proposal for going beyond critique is some synthesis within a social constructionist framework of the three traditions. As we have made plain, Gergen's primary concern is how these critiques challenge the modern notion of *individual* knowledge; ours is with knowing *of any kind*. Yet, as we assess attempts to reform modern epistemology, we will on occasion find it useful to use Gergen's classification of these intellectual traditions.

DISCOURSE, TEXT, CONVERSATION—AND ANALYSIS

The backgrounds from which we (the authors) come—philosophy of science (Newman) and developmental psychology, psycholinguistics, and sociolinguistics (Holzman)—no doubt contribute to our reading of the voluminous writings on methods of analyzing language. Having done our share of linguistic analysis (utilizing very different methods), both of us can, without much difficulty, "get into" this fundamentally reformist activity. At the same time, there is a way neither of us comprehend what is being done and why. As an intellectual pursuit-in-itself, such work seems to us as reasonable and justifiable as any other, but as an approach to transforming human life it seems to miss the mark completely. To put it simply, if the premises of such studies are: (1) that we construct our lives (accomplish social activities, create reality and so on) through language (conversation, discourse, dialogue, narrative); and (2) that our lives as constructed constrain us (are nondevelopmental and so on) and therefore could be substantially improved, then shouldn't we (practically-critically, that is, revolutionarily, speaking) work to help people create new language (conversation, discourse, dialogue, narrative)?

But in the hands of the reformists, the insight that human beings "do things with words" has led to analysts of conversation, discourse, and text describing and analyzing the things people (usually others, but sometimes they themselves) *already* do with words, two of those things being analyzing and describing. Austin's (1962) formulation and the many that have followed from it are troublesome to us, for in debunking a representational view of language without a revolutionary practice and environment, they seem to offer yet another dualistic and instrumental conception: words exist and we use them for different purposes. Questions remain: What does it mean to do things with words? Are the things we do with words ultimately mentalistic? What are these words that we do things with? Do we do things to create them or do we just do things *with* them? What is a word? What is *with*? In discovering and delineating the significance of language use, is the linguistic (discursive, dialogic, narrative) turn that characterizes much of postmodern philosophy, social science, and cultural studies leading us down still another epistemic road?

Few disciplines have been untouched these past fifty years by the linguistic turn; indeed, the focus on language has blurred the traditional distinctions between disciplines and disrupted the existing order of academia. New kinds of inquiry—descriptive/analytic studies of how knowledge (especially scientific knowledge) is created; recharacterizations of the subject matter of psychology, anthropology, history, and sociology; and new ways to practice (for example, psychotherapy and pedagogy)—no longer fit neatly into university departments. The relatively new academic disciplines of cultural, rhetorical, and communication studies are at once philosophical, psychological, historical, linguistic, and political. In our view, that they constitute a reshaping of traditional bodies of knowledge is a source simultaneously of their most important contributions, their institutional pervasiveness, and their practical-critical limitations.

The turn to language in the field of psychology came, not surprisingly, mainly from influences outside it—most notably from Wittgensteinian-influenced analytic philosophy, philosophy of science, ethnomethodology, poststructuralist writings by historians, philosophers, and cultural theorists, and the rediscovery of the work of Lev Vygotsky and his contemporary, Mikhail Bakhtin. To varying degrees, these works have contributed to studies that examine psychology as metaphor (Soyland, 1994), narrative, or discourse (Harré and Gillett, 1994; Parker, 1992), ideology (Burman, 1994; Henriques *et al.*, 1984; Morss, 1990), and myth (Newman and Holzman, 1996). These approaches are historical and discursive; that is, their premise (and method) is that what psychology is—what it says, how it conducts its business, what it claims to have discovered—is inseparable from how psychology has constructed itself through the texts, stories, narratives, rhetorical devices, genres of discourse, and so on that it has produced and continues to produce. (Rather unusual is Danziger's historiography, which attempts to redress the neglect of the history of discourse in psychology; see Danziger, 1994 and his forthcoming *Naming the Mind: How Psychology Found Its Language*.)

These writings have produced valuable insights into the increasingly regulatory and propagandistic function of psychology over the century. Most recently, Wittgenstein's later writings have guided psychologists sympathetic to the turn to language in formulating a critical deconstruction (and, in some cases, in formulating how to create a positive reconstruction) of psychology. His work has provided an impetus to investigate not only the ideological functions of psychology but also to take a closer look at its methodological presuppositions, especially those concerning explanation and interpretation. Whether calling for an emancipatory psychology, a more ethical psychology, a radical psychology, or even a revolutionary psychology, their investigations are based on the belief that psychology, like all modern disciplines and institutions, is a particular societal arrangement of language, knowledge, and power. Its "fatal flaw" is the pseudoscientific (perhaps unintentional but nevertheless ideologically driven) assumption that human life is of the same nature as the physical world and/or that it can be studied in the same manner. These critical psychologists insist that psychology can and must be reformed if further human development (progress, emancipation, discovery) is to take place (be possible). Curiously, very few (we are among them) call for abandoning psychology altogether. Instead, the linguistic turn has prompted a reorientation of psychology from an explanatory to an interpretive science.

Conversational analysis

We begin our discussion of reforms not with psychology, but with sociology. The notion of *context* is central to the approach to social interaction and language use known as conversational analysis. Drawing upon conceptions arising from sociology, linguistics, and anthropology since the 1960s, especially the groundbreaking work of the American sociologists and ethnomethodologists Garfinkel (1967), Goffman (1974), Gumperz (1982), Hymes (1962), Sacks (see Jefferson, 1992), and Schegloff (1972), it is an attempt to describe "talk-in-context" empirically. According to Drew and Heritage (1992), conversational analysis synthesizes the rich cultural contextualization of the ethnography of speaking with the formal approach of speech act theory to the sequence of utterances and actions. Rather than beginning with either culture or social identity, on the one hand, or, on the other hand, with linguistic variables such as word selection or syntax, "CA [conversational analysis] begins with a consideration of the *interactional accomplishment of particular social activities* . . . embodied in specific social actions and sequences of social actions" (Drew and Heritage, 1992, p. 17).

To conversational analysts, talk or conversation is social action. While Drew and Heritage, drawing upon classic work by Sacks, speak of "activity," they appear to mean what others mean by "action" rather than what Marx, Vygotsky, and we mean by "activity." They are concerned to show how interactional "work"—telling a joke, giving advice, examining a baby, doing a psychiatric intake—is "managed" through talk. They are equally concerned with showing how features of social structure such as race, class, and gender are produced through talk.

According to Edwards (1995), this approach challenges mentalism and a representationalist view of language. In his thoughtful and admiring review of a collection of lectures delivered by Harvey Sacks which provide the historical foundation of conversational analysis (Jefferson, 1992), Edwards notes that, at least for Sacks, "talk is *action, not communication*" (Edwards, 1995, p. 585). Focusing on talk as action rather than communication is, according to Edwards, an essentially anti-psychological approach to social interaction; it does not presume that conversation is the consequence of some mental state. It is not that the mind (which mentally represents, has a symbol system which it shares with other minds, stores information, and so on) is made visible *through* talk; rather, social interaction (that is, talk) *is essentially visible* (Edwards, 1995, p. 585).

An essay by Schegloff (1992) defending conversational analysis as being solidly located within the tradition of sociology makes clearer how conversational analysis attempts to be an alternative epistemology—a challenge to cognitivism—within the modernist paradigm. While concerned with one of the long-standing themes in social analysis— "action in interaction" (p. 105)—its approach to social structure is anti-positivist. It rejects the positivist "criteria of relevance" traditionally used to evaluate analytic characterizations—for example, that the analysis is theoretically reasonable or that it is justified by statistical significance or historical evidence. Rather, Schegloff says, the criterion utilized by conversational analysis is that the term or categorization must be shown to be relevant *to the participants*. In other words, in order to claim that a certain characterization (such as "student," "black," "white," "man," or "woman") or context (the institutional location in which the talk is occurring, such as a classroom, hospital, or office) is relevant in the conversational analysis, one must account for its relevance to those who are conversing—when they are conversing:

> The point is not that persons are somehow *not* male or female, upper or lower class, with or without power, professors and/or students. They may be, on some occasion, demonstrably members of one or another of those categories. Nor is the issue that those aspects of the society do not matter, or did not matter on that occasion. We may share a lively sense that indeed they do matter, and that they mattered on that occasion, and mattered for just that aspect of some interaction on which we are focusing. There is still the problem of *showing from the details of the talk or other conduct in the materials* that we are analyzing that those aspects of the scene are what the *parties* are oriented to. *For that is to show how the parties are embodying for one another the relevancies of the interaction and are thereby producing the social structure.*
>
> (Schegloff, 1992, pp. 109–10)

Schegloff is arguing here both for and against traditional criteria of knowledge. He rejects the objectivist modernist paradigm and principles of relevance, yet holds fast to accountability. At all costs, we must be able to account for the conversational moves that people make. Unless our observations about social organization (for example, about race, class, gender, status) are successfully translated into "defensible, empirically based analyses that help us to get access to previously unnoticed particular details of talk-in-interaction, and appreciate their significance," we have only " 'a *sense* of how the world works' . . . without its detailed explication" (Schegloff, 1992, p. 106). And, in spite of the insistence that such explication is made on the participants' "own terms" (what is relevant to them on the occasion of their actions), accountability is actually to be found outside and distant from the occasion and the participants. And so it must be, for the only actual (if you will, real) "accountability on their own terms" is in the very activity of their speaking. It seems to us, then, that an ecologically valid challenge to accountability would be no analysis whatsoever. Accountability is a mapping, an explanation, a description, an after-the-fact analysis. It is a, if not *the*, major feature of the knowing paradigm. By purporting to be an alternative and superior source of knowledge claims about what people do, conversational analysis fits comfortably within that paradigm.

The modern conception of language (as both the source of and the evidence for knowing) is only partially challenged by this approach.

Hailing talk as social action does not make it any less knowledge-based, interpretive, or instrumental. While we may have gotten rid of the mind, we still have *aboutness* (and, thereby, knowledge)—that which generated the need for a mind in the first place—to contend with. Conversational analysts make several assumptions that link knowing and meaning and speaking. They assume that they can know what people are doing from what they are saying; they assume that what people say must mean something; they assume that what people say must be interpreted; and they assume that talk must accomplish something(s). In this case, the meaning, interpretation, and accomplishment are "social" rather than individualized mental acts. What people say means (and is interpreted to mean) what they are "orienting to" and what they are "embodying for one another." What people say produces social structure. Yet such epistemic assumptions are for the most part unexamined.

We have taken the time to discuss conversational analysis in spite of the fact that, being structuralist and empiricist, it is not an approach within the postmodern camp, nor even a critical tradition in Gergen's (1994) scheme. Yet we think it shares some presuppositions about knowledge and language with other types of language analysis and that the above deconstruction, modest as it is, will be useful as we proceed to examine poststructuralist and postmodern approaches.

Discourse analysis

Conversation, however, is not all there is. Conversation is intimately tied to discourse. While some analysts define discourse loosely as any linguistic interaction (either spoken or written) that follows some pattern and has some function, the more interesting use of the term is that which ties it to a critical perspective.

The social psychologist Ian Parker advocates for politicizing discourse analysis in the effort to create an emancipatory psychology. In *Discourse Dynamics: Critical Analysis for Social and Individual Psychology* (1992), Parker summarizes the way discourse analysis has been conducted and how he thinks it needs to be changed. Discourses are systems of statements that construct an object (Parker, 1992, p. 5) produced and reproduced in conversation and written text. An example of "a discourse" of the discipline of social psychology is the following:

> Social psychologists may draw upon a discourse of "authoritarianism" and they will use the notion of "authoritarianism," which has been constructed as an object by that discourse, to explain different social and political phenomena. Each time they use the term they will, by the same token, be reproducing the discourse.
>
> (Parker, 1989, p. 62)

The distinction between conversational analysis and discourse analysis is not always clear from the literature. What looks like conversational analysis is sometimes called discourse analysis (for example, Ferrara, 1994), and most discourse analysis does not acknowledge the contribution of conversational analysis, although that influence is apparent (at least to us). In an essay on discourse and uncertainty, Michael (1994) makes a distinction between ways of analyzing discourse that is helpful in understanding the relationship between these two research traditions. One (what we refer to as conversational analysis) is concerned with process, with the ongoing production of social interaction and meaning in an immediate situation. The other (what we will discuss here as discourse analysis) is concerned with the historical-societal-cultural discursive and institutional context from which such local discursive events are derived and in which they occur.

The recognition of the social, psychological, and political significance of discourse is commonly attributed to Michel Foucault's studies of the history of institutions of Western culture, including sexuality, madness, and medicine (Foucault, 1965, 1972, 1973, 1975, 1979). His unique method of historical analysis reveals how particular systems of discourse—which not only determine how we speak but how we think, feel, and see—were created simultaneously with modern culture, including such elements of it as the scientific method, hospitals and clinics, prisons, and conceptions of madness and sanity. Following Foucault, in discourse analysis, the meanings of the symbols people use in speaking and writing are understood to be a function of how they are used in discourses; their uses, in turn, are constrained and interconnected in certain ways by informal rules and unstated conventions that create and reflect what Foucault called "the order of things." Foucault's notion of discourse as producer and perpetuator of "regimes of truth," the site of both power and resistance to power, has been taken up by contemporary critics who see psychology as ideology, including many feminists and others who focus on gender inequality (for example, Diamond and Quimby, 1988; Henriques *et al.*, 1984; Henwood, 1995; Walkerdine and Lucey, 1989; Walkerdine, 1993).

Following Foucault, the power of discourse analysis lies in its potential to expose the relationship between language, knowledge, and power. Thus, Parker further defines discourses as "systems of meaning which offer positions of power to some categories of people and disempower others" (Parker, 1992, p. 10). The dynamics of discourse reproduce power relations and the interconnectedness of power to knowledge. Knowing the history of the discourses of the *self-contained individual*, the *rational mind*, or the *developing child*, for example, can help to reframe these psychological objects; it can change their location from truths about the world that psychology has discovered to " 'truth' held in place by language and power" (Parker, 1992, p. 22). Discourses, then, are not descriptions of naturally occurring phenomena, nor are they "just how we talk." They are political-social-ideological frameworks, and discourse analysis is the self-conscious effort to systematize ways of talking in order to understand them better.

This approach to talk has had considerable impact on psychological and interdisciplinary research concerned with power relations and inequality, and the ideological biases of modern disciplines and systems of knowledge. Parker (1992) provides an excellent guide to books, journals, and ongoing research institutes in the discourse analytic tradition. The discourses of science, psychology, race, gender, and sexuality are among those that have been examined empirically.[2]

In our view, Parker's agenda—politicizing discourse analysis—should be admired. He is concerned that too many proponents of discourse analysis ignore social structure and, in particular, are insensitive to power relations (and thereby, the possibility of resistance). In delineating the criteria an analyst might employ for discovering discourses, he adds to the commonly noted ones (for example, that a discourse is realized in texts) three "auxiliary criteria": discourses support institutions; they reproduce power relations; and they have ideological effects (1992, pp. 17–20). These criteria, according to Parker, are necessary to save discourse analysis from being just an intellectual enterprise—the accumulation of bits of information that may be knowledge-producing and "edifying," but not emancipatory (p. 21). He says that discourse analysis should challenge and disrupt, that it itself can change the way discourse is used and, in doing so, open up "space for manoeuvre and resistance" (p. 21).

Parker is also making a case against postmodernism, particularly social constructionist approaches (1992; see also Parker, 1996), which he says hold to an anti-realist view of the social world—a position that, as a Marxist, he considers untenable. He targets two features of postmodern critiques (as exemplified in the turn to language) that he sees as dangerously undermining a radical political agenda—relativism and an insistence on reflexivity. In place of a material world, to social constructionists there are only sets of competing discourses; conceptions of social structure (such as the Enlightenment belief in emancipation and Marx's notions of class and political economy) are themselves discourses (grand narratives). Parker interprets this postmodern relativism as the giving up of a critical standpoint and any hope or desire to change the world in favor of a view that "celebrates the way things are because any other way is as unreal" (1992, p. 70). With respect to the problem of reflexivity, he comments,

> There is something odd going on when the connection between the individual and the social is made in terms of "reflexivity" instead of political practice. My caution is that we have to understand the political functions of that connection instead of heaving a sigh of relief because a connection has been made. Reflexivity is an attempt, well suited to the postmodern condition, to connect which is *depoliticised.*
>
> (Parker, 1992, p. 80)

As sympathetic as we might be to Parker's radical political goals, we have problems with the psychology and philosophy (and practice) that underlie (or, more precisely, overdetermine) it. For Parker is upholding a modern (and, we would argue, distinctly non-Marxist) duality between the individual and the social; why else would he be concerned with how the "connection" is made (by either reflexivity or political practice) if he were not presupposing their separation? For Parker and other orthodox Marxists (but not for the early methodological Marx), social structure is the "cement" that holds together individual and society, text and the world.

What is the practical-critical nature of this "individual" for whom, presumably, we must find a way of connecting to the world? For Parker, the individual is inextricably connected to materiality. He tells us that the experience of individuality in contemporary culture (as private, isolated, and dehumanized) cannot be wished away, with which we strongly agree; it is social and not just formal.The attempt to do so as if that experience "rested on nothing, as if there was no material basis, no human nature, would be as bad as behaviourism or as bankrupt as the promises of the postmodernists" (1992, p. 81). For Parker, evidently it is only the "experience" of individuality that can be altered by revolutionary practice, not our material-ontological status as "individuals." Parker's use of *material basis* here is curious to us. He seems to imply that individuality is unalterable by virtue of it being materially based, a position in contradiction to dialectical-historical materialism practically-critically understood. His claim that individuality is materially based rests on a reading of Marx that is, to us, insufficiently dialectical in that it appears to presume that since *everything* is materially based, any *thing* is materially based. But the materiality of the world, Marx tells us, does not come to (impact upon) human beings particularized and individuated, but *as totality* (that is, as "everything"). It is epistemology that comes to us individuated (and individuating), and creates the experience of the materiality of the world (including ourselves) as individuated. Far from being materially based, individuality is thoroughly *epistemologically based*. To gain understanding of individuality, we need to look at the family of concepts with which it is associated rather than seek something beyond it (either in the superstructure or base).

Discursive psychology

Parker's materially based individual is only one of many attempts to gain an understanding of individuality—and *sense of self* and *identity* (which are part of the family of concepts with which individuality is associated in modern culture)—through adding a discursive or textual perspective to a realist framework. Another is the work of Rom Harré. In a series of writings since the late 1970s (Harré, 1979, 1983, 1986; Harré *et al.*, 1985; Harré and Secord, 1972), he and his colleagues have argued that the discursive turn in psychology provides alternative grounds for understanding cognition and emotion. His latest work, *The Discursive Mind* (Harré and Gillett, 1994), is an introduction to ways of understanding *the mind* (a psychological object, closely related to the isolated individual and individual knowledge) as discursively constructed: "Only by adopting the discursive viewpoint will it be possible to develop a psychology of the self directed to the question of our sense of personal individuality and to undertake a study of how we acquire it" (p. 102). Note that this project, in accepting the need to account for the mind, differs in a most important way from the conversational analysis of Sacks and Schegloff. It is yet another attempt to reform—and therefore hold on to—psychology.

According to Harré and Gillett (1994), the discursive viewpoint (or "discursive psychology," which they call the new paradigm for cognitive psychology) holds to three principles: many psychological phenomena should be interpreted as features of discourse which may be public (behavior) or private (thought); individual and private uses of symbolic systems (thinking) are derived from interpersonal discursive processes; and the production of emotions, decisions, attitudes, and so on depends on the skill of the actors, their relative standing in the community, and the story lines that unfold (p. 27). Harré and Gillett use these principles to account for key psychological objects, including sense of self and personal identity, personality, perception, consciousness, motivation, and emotion.

Harré and Gillett insist throughout that they reject Cartesianism: the mind is not a substance; the dual nature of human existence need not be accounted for in the way it has been for centuries, that is in terms of mind–body or mental–material dualism. Yet they do accept the dual nature of human existence and, moreover, that there must be *some* accounting for it. Their "anti-Cartesianism" consists of replacing the mental with the discursive:

> Human beings live in two worlds. One is essentially discursive in character; that is, it is a world of signs and symbols subject to normative constraints. It comes into being through intentional action. . . . The other world in which we live, the physical or material world, is structured by causal processes.
>
> (Harré and Gillett, 1994, pp. 99–100)

Human beings are "always trying to make sense of their life and the situations around them" (p. 127), and using language is how we do it, for language is the major means for "managing in the world of symbols," while our hands and brains are "in the material world" (p. 100). Apparently uninterested in how human beings manage in these "two worlds" (how we organize their relationship), Harré and Gillett focus on the discursive world. Mental life, by their account, becomes "a dynamic activity, engaged in by people, who are located in a range of interacting discourses and at certain positions in those discourses and who, from the possibilities they make available, attempt to fashion relatively integrated and coherent subjectivities for themselves" (p. 180).

Harré and Gillett offer this accounting as a challenge to the long-standing philosophical and psychological assumption that there must be "mental states or processes 'behind' the mental states and processes of our discursive activities" and the concomitant need to invoke such "mystery processes" to explain our "discursive and practical activities", (p. 60). It might well be, yet it seems to us to reintroduce Cartesian dualism—aren't they trying to account for "what's behind" the *cogito*? In positing the existence of "discursive and practical activities" on the one hand and, on the other hand, "the mental states and processes of our discursive activities," they create, it seems to us, a discursive revision of Descartes along the lines of "I speak, therefore I think, therefore I am." In holding to the reality of private mental life in this way, in accepting individual subjectivity as an intentional, self-conscious creation of each human being "individually" (each of us "attempt[s] to fashion . . . subjectivities"), in positing discourse as context (where human beings are "located" and "positioned"), they undermine the very project they claim to have undertaken—charting a new psychology. For they merely provide alternative grounds with which to account for "rational man"—who is, after all, the subject and object of modern epistemology, including psychology.

In building their case for a discursive psychology and epistemology, Harré and Gillett appeal to both Vygotsky and Wittgenstein in ways that, from our practical-critical, activity-theoretic perspective, distort the radical (revolutionary) views on language of both these preeminent pre-postmodernists. For example, Harré and Gillett put forth the "new ontology" of discursive psychology as Vygotskian, but not only are its elements—"arrays of people," "speech acts," and "rules and story lines" (pp. 29–30)—not the sort of units of analysis with which Vygotsky worked, the enterprise of replacing the elements of traditional psychology with new ones is not in keeping with Vygotsky's revolutionary tool-and-result methodology. Furthermore, they claim that their discursive model accounts for how language expresses thought—a position counter to Vygotsky's formulation that speaking and thinking are a dialectical unity in which language completes—rather than expresses—thought. Similarly, they invoke Wittgenstein to support their view that language be used as a model for nonlinguistic behaviors such as gestures and facial expressions. Yet the position that such behaviors "should be analyzed as if they were through and through linguistic" (p. 99) flies in the face of Wittgenstein's anti-foundationalism and abhorrence of systemization. Like many other revisionists who pragmatize Wittgenstein and Vygotsky, Harré and Gillett miss their understanding of language as *activity*.

Indeed, one of the problems we have with nearly all language-based critiques of modernist epistemology, including conversational and discourse analysis, is their equation of meaning with use (which makes it difficult, if not impossible, to do what Wittgenstein urged—to see language "as activity, or a form of life"). As we have seen, the dominant reform of representationalism (often attributed to Wittgenstein!) is to locate the meaning of language in its use—discursively, rhetorically, conversationally. Meaning has effectively been taken out of the heads of individuals and placed in *relationship*—of person to person, conversation to discourse, discourse to power or ideology. As reasonable as this reform is, given the pervasiveness of a representationalist view of meaning, we think it keeps meaning as an epistemic category. For none of the creative analysts and critics we have discussed thus far relates to meaning as human activity, that is, without an aboutness, purpose, product, or result of the meaning-making activity itself. Rather, the various strains of discursive psychology all give primacy to the meaning language has, to what gets produced through discourse, text, conversation, or narrative. Whether it is one's personality or sense of self (Harré and Gillett), positions of privilege and marginalization (Parker), or social structure (Schegloff), the significance of meaning winds up being located not in its activityness but in its purpose or instrumentality.

Shotter's work

We turn now to a body of work that moves much closer to our own and some distance away from a simplistic meaning–use equation but does not (as we see it) go all the way to revolutionary activity. John Shotter, one of the first psychologists to look seriously at what a synthesis of Vygotsky and Wittgenstein might produce, has been more sensitive than most of his colleagues to the problems of the meaning–use equation common to Wittgensteinian-influenced psychologists. He considers use, correctly, in our view, to be only one among many means of making meaning (1993a, p. 28).

Since the 1980s, Shotter has made an important contribution to the post-modern movement. Like many of his colleagues, he points (in a practical-critical posture) to the dilemma in which the modern science paradigm has placed us: "everyday social life still continues in spite of its disorderliness" (Shotter, 1992, p. 69). According to Shotter, our continued failure to understand how this is possible has to do with the fact that we confuse questions of being (ontological questions) with questions of our knowledge of being (epistemological questions). But it is the *nature* of social life, not how we might come to know it, that is the critical issue. Social scientists have related to the world, including social life, as if it were a "natural" and lawful phenomenon capable of being individually investigated. Postmodernism, in part, is the dual recognition that "we now must begin to face the fact that such an activity is only possible if what we study is already ordered" (1993a, p. 60), and that such an assumption is untenable. Ontologically, both our own "being" and the "being of the world" are, says Shotter, "determined by us and for us in all the self–other relationships in which we are involved" (1993a, p. 60).

In his most recent books, *Conversational Realities: Constructing Life Through Language* (1993a) and *Cultural Politics of Everyday Life: Social*

Constructionism, Rhetoric and Knowing of the Third Kind (1993b), and articles, Shotter urges that living in the postmodern world as a "full political member" requires that we give up modern assumptions about knowledge, reality, the orderliness of the world, universals, and underlying appearances, and create a new stance toward ourselves and our world. He calls this new stance *knowing of the third kind* and *practical-moral knowledge* (we call it practical-critical, revolutionary activity); it is a version of social constructionism, that takes the terms in which human conversations, traditions of argumentation and debate are conducted, to be Central (1993b). We constitute ourselves and our world through our conversational activity and it is within such activity that practical-moral knowledge is embodied. Yet precisely how we conduct our conversations—the vocabulary we use, the way we understand what language is—makes this kind of knowing invisible. Shotter argues that it need not remain so: we can change our conversational activity in a way that highlights our practical-moral knowledge. Central to his argument is his view that language is primarily "responsive" and "rhetorical" rather than representational.

Shotter is not merely restating speech act theory nor adding to the list of how we "do things with words." Rather, he is attempting to get a handle on the peculiarities of conversational activity and, by extension, the nature of social life. The referential, representational use of language that we typically take to be its only or major function is, in fact, derived from responsive-rhetorical forms of talk (Shotter, 1993a). That these forms of talk are invisible—in the background of our lives—has consequences for how we live our lives. For within them is embodied that special kind of knowledge having to do with "how *to be* a person of this or that particular kind. . . ." Knowing of the third kind is "knowing *from within* a situation, a group, social institution, or society" rather than knowing-what or knowing-how; it is "knowledge-in-practice" and "knowledge-held-in-common with others" (1993a, p. 19). It is this knowledge, inseparable from our constitution of it in conversational activity, that creates the "disorderliness of everyday social life." We think this is enormously perceptive, as far as it goes. To us, however, it is not a matter of knowing (knowledge) at all.

In a recent article, Shotter (1995) further delineates both the origins and implications of responsive–rhetorical forms of talk. Drawing on Bakhtin (1981, 1986), he argues that all human social action is *dialogically* linked to both previous actions and possible future actions. To Shotter, it is its dialogic nature that makes conversation peculiar, for as speakers we are responsive not only to the others in the conversation but also to "a strange ethical Otherness in our surroundings we construct between us" (1995, p. 55). In other words, being responsive cannot be reduced to communicating. Thus Shotter rejects the notion that conversation is primarily communicative and/or rule-governed (and thereby cognitive). On the contrary, conversation is "a structure of presuppositions and expectations of a non-cognitive, gestural kind that unfolds in the 'temporal movement' of the speaker's voice ... a joint action" (p. 66)—in our language, a revolutionary activity.

Shotter offers this rhetorical-responsive approach to language as a way out of the dichotomous alternatives that cognitivism requires. Speaking, he says, is neither an individual act (a phenomenon of individual creativity) nor is it located in society (as a system of normative rules). Rather, "the organizing center ... of the act of speaking" lies "precisely upon the boundary between the two, in the interactive moment of speaking, as speakers are making connections between themselves and their surroundings" (p. 67) (this is what we mean by doing politics). Shotter explores the implications of this kind of knowledge both for how we currently experience and talk about ourselves and the world and also for how we might come to talk differently. Making rhetorical-responsive talk visible is to speak in *relational* rather than individualistic terms; it is changing how we interrelate from an individualistic to a relational manner as a way to "begin to 'socially construct' a relational society" (1993a, p. 182; see also Shotter, 1996).

To us, it is a non-relational, non-rhetorical revolutionary activity. But these differences with Shotter, we suspect, are not merely rhetorical; to us, his reformist location within an institution of knowing (to which, therefore, he must maintain a *relationship*) ultimately overdetermines his insights, brilliant though they are. Thus, in contrasting a relational way of talking with an individualistic way of talking, he is focused on "doing in" the individual (the individuated self)—that is, dualism in its substantive form—and less than attentive to formal dualism (the thing and the relationship).

Forms of life (language-games, conversations, creative completions, and so on) may well have family resemblances (in Wittgenstein's sense) but, to us, there is no identity or sameness relationship between them. They are activities. As such, they are at once what they are and other than what they are. Identity does not (and need not) apply. Non-epistemic understanding is indistinguishable from participation in the life process. The changing and the understanding are not identical but *indistinguishable*. Children come to be knowers at a relatively late point in the process of societal adaptation. The social (which, according to Vygotsky, precedes the individuated societal) does not include the intrapsychical epistemological alienation (distance between knower and known) necessary to be a knower (Bakhurst, 1991). And even as adults our capacity to perform, when it is reinitiated, makes it possible for us to understand (that is, change) without knowing. Growing without knowing is indeed critical for the early childhood development necessary for societal adaptation, including, ironically, adaptation to knowing. Continued development, in our opinion, demands a rejection of knowing as the sole or dominant form of understanding. Activity must replace reality, even as performing replaces knowing in the practice and understanding of human life.

For all the differences between conversational analysts, discourse analysts, social constructionists, narrative therapists, discursive psychologists, and the like, there seems to be an overriding similarity in their enterprises. Their varying attempts to change the understanding and status of language within psychology, to expose the pseudoscientific nature of psychology, and to refute the modern belief in objective knowledge and truth (with or without a capital T), are constrained, as Gergen has acknowledged, by virtue of their being reactions to "prevailing assertions of truth" and, as we have said, by being *institutionally*—epistemologically and ultimately revisionistically—overdetermined. The turn to language within psychology is a good reform of modernist epistemology—an argument against a causal-explanatory scientific paradigm and for an interpretive one. The claim that psychology is an interpretive science is twofold. First, human life cannot be understood using an explanatory (hard) scientific framework; rather it requires an interpretive science. Second, the critical developmental characteristic of human beings is not that we are an explaining or deducing species (although surely we do explain and deduce), but that we are an interpreting species. Understanding human life, on this account, requires that we view the acquisition of knowledge about the world (which is inseparable from knowledge about ourselves) to be an active, creative, emergent, relational process of *jointly constructed interpretations*.

Our ongoing conversation with these and other critical and postmodern researchers reflects and continues our activity of gaining clarity on the limitations of efforts to reform psychology and modern epistemology. An interpretive species? Undoubtedly, "our" Marx (the early Marx of *The German Ideology*) would be dismayed to hear such a perspective put forth in the name of human emancipation! It was the *practical-critical, revolutionary activity* of human beings that Marx took to be necessary for profound social change. (See Marx's First Thesis on Feuerbach in note 10, Chapter 2.) His disdain for "interpreting the world" could not be clearer; while he was overly enamored of the explanatory power of modern science, interpretation was anathema to him. Yet, as we will discuss more extensively in Chapter 4, there is a tendency within neo-Marxism to revise his strong position on interpretation.

In invoking Marx, perhaps we are being unfair to those colleagues whose work we have been discussing, most of whom do not consider themselves followers of Marx or even appeal to his worldview or methodology. However, they do draw to varying degrees upon the works of Vygotsky and Wittgenstein, both of whom were similarly hostile toward interpretation. In Vygotsky's case, his Marxism and his revolutionaryness were integral to his psychology (Holzman, 1990; Joravsky, 1989; Newman and Holzman, 1993). Most important, the polemics of all three—Marx, Vygotsky, and Wittgenstein—included formulating a non-interpretive conception of language. In positing activity, they point the way for the linguistic turn to become practical-critical revolutionary activity.

MOVING BEYOND THE RATIONAL (BOTH THE EXPLANATORY AND THE INTERPRETIVE VARIETY)

We turn next to European postmodern theorists, in particular French philosophers and psychologists, whose "epistemological footing" is not so much in *the self* (and the related conceptions of identity and the individual) as it is in human *experience*. The Continental philosophical tradition has generally been more fascinated by this aspect of the paradox of subjectivity—the experience of self-conscious abstracting, the experience of knowing, the experience of experiencing—than the Anglo-American tradition which has concerned itself primarily with delineating (reductionistically) the causal mechanisms of subjectivity, knowing, and experience. In urging that postmodernism "go beyond itself" we believe that positing alternative ways of knowing (or new epistemologies) brings us no closer to understanding subjectivity than the modern way. In Chapter 2 and our just completed discussion of the linguistic turn, we focused on postmodern critiques of modern epistemology that draw primarily on the Anglo-American philosophical tradition and argued that current attempts to eliminate "the self," "the individual knower," and "the mind"—without eliminating knowing—leave epistemological dualism intact. Taking what was previously considered individual (private, mental) and making it relational (visible, constitutive, socially constructed) is a reasonable reform, but it does not challenge the knowing paradigm at its Greek roots. Neither does replacing modernism's Truth with postmodernism's interpretive or narrative truths. In exploring and summarizing the ideas of some of the leading European postmodern thinkers, our concern is likewise with the extent to which their critiques of modern conceptions of human experience (including what it is we are experiencing) challenge not merely modern epistemology, but the epistemological posture itself.

European philosophy did not become the servant of science in the same way that American philosophy did in the twentieth century; the transformation of philosophy into epistemology (methodology and modern science) did not occur. For better or worse, on the Continent metaphysics remained a bona fide tradition and alternative philosophical approaches such as phenomenology, hermeneutics, and existentialism, while arguably never dominant, did continue to flourish. Consequently, postmodern European philosophy has tended to be less focused on debunking objective knowledge and truth, the hallmarks of the modern scientific paradigm.

The historical division between the Anglo-American and Continental philosophical traditions has, to a large extent, continued—philosophy of science and analytic philosophy being the first and most significant influences on Anglo-American philosophical psychologists, and Hegel, Marx, phenomenology, and hermeneutics being major influences on European postmodernists. While Kant, of course, influenced both traditions (he transformed/redefined the study of subjectivity), it is his constructionist tendencies and writings on aesthetics, judgment, and morals that mainly interest the Europeans, the Anglo-Americans seeing primarily the categorical, epistemological Kant. (The Swiss philosopher/psychologist Jean Piaget, who took Kant's categories as the basis for his life-long study of genetic episte- mology, is an important exception.) Ironically, some American and British philosophical psychologists are more and more turning to the European post- modernists, having seen the problems of extreme reductionism in the Anglo-American philosophical tradition. The deconstructionist writings of Michel Foucault and Jacques Derrida, considered postmodern by some and not by others, have been major influences on current postmodern theorizing. We have already seen that Foucault is, at a minimum, in the background of most discourse analysis and social critiques of language and power. Derrida's ironic approach to intellectual discourse (1976; 1978) has been the catalyst for deconstructionist studies in just about all fields of inquiry. His understanding of text—in particular, his deconstruction of the traditional distinction between speaking and writing which privileges speaking, and his identification of illusions or myths of Western thought such as the belief in origins or begin- nings—has been widely cited and incorporated into a variety of ideological, literary, and social critique, including recent critical developmental psychology (see, for example, Bradley, 1989; Morss, 1992; and Shotter, 1986, 1990).

Interestingly, it is a semi-popular book by an American and mostly about the American postmodern experience that, in our opinion, best brings together the concerns and contributions of both the Anglo-American and Continental traditions. Gergen's *The Saturated Self: Dilemmas of Identity in Contemporary Life* (1991) describes how the contemporary self is "under siege" (an American concern)—how our daily experiences of self and others are radically changing as part of the social upheaval engendered by, among other things, technological inventions and achievements, the transformation of knowledge, and increasing skepticism toward the Western traditions of truth, knowledge, and the good. It is Gergen's linking of changes in the quality of everyday life with these social-cultural transformations that is reminiscent of contemporary European postmodern theorizing about the nature of reality and our experiences of reality.

The French social theorists Jean Baudrillard and Jean-François Lyotard are cases in point. Both follow in the French tradition—exemplified in the work of Foucault, Derrida, and anti-psychiatrists Deleuze and Guattari—of analyzing modernity in political-cultural-discursive terms. At the same time, in carving out their particular niches both Baudrillard and Lyotard have also distanced themselves from those whom they followed earlier. For example, Baudrillard's early works championed Foucault, yet in *Forget Foucault* (1987; originally published in French in 1977) he charges that the theory of his former colleague is obsolete; Foucault's eloquent and even bril- liant analysis of knowledge, power, and disciplinary mechanisms and institutions is no longer relevant. According to Baudrillard, power has become a complete abstraction, no longer located in any societal institutions but now "invented on the basis of signs" (1987, p. 59). In similar fashion, in the early 1970s Lyotard (1977) incorporated the view of Deleuze and Guattari that modernity is characterized by the "territorialization of desire" (1977) in oppressive social institutions, only to abandon a philosophy and politics of desire later on and—like Baudrillard—immerse himself in semiotic theory and philosophy of language and communication.

Jean Baudrillard, one of the most frequently cited contemporary social theorists, has been called "*the* supertheorist of a new postmodernity" (Best and Kellner, 1991, p. 111) and "a sort of academic Jimi Hendrix" (Levin, 1996, p. 25). His writings over three decades (nearly twenty full-length books and numerous articles, essays, and interviews) have been translated from the original French into English, German, Spanish, and several other languages. In addition, books and electronic discussion groups devoted to his work abound (one search engine turned up thousands of Web sites pertaining to Baudrillard). Still relatively unknown among social scientists, he is a leading figure in cultural studies and political theory.

Baudrillard's work has undergone significant changes since his first published book, *Le Système des Objets* (1968). Yet the central theme remains: techno-capitalism has created a rupture in history. The modern era was characterized by the *demystification of reality*, a period in which various depth models (such as Marxism and Freudianism) were used to reveal the realities that lay beneath appearances. Modernity was "the radical destruction of appearances, the disenchantment of the world and its abandonment to the violence of interpretation and history" (Baudrillard, 1984b, p.38), "a revolution in meaning" grounded in the dialectics of history, economics, or desire (Best and Kellner, 1991, p. 127). Postmodernity, by contrast, is characterized by the *absence of meaning*—"the immense process of the destruction of meaning, equal to the earlier destruction of appearances" (Baudrillard, 1984b, pp. 38–9).

We now live in a world of *hyperreality* and *simulation*. What has occurred is a blurring of heretofore clear distinctions between the real and the unreal, the image and reality. TV personalities and actors receive letters not only to themselves but to the characters they play; *models* of reality (the ideal man, woman, home, or sex life) are used to determine and judge what is real; entertainment bytes have become the day's news; simulations of real life situations (for example, *Court TV*) are a new and highly popular form of entertainment. It is not simply that we cannot tell the difference between what is real and what is not, Baudrillard says. Our postmodern world is marked by "implosion," a process of social entropy: dead meanings and frozen forms mutate into new combinations and permutations; there is growth beyond limits; the universe turns in on itself, and collapses into inertia (Best and Kellner, 1991, p. 126). Simulation, experienced as more real than actual institutions, has become reality. All sorts of boundaries—including those between politics and entertainment, popular and high culture, facts and hype—have crumbled. Signs have taken on a life of their own and constitute a new social order. The respective roles of subject and object have reversed themselves; objects (commodities, information, media) are now fully in control. Nothing new is possible in art or theory: "It has all been done. . . . So all that are left are pieces. All that remains to be done is to play with the pieces" (Baudrillard, 1984a, p. 24).

The subject/object dichotomy—and the clear superiority of the subject— has been the basis of Western philosophy from Plato through modern science. If Baudrillard is correct that the image and the real have imploded, that there is no meaning but only signs, information, and simulation, and that "the object" has triumphed over "the subject"—that we human beings are now dominated by our fetishized creations—then philosophy (and much else) are certainly dead. What becomes of subjectivity? It too is dead. In his recent writings, Baudrillard recommends (partly in jest, partly seriously) that we give up "the hubris of subjectivity" and any illusion that we have control over things or can change the world. We should submit to and become more like the hyperreal objects we created. This is Baudrillard's "fatal strategy," described by Levin (1996) as

> a conscious and systematic perversion of the Hegelian subject-object dialectic, in which the outcome of the history of the Spirit is no longer conceived as a triumph of the concrete universal, but as a kind of squalid failure of transcendence and collapse into the abstract particular.
>
> (Levin, 1996, p. 27)

The only way out is to pursue an extreme course of action, to go beyond all limits (for example, to consume always and anything toward no purpose), to push the system beyond itself ("into hyperlogic") and thereby produce something new (Baudrillard, 1987, 1988a, 1988b, 1988c, 1989, 1990, 1994). Although subjectivity has been destroyed, Baudrillard never- theless describes the subjective state engendered by living in the postmodern hyperreal world. The masses, he says, become bored, restless, apathetic; they are sometimes inert and sometimes giddy. But the over- riding experience is melancholy.

Baudrillard is a controversial figure. Nearly a decade ago he began to withdraw from academic life, while continuing to write as a journalist and "professional intellectual." As the first and still most prominent "high-tech" social theorist, he has been praised for his trenchant analyses of consumer society, cybernetics, the media, art, and popular culture. He has also been scorned for having abandoned a progressive political or social theory, for his retreat into metaphysics, and for certain statements appearing in recent satir- ical essays that align him with neo-conservative positions (for example, that history has ended and that the Gulf War never happened). His writings— increasingly obscure, poetic, and bizarre (by academic standards) and including travelogues, anecdotes, and memoirs—are considered rhetorical and banal by some and brilliant by others. According to Levin, Baudrillard has turned himself into a "bizarre object" whose "repudiation of intellectual tradition has already become part of that tradition" (1996, p. 27).

It might appear, from this brief and selective summary of his work, that Baudrillard is radically non-epistemological. Certainly, he is not recommending anything like a new epistemology. "Knowing" does not seem to play a part either in his description of postmodern culture nor in the few recommendations he makes about what we can do. But what *is* he doing? Why is he so concerned to describe, analyze, and understand the current state and status of reality, and how are they qualitatively different from modern reality? Why is he so despairing about the disappearance of meaning in all its manifestations? Both concerns imply, to us, a vantage point from which he is stepping back and viewing the world—a hallmark of the epistemological posture or gaze.

The form of his writing also suggests that modernity still has a hold on him. On the one hand, it is understandable that Baudrillard would struggle to give up denotative language and create ways of speaking and writing that are more consistent with hyperreality, that is, a world where language *in fact* (or, in his view) does not denote (because there is nothing *to* denote). On the other hand, to paraphrase Quine, from the point of epistemological footing "hyperreality" is no less "reality" for being "hyper"—the more-real-than-real is still reality-based. In his attempt to create language that has a closer proximity to "(hyper)reality," Baudrillard reveals an allegiance to reality, not to activity.

Jean-François Lyotard, Baudrillard's contemporary, has been equally prolific and influential in shaping the dialogue on postmodernity. From his first book, an introduction to phenomenology (1954), through his best-known work, *The Postmodern Condition: A Report on Knowledge* (1984, originally published in French in 1979), to his most recent essays and interviews, Lyotard's critiques of modernity have emphasized the oppression and coercion of the hegemonic philosophy. Trained in philosophy at the Sorbonne, he has, over four decades, grounded his theoretical work in one or another philosophical school. Husserl, Kant, Marx, Nietzsche, and Wittgenstein are among those whom he has followed at one time or another.

Lyotard was also a leading figure in the French academic left, having been politically active during the 1950s and 1960s, first in trade union politics, then in the movement for Algerian independence, the anti-war movement, and the May 1968 student movement. He wrote for left journals, was a member of the French group *Socialisme ou Barbarie* through the mid-1960s, and briefly formed his own political organization before abandoning Marxism in the early 1970s.

Lyotard came to see Marxism and other Enlightenment theories as historical narratives—stories about historical process presented as the truth of history. Influenced by the works of Kuhn, Feyerabend and Anglo-American philosophy of language and linguistics (discourse and narrative analysis and speech act theory, especially J. L. Austin's notion of the *performative*), Lyotard approaches the cultural transformations of post-industrial societies—in particular, transformations in science and knowledge—in "the context of the crisis in narratives" (1984, p. xxiii).

In *The Postmodern Condition* he explores the nature of scientific knowledge. Science, Lyotard says, has always distinguished itself from narratives, judging them to be fables. However, to the extent that science seeks the truth,

> it is obliged to legitimate the rules of its own game. It then produces a discourse of legitimation with respect to its own status, a discourse called philosophy. I will use the term *modern* to designate any science that legitimates itself with reference to a metadiscourse of this kind making an explicit appeal to some grand narrative.
>
> (Lyotard, 1984, p. xxiii)

Liberation from superstition and ignorance and the production of wealth, truth, and progress are part of the grand narrative of modern science.

Lyotard likens the legitimation of science to legitimation in the legal arena; it is

> the process by which a "legislator" dealing with scientific discourse is authorized to prescribe the stated conditions (in general, conditions of internal consistency and experimental verification) determining whether a statement is to be included in that discourse for consideration by the scientific community.
>
> (Lyotard, 1984, p. 8)

As he continues this argument, Lyotard makes an important link between science and morality—at the level of discourse:

> The parallel may appear forced. But as we will see, it is not. The question of the legitimacy of science has been indissociably linked to that of the legitimation of the legislator since the time of Plato. From this point of view, the right to decide what is true is not independent of the right to decide what is just, even if the statements consigned to the two authorities differ in nature. The point is that there is a strict interlinkage between the kind of language called science and the kind called ethics and politics; they both stem from the same perspective, the same "choice" if you will— the choice called the Occident.
>
> (Lyotard, 1984, p. 8)

With the loss of grand (or meta) narratives that characterize postmodernity ("Simplifying to the extreme, I define *postmodern* as incredulity toward metanarratives," Lyotard, 1984, p. xxiv), science has lost its means of legitimation.

Lyotard is especially concerned to understand the current status of scientific knowledge, given the way in which it has become increasingly subordinate to new technologies. Cybernetics, informatics, and the growth of computer languages, he argues, have transformed the nature of knowledge into "an informational commodity indispensable to productive power" for which nations compete (1984, p. 5). This change has important repercussions for science and education; now devoid of grand narratives, both become completely pragmatic. As Lyotard puts it:

> The question (overt or implied) now asked by the professionalist student, the State, or institutions of higher education is no longer "Is it true?" but "What use is it?" In the context of the mercantilization of knowledge, more often than not this question is equivalent to: "Is it saleable?"
>
> (Lyotard, 1984, p. 51)

Such an environment of delegitimation on the one hand and pragmatics on the other is "sounding the knell of the age of the Professor: a professor is no more competent than memory bank networks in transmitting established knowledge" (p. 53). As we saw earlier, this is precisely the kind of thing that worries the neo-liberal pragmatists like Menand, who reduce postmodernism to bad marketing for the university (see Chapter 2). Lyotard, however, is neither so pragmatic nor so pessimistic. For, as he sees it, the science activity (the game of science) itself is changing—and with it the very meaning of knowledge. Scientific knowledge has historically been privileged over and distinguished from nonscientific knowledge (narrative knowledge) by virtue of the fact that it gave priority to its own legitimation and certified itself through argumentation and proof. These two kinds of knowledge are really two different discourses, and their unequal relationship is "an intrinsic effect of the rules specific to each game" (Lyotard, 1984, p. 27).

Following Lyotard's argument, all science is discourse, story or language-game; postmodern science is recognized as such. Only the rules of the science game have changed with the "return of the narrative in the non-narrative" (p. 27). Theory, for Lyotard, is "a narrative which claims not to be one by virtue of a pretension to omnitemporality" (that is, a "forgetting" of its own temporality as a narrative act) (1977, p. 67). Invoking Wittgenstein (to whom he refers, along with Kant, as "epilogues to modernity and prologues to an honourable postmodernity" (1988a, p. xiii), Lyotard decries the pessimism that, for many philosophers and others, accompanies the loss of a universal metalanguage, the grand narrative, the privileging of scientific knowledge, and the recognition of the indeterminacy and infinite possibility of new language-games:

> Wittgenstein's strength is that he did not opt for the positivism that was being developed by the Vienna Circle but outlined in his investigations of language-games a kind of legitimation not based on performativity [pragmatic efficiency]. That is what the postmodern world is all about. Many people have lost the nostalgia for the lost narrative. It in no way follows that they are reduced to barbarity. What saves them from it is their

knowledge that their legitimation can only spring from their own linguistic practice and communicational interaction.

(Lyotard, 1984, p. 41)

The postmodern science game is open-ended in part because language-games are heterogeneous. The goals of science are no longer (if they ever were) discovering what was previously unknown and communicating to reach consensus. Scientists are no longer producers of the known, but of *the unknown*. Citing numerous examples from foundations of mathematics, quantum theory, microphysics, and quantum mechanics as instances of post-modern science, Lyotard describes science as now concerned with paradox, the undecidable, catastrophe, and the limits of control and prediction. The goal of scientific (indeed, all postmodern) dialogue for Lyotard is not consensus, for that would violate language—language is heteronymous (one game is not translatable into another) and paralogous (there is no model for determining the limits of what is tolerable as a move in any particular game). The concept *paralogism* is important in Lyotard's characterization of post-modernity. Unlike the *innovation* of modernity—making new moves within the rules of a particular language-game—paralogism is the "impossible" move, the move that displaces the rule of the game, creating the possibility of nonrepresentation.

This, then, is the position Lyotard laid out in *The Postmodern Condition*. Since then, he has developed some of these ideas and altered others. (Some of his followers and interpreters, for example, Bennington, 1988, believe there is little continuity in his work.) In place of Wittgenstein's notion of language-games, in *Le Differend* (1988a, originally published in French in 1983) Lyotard begins to use the terms "phrase regimens" and "genres of discourse" to convey (show) that knowledge, truth, opinions, politics, history, and so on are discursive. Here and in subsequent writings he aims to develop modes of language that disrupt abstract genres of discourse through employing imagery, poetics, and ambiguity—to "paint with and in words" (Lyotard, 1971). In *Le Differend* he makes much more of the tyranny in the hegemony of "the economic genre" (the efficiency-driven mode of consumerist, technological society) and how it is destroying subjectivity. Drawing on Kant's writings on judgment, the beautiful and the sublime, and the metaphysics of morals, Lyotard bemoans the loss of "sublime feelings" such as enthusiasm, respect, admiration, and sorrow (1988a, p. 179); the postmodern experience is marked, for Lyotard, by the absence of such "vigorous emotions." (Like Baudrillard, he refers to contemporary humanity as melancholy.)

The only hope we have lies in our language. Language inevitably contains and produces conflict—Lyotard's *differend*—because different genres of discourse have different, non-overlapping, rules. It is this that gives us the potential to create new moves, new rules, and perhaps new games. In the *differend* is the possibility for plurality of voice, for differences to be articulated, for all to enter the terrain and speak.

Lyotard concludes what is for the most part a poetics of despair in this way:

> The only insurmountable obstacle that the hegemony of the economic genre comes up against is the heterogeneity of phrase regimens and of genres of discourse. This is because there is not "language" and "Being," but occurrences. The obstacle does not depend on the "will" of human beings in one sense or in another, but on the differend.... [which] summons humans to situate themselves in unknown phrase universes, even if they don't have the feeling that something has to be phrased.
>
> (Lyotard, 1988a, p. 181)

By insisting on *occurrences*, or *events*, as "what there is," Lyotard rejects critical features of modern epistemology. For example, he resurrects the important distinction between an event and the representation of an event: "There are events: something happens which is not tautological with what has happened" (Lyotard, 1988a, p. 79). But modernity blurs the distinction between "It happens" and "What happens," making the event invisible by reducing it to what it "means." To escape representationalism, Lyotard introduces the concepts *figure* and *figural*. The postmodern is the *figural other* that necessarily accompanies modernism and modernist discourse. An event cannot be understood at the time it happens "because its singularity is alien to the language or structure of understanding to which it occurs" (Readings, 1996, p. 57). The value of narratives, for Lyotard, is as *figure*—not, as it is for some discourse analysts, a representation, an accounting, or even a construction of self. Narrative can "testify to the force of the event.... Postmodernism is the attempt rigorously to think the eventhood of the narratives of culture" (Readings, 1996, p. 83). It is the figural force of the event that disrupts modern thinking, the time of an event marking a "figural incommensurability" between the eventhood and the meaning of the event. The figural makes us aware, in representation, that there is something that cannot be represented.

In showing how representation overdetermines what an event "is"—how it necessarily excludes the other—Lyotard makes, we think, a valuable contribution to understanding the constraints of modern epistemology. In our activity-theoretic language, he shows that the "activityness" of an event (a happening, the figural) is distorted not only within and by a representationalist paradigm but also within and by an interpretive one. We think it reasonable, however, to ask what his activity is. In certain respects Lyotard has gone beyond the reformism of relational knowing; "it happens" appears to reject the age-old belief that since the world consists of things and relations between them, we must have things and relationality in order to know about the world. And yet his very argumentation against representation and relationality invokes, it seems to us, relational dualism. For both the paradox of eventhood (only in its representation is it revealed that it is not representable) and its singularity rest, ultimately, upon an epistemologically relational world. To assert that this event is not the same as that event requires the conception of particulars (formal identity) that, as we have seen, is the "cement" of relational models of knowing. Like the social constructionists, Lyotard tries to do away with epistemology but without getting rid of dualism—which is what the activity of doing away with epistemology entails.

We admire Lyotard's effort to give expression to the inexpressible (that which cannot be represented or interpreted). Yet we do not think this effort can take us "from here to there." As we shall attempt to show later in this chapter and in Chapter 4, it is (non-relational, political) *activity*—and not just *experience*—that breaks with epistemological dualism. This activity, we believe, is what is required if we are to escape from the modern paralysis of non-development. So while it is reasonable to ask (although we think the question unanswerable) whether *this* event (action) is the same as *that* event (action), it makes no sense to ask that question about *activity*; the historically monistic practice of human activity is radically non-relational. Activity-theoretic, practical-critical understanding renders the need for, and application of, relationality obsolete. We can see that even in Marx's classic statement, at the same time methodologically insightful and flawed (see Chapter 4 and Newman and Holzman, 1996), about dialectical–historical materialism:

> This method . . . starts out from the real premises and does not abandon them for a moment. Its premises are men, not in any fantastic isolation and rigidity, but in their actual, empirically perceptible process of development under definite conditions.
>
> (Marx and Engels, 1973, pp. 47–8)

We think it is significant that both Baudrillard and Lyotard radically reject the meaning–use equation that, as we have said, is prevalent (and usually unexamined) in Anglo-American language-based critiques of modern epistemology. They not only refuse to accept the view that language represents and denotes (inner feelings and/or outer reality); they deny that language *means*, period. In different ways, they argue that the modern conception of meaning (and here we include the overidentification of meaning with use) has been or must be abandoned. Lyotard's figural is an attempt to break from "the revelation of meaning" that characterizes both myth and narratology; the figural is not cognitively based, but experience- (if not yet activity-) based, while for Baudrillard postmodernity is nothing less than the destruction of meaning. Yet, sympathetic as we are to their insistence on throwing out the cognitive, pragmatic, and interpretive conceptions of meaning, we cannot approve of their inclination to abandon the human *meaning-making activity* along with it. Without an activity-theoretic methodology, it is probably impossible to get rid of the former and still hold on to the latter. Within the framework of practical-critical, revolutionary activity, however, the meaning-making activity is no trouble, since it does not produce meaning. Activity is not productive; it is the tool-and-result-ish, ontological-dialectical unity of a post-postmodern world.

DEVELOPING DEVELOPMENT

We also admire, and have reservations concerning, a growing body of work that, in its attempt to rid developmental psychology of its modern metaphysics, abandons the activity of human development. Recent deconstructionist and social constructionist analyses have shown developmental psychology and its conceptions of growth, normality, children, childhood, and the like to be ideologically biased, political, rhetorical, and pseudoscientific (for example, Burman, 1994; Bradley, 1989, 1991; Henriques *et al.*, 1984; Morss, 1990, 1993, 1996; Walkerdine, 1993). These critiques leave little doubt that psychology's notion of development as a continuous, linear, evolutionary, universal, and individual process is not only theoretically untenable but practically-critically anti-developmental (Newman and Holzman, 1996). We agree with our fellow critical developmental psychologists that the modern construction of development should be abandoned. However, we do not agree with their claim that the actual process of *human beings developing* ("people in their [sometimes] empirically perceptible process of development under definite conditions," as Marx put it) is nothing more than a Euro-American fiction. We search instead for a form of life (a form of activity) in which development does not produce development.

We can illustrate our concerns with some recent work by Walkerdine (1993). It seems to us that she is rightly uncomfortable with psychology's insistence on a universal course of development because of how exceptions to it are explained away as deviance or pathology, thereby serving to keep oppression hidden and to marginalize those who are not developing "naturally." We can even agree with the thrust of her recommendation that it is necessary "to account for the production of subjectivity within historically and geographically specific practices, with no clear developmental sequences at all" (Walkerdine, 1993, p. 461). It is in her denial of *developing* that we discern a conflation of the map (the psychologist's account of developmental sequences) with the mapped (people's emergent life activity), and the problems such conflation poses.

In the name of historically specific practices and in defense of the oppressed and marginalized, Walkerdine winds up, ironically, glossing over the significance of specific practices, denying qualitative change and difference, and replacing the universals of psychology with still another set of identity-political universals (see Chapter 4), in this case, her own class- and gender-analytic abstractions. Much of Walkerdine's research has been an effort to show that what psychology labels pathology (poor cognitive functioning, for example) is in fact oppression (Walkerdine, 1984, 1988, 1989, 1991; Walkerdine and Lucey, 1989). Typically, she presents a traditional pathologizing research account and shows how it ignores issues of class, race, and/or gender. She then concludes—incorrectly, in our view— that because it mystifies in this way, psychology has not profoundly shaped the lives of people "on the periphery."

For example, Walkerdine's argument against a research study premised on the developmental universal of "the power of the puzzling mind of the four year old" consists in pointing out that a working-class child who was pathologized for "lacking puzzlement" about money (in contrast to a middle-class white child who did puzzle about it) should not be pathologized because the conditions of her life—money is always scarce—are such that she has "no grounds for puzzlement" (1993, p. 461). No doubt the girl should not be pathologized, but neither should she be reductionistically explained by vulgar materialism.

In another instance Walkerdine tells us that the precocious sexuality of working-class girls "threatens the idea of a natural childhood innocence" (1993, p. 459). She refuses to see the girls in the terms set up by developmental psychology—for example, as being deprived of "childhood"—because that would pathologize them. So far, so good. But she goes on to insist that "childhood" is a fiction and that the *idea of development* is the problem. We are unconvinced. If anything, it is *ideas* (including the idea of development) that are the problem—not developing. The concern and conflictedness that parents, teachers, and pre-adolescent and adolescent working-class girls themselves experience toward their sexuality probably have nothing to do with the *idea of natural childhood innocence* and everything to do with the quality of their lives, notions of upward mobility, self-esteem, sense of self, and morality—in short, the complex interplay of an infinitude of social-cultural practices.

Walkerdine's allegiance to ideas (more precisely, to the ideas of intellectuals) is revealed even more in her assessment of the current relationship between the center and the periphery (the marginalized, like working-class girls). Modernity's biggest challenge, she believes, is the threat posed by the periphery to the center: "That peripheral subjects are *not willing to be defined* as regulated according to the pathologizing models accorded to them is what most threatens the power of developmental orthodoxy" (Walkerdine, 1993, p. 461, emphasis added). We find this statement to be quite peculiar. For one thing, during the latter half of this century there has been nearly a wholesale acceptance of pathologizing models and institutional practices by all classes in the highly industrialized countries. There is, in fact, evidence that those "on the periphery" have been the *most* accepting of such models and practices by virtue of being subject to their institutionalization through psychiatric and educational diagnosis. Since those in power do the defining (they are the ones, after all, who invented *definition*!), it is difficult to see how it could be otherwise unless and until the definition of definition is transformed—through collective revolutionary activity. For another thing, if there were such unwillingness on the part of "peripheral subjects" to be pathologized, then Walkerdine would not—could not—be engaged in the research she does!

How is it, then, that she can make such a claim? We cannot know, of course, but Walkerdine herself implicates the privileged and revisionist political position of the academic: "It is feminist and black work, for example, that has been most vociferous in attempting both to demonstrate the problems in modern developmental psychology and to put forth other possibilities" (Walkerdine, 1993, p. 461). So it is really those on the periphery *within academia* who are "unwilling" to accept pathologizing models and who are, consequently, threatening to modernity.

We have tried to show the insidiousness of epistemology. The confusion of the map with the mapped, the substituting of oneself for the Other, the exempting of one's own environment from critical deconstruction, are as pervasive in politically motivated progressive and postmodern research as they are in modern social science. We think this is largely due to the institutional environment in which research, critique, and theorizing are done. Academia cannot help but be overdetermined by epistemology. It is, ultimately, a non-growthful environment. Perhaps it is the critical psychologists who want to discard developing as a non-issue who themselves have stopped developing. We do not say this to be unfriendly, but rather to point to an unself-consciousness on the part of our colleagues concerning their own historical-political-discursive context. For while their deconstruction of developmental psychology as discourse is finely attuned to the specifics of the context (determined by the Age of Enlightenment's grand narrative of progress and the growth of free market capitalism) in which it emerged, there is no parallel deconstruction, no critical self-reflexive examination of the environment (discourse and otherwise) of *their* discourse. From our revolutionary location, we cannot help but think that it may perhaps be self-serving to make one's living, and reputation, by arguing that there is no such thing as developing at the very moment in human history when development is on the verge of ending.

John Morss, arguably the most eloquent spokesperson for *and* critic of critical developmental psychology, has taken an important step in the direction of self-reflexivity. In *Growing Critical: Alternatives to Developmental Psychology* (1996), he reviews and evaluates critical psychological theorizing because

> If human development is too important to be left to orthodox psychology, it is also too important to be left to critical psychology. . . . We must submit the claims of the critics to an examination every bit as rigorous as their examination of the orthodoxy.
>
> (Morss, 1996, p. ix)

Morss is conflicted about the issue of development (the human activity); he also calls for an "anti-developmental" point of view: "the search for anti-developmental alternatives must therefore be seen as an emancipatory project" (Morss, 1996, p. 1). It is not clear to us why he holds on to emancipation and gives up developing, nor how human emancipation could be created *without* further human developing.

We think that the constraints of the overly cognitive environment of academic intellectual debate produce such paradoxes. Societal transformation is an extended historical process of human revolutionary activity, not the result of a theoretical statement or critical deconstruction. Yet the way in which critical psychologists argue against the Enlightenment bias of grand narratives, against theory as Truth, against universals and models (pathologizing and otherwise), repeats these very biases. Morss reviews our work (Newman and Holzman, 1993) favorably. He calls it anti-developmental and, from the vantage point of his location, it is. We, on the other hand, consider it ever-developing—developing in a way and in a place which does not produce development. Within an epistemologically overdetermined environment of ideas, it is—perhaps—anti-developmental, but within a developing community and as the practice of method (revolutionary activity), it is developmental.

WHAT IS THE PRACTICE OF METHOD?

What we now call the development community (a community that develops without producing development) is a new *kind* of community. Somewhat formalistically, we recently described it as "a community which at once supports development and has as its non-instrumental, non-pragmatic (tool-and-result) activity the development it supports" (Newman and Holzman, 1996, p. 151). Here we want to tell the story of how we practice method, of how our developing (development) community was and continues to be built, of how we have created a unique environment in which, among other things, Vygotsky, Wittgenstein, and Marx speak to us in the way they do. How do we tell this story without distorting the actual process we and hundreds of co-workers (as well as thousands who have participated along the way) have been going through? After all, we are in the midst of our practice; perhaps we are too close to see very much. On the other hand, we have lived it; perhaps we are already too distanced by the process of continuous assessment and transformation. These complex social activities (like any other) can be described in an infinite number of ways, none more valid than any other. Our concern is not to "tell the truth"—neither as ethnographers, historians, novelists, or social critics—but to speak as revolutionary activists.

We have begun to write this section several times, only to discard (more accurately, delete) what we have written as a *cognitivist revision* of our history. From where we are now, it is extremely difficult to refrain from imposing a structure or order, smoothing over chaos, interpreting our deconstructive-reconstructive *anti-institution/development community-building activity* as derived from either intellectual curiosity or theoretical commitment, presenting our activity as guided by what we knew (or thought we knew) or know (or think we know)—in short, it is hard not to epistemologize our history/work/lives-as-lived. Perhaps a non-chronological, non-systematic telling—a multi-level description—will keep us from deviating too far.

One of us (Holzman) recently returned from an international conference in Geneva sponsored by the Society for Sociocultural Research. The theme, Piaget–Vygotsky: 1896–1996 (in commemoration of the centennial of their birth), drew nearly one thousand people from forty countries, the majority more "Vygotskian" than "Piagetian." In a conversation about the conference back in New York City, Holzman was asked (by a woman who studies at the Center for Developmental Learning and is familiar with the Vygotskian Barbara Taylor School—both projects of our development community), "Oh, so you got to meet people from Vygotskian schools all over the world! How wonderful! How many are there?" Delightedly surprised to hear that there were so many Vygotskians present, she assumed—being unfamiliar with academia and the world of institutionalized research—that a gathering of Vygotskians would be a gathering of practitioners.

There are, as far as we know, barely a handful of schools in the world that identify themselves as Vygotskian (along with a hundred or so demonstration projects in existing school systems). There is, as far as we know, no Vygotskian-influenced psychotherapeutic approach other than social therapy, the one we practice. However, the number of funded research projects (both theoretical and experimental) described as Vygotskian being carried out by university professors and graduate students around the world is in the thousands. As the work of this early Soviet revolutionary thinker becomes increasingly well known within the university, it is fast being turned into a bona fide research paradigm, and losing both its critical and practical-critical, revolutionary edge.

One would be hard pressed to find an environment more alienated and epistemologically overdetermined than the academic conference. That this particular conference was devoted to "sociocultural research" and held in honor of an early Soviet, a Russian Jewish Marxist whose revolutionary psychological-methodological work was suppressed under Stalin, just made that alienation and epistemological overdetermination all the more glaring. We are speaking here of a few hundred young Brazilian psychologists, obviously committed to transforming their country's anachronistic European-style school system, presenting research results without ever mentioning that their work environment is a country in which a small percentage of children attend school and where each week hundreds of homeless children are gunned down in the streets by the police. We are also speaking of a dozen or so Yugoslavian psychologists reporting, with sadness in their voices, on what they have learned about the impact of war on Serbian and Muslim children—a war that is matter-of-factly referred to in the media, in passing, as "ethnic cleansing." We are speaking of psychologists from countries, cultures—indeed, a world—in crisis, where people daily destroy each other (psychically if not physically) who gathered together for five days to speak *at each other about ideas*. And we are speaking about caring, committed, intelligent people with the best of intentions.

Vygotsky himself did not live into the mid-twentieth century, when talk of paradigms and paradigm shifts entered intellectual circles. But he was keenly aware that human activity all too easily becomes severed into process and product, that product becomes reified as the history of its production is forgotten. He spoke of "fossilized behavior" both within human development and in psychological research (as when initial data are discarded from a study). We prefer to speak of fetishized objects. The practice of method is a moving about around and beyond the fetishized objects we human beings have created—especially fetishized knowing and language. Vygotsky's revolutionary brilliance was his recognition that human life (including the study of human life) requires that method be practiced, not applied. The science activity, like all human activity, embodies its own paradox—it must create its object of investigation. Here is how he put it:

> The search for method becomes one of the most important problems of the entire enterprise of understanding the uniquely human forms of psychological activity. In this case, the method is simultaneously prerequisite and product, the tool and the result of the study.
>
> (Vygotsky, 1978, p. 65)

Vygotsky is offering a new conception of methodology here. In traditional scientific and philosophical terms, method is separate from the substance and results of the inquiry. It is something to be applied to objects (particulars) in order to yield results; it is instrumental and pragmatic, a functional means to an end. Using Vygotsky's language, we can say that traditional scientific method is not "simultaneously . . . the tool and the result" but the tool *for* result (Newman and Holzman, 1993). Such a dualistic conception of method is epistemologically overdetermined, for it requires, on the one hand, objects of knowledge and, on the other, tools (method) for attaining knowledge about the objects.

Vygotsky's method is dialectical rather than dualistic. It is activity-based rather than cognition-based. Method is practiced, not applied. Whatever is to be discovered is not separate from the activity of *practicing method*; it is not "out there" awaiting the application of an already made tool, but is dialectically inseparable (that is, neither idealistically indistinguishable, nor materially distinguishable) from the activity of discovery. Practice, for Vygotsky, does not derive from theory. Rather, it is practice that restructures science "from beginning to end," that "poses the task and is the supreme judge of theory" (1982, pp. 388–9). *Practicing method* simultaneously creates the object of knowledge and the tool by which that knowledge might be known. Tool and result come into existence together; their relationship is one of *dialectical unit*, not instrumental duality (Newman and Holzman, 1993, 1996).

In making this methodological break with the dominant dualistic, instrumental and reductionistic scientific paradigm, Vygotsky planted the seeds of a new psychology (really an anti-psychology), one without a sharp distinction between what psychology is about (its substance) and how it is done (its method, or what is sometimes called metapsychology). He engaged in psychological investigation in the interest of discovering/creating what psychology is.

Not everyone sees Vygotsky in these revolutionary terms. In fact, the point we are making about method—the critically important distinction between tool-and-result and tool-for-result methodology—is, for the most part, overlooked by his interpreters and followers alike. Most contemporary Vygotskians regard him primarily as a psychologist, specifically an educational or cognitive psychologist, and use his conceptions and substantive findings as instrumental tools to advance current psychological research about learning. His work is thus used to breathe some new life into the traditional psychological paradigm. This reformist application violates Vygotsky's revolutionary enterprise and life-as-lived; his own practice of method is paradigmized, fossilized, and fetishized.

In 1968, Newman and a handful of others set up an apartment commune in the Bronx, a borough of New York City. "Knowing" only that they wanted to build something different together—an environment that was not hypocritical or intentionally hierarchical, a kind of political, educational, and psychological center, something that might turn out to have some meaning for people—they hadn't a clue, much less a plan, as to how to do it. The main concern in these early years of the development (developing) community, as it is now, was the social process by which such an environment could and would be built. Great attention was consequently paid to what and how everything was being done; in the effort to prevent unexamined societal assumptions from overdetermining the environment, every activity was of equal importance. How to pay the rent, teach symbolic logic, organize a free health clinic, and clean the bathroom were inseparable activities in creating a new kind of environment. The ongoing process could be described, in postmodern language, as a radical political deconstruction.

Newman had worked as a machinist and served in Korea before completing an undergraduate degree in philosophy at the City College of New York in 1959 and a PhD in philosophy of science at Stanford University in 1962. For the next few years, he taught philosophy at a number of colleges and universities around the country—getting fired from many for giving As to all his students to keep the men from being drafted into the armed services during the Vietnam War. In 1968, he left his last academic position at the City College of New York and began doing community organizing and radical politics. He and the others in the Bronx commune believed that changing society—schools, health and mental health treatment, and politics—had more to do with building new kinds of institutions and community organizing than with having the correct critical analysis. They believed that *how* we do things—the social process— mattered more in a human sense (that is, in terms of development) than what we know or even what we are doing. They believed that environments are not neutral contexts; they overdetermine social activity—*unless they are created, continuously, along with the activity*. This non-epistemological activity of practicing method engaged (and engages) people from all walks of life and every class and ethnic background, giving them the opportunity to participate, to the extent that they choose to, in "changing the world" by helping to create new kinds of political organizations, schools, medical care, psychotherapeutic practices, and culture.

We first described this process as *the practice of method* eleven years later in our first written collaboration (Holzman and Newman, 1979); fourteen years after that (Newman and Holzman, 1993), we called it *tool-and-result methodology* and *revolutionary activity*; another three years later on (Newman and Holzman, 1996) we referred to it as *the development commu-nity*. Our changing language (games) have more to do with the developmental process of reconstruction than with any change in activity, belief, or posture. For it was only after we (now numbering in the hundreds) had not only kept our non-knowing environment going but had created a viable practice of building community that included a network of indepen-dent psychotherapeutic, educational, political, and cultural organizations (financially supported and patronized by poor, working-class, and middle-class communities) that our intellectual interests and academic histories began to play a significant role. In this non-epistemological environment, Marx could be appreciated for the relevance of his revolutionary philosoph-ical writings; Wittgenstein (whom Newman had studied at Stanford) could be seen as therapeutic and practical; Vygotsky (whose work Holzman had become familiar with as a researcher at Rockefeller University) could be read as a Marxist revolutionary scientist. We have also been able to see and say some things developmental concerning other intellectual and political traditions—including Black psychology, lesbian and gay liberation, feminist studies, ethnography and cultural anthropology, systems therapy, political and avant-garde theatre—as they too have been included in and reshaped by our practice.[3] Since we are neither knowledge-seeking nor knowledge-producing, we are collectively able to use what we learn to continue creating the developmental developing environment.

Perhaps we are saying nothing more than, "We say and write what we do because of what and how we do." Banal as this may sound, we think it needs to be said, for the importance of activity and institutional location, including the history of one's cultural-political process of production (that is, politics) is so often overlooked. Indeed, had they not been ignored for most of this century, there would have been no need for critical social science or the sociology of knowledge. In our case, there is the further point that we would have nothing to say or write were it not for the - community-building activity we have been part of. Having created, to the extent possible in contemporary culture, an ecologically and historically valid experiment in the collective activity of practicing method (as opposed to an institutionally sanctioned experiment in the application of a fixed method), it would be surprising, we think, if we did not see things somewhat differently.

Vygotsky is transformed in this environment from a cognitive psychologist and mediation theorist to a therapeutic developmentalist and practicing methodologist. As revolutionary activists (developmentalists), it seems to us that what he called "learning that leads development" requires an activity-theoretic practice of method to build and sustain an environment conducive to growth. Wittgenstein is transformed in this environment from a father of ordinary language philosophy into a therapist who helps "make the problem vanish." He too is a therapeutic developmentalist and practicing methodologist. Creating and playing language-games frees us from fossilized, fetishized language use and involves us in the developmental activity of language making, completing each other in conversation, making meaning. Marx too is transformed in this environment. In no longer having to speak the Truth, his historically monistic dialectical-historical methodology is developmentally useful.

Over nearly thirty years, the development community of independent institutions has grown dramatically: from one apartment complex in New York City to social therapy centers in several American cities; from a handful of people to tens of thousands. Its work is now multifaceted and includes a training and education center (the East Side Institute for Short Term Psychotherapy and its Center for Developmental Learning); the largest community-based cultural organization for inner-city youth in the USA (the All Stars Talent Show Network); a highly respected multicultural Off-Off-Broadway theatre (the Castillo Theatre); a small press (Castillo International); a Vygotskian-influenced laboratory elementary school (the Barbara Taylor School); teen pregnancy and abuse prevention programs in preschools and public schools; and more. Significantly, it also includes a contributor base of 200,000 individuals who participate by giving their financial support to these ongoing projects.

From our societal-historical location, the human capacity for practical-critical, revolutionary activity that Marx identified is not "expressed" in our actions as thinkers, perceivers, conceivers, constructors, or interpreters (even if relational and situated), but completed in our creative performance as collective developers of our lives. Our developing community is not a version of a sixties-style "university without walls" but walls without a university. In *Lev Vygotsky: Revolutionary Scientist*, we spoke of it this way:

The creation of "history zones" where history games (and, as an element thereof, language-games) can be played (performed, we prefer to say) is somewhat analogous to the creation of the European-style university relative to the explosion of discoveries (mainly in the natural sciences) called modern science. That "universal zone" served a particular class at a particular historical moment. The "ZBD" ("Zone of Bourgeois Development") required an urban-based research-educational community directly connected to the most progressive forces in the social environment (the bourgeoisie) while simultaneously being protected from the most regressive (the church and the nobility). The European-style university ("ZBD") played such a bourgeois revolutionary role. But the "ZPD" ("Zone of Proletarian Development") could not, ultimately, be the "ZBD." Thus, while the European-style university has been the home of many a proletarian revolution-in-name, it has also been the site of the most tragic sellouts of the working class. In this century traditional psychologists have often been in the forefront of both.

(Newman and Holzman, 1993, p. 91)

4   Deliberately unsystematic thoughts on a new way of running a country

The conclusion to Gergen's succinct characterization of the postmodern era that we quoted in Chapter 2 (p. 23) is the distinctly political metaphor, "The center fails to hold." The formulation (from Yeats's "The Second Coming") is in this context *substantively* apt, for postmodernism makes "compromise as Truth" structurally meaningless (given that there is no Truth). Furthermore, it is *formally* appropriate in the sense that the issue of whether there can be a developmental way to continue knowing and, if not, what lies ahead for our species is, in our opinion, ultimately a political matter.

The search for the center has not only guided the practice of politics in liberal democratic society these past few hundred years, it has shaped our very way of thinking and talking about politics. Left and right projected on to the ends of a finite and fixed horizontal line—with the center that this model logically, geometrically, necessitates—have come to mean much, much more than which side of the aisle someone sits on in the French (or any other) national assembly; this horizontal model has come to define programmatically oriented democratic compromise politics. Thus, the postmodern suggestion that the center fails to hold is viewed by many with great alarm; it seems to imply the end of compromise and the emergence of one form or another of extremism. Such radical relativism—tantamount to either some kind of authoritarianism or anarchism, politically speaking—understandably shakes liberal sensibility to its roots. Nevertheless, to many, Gergen's descriptive (not prescriptive) observation about the collapse of the center seems increasingly to be the basis of the emerging social and political pragmatics of our time and our society.

Not only political scientists (so-called) and philosophically oriented thinkers on such matters but, more importantly, political players are coming to see things this way. Amid eight days of Republican Party and Democratic Party nominating conventions in the US in the late summer of 1996 (nothing very much happened during these multi-million dollar post-modern—in the critical sense of the term—extravaganzas except for thousands of hours of media coverage and commentary on "what happened"), a Democratic Party advisor (an insider) made an unusually pithy and honest comment in responding to a typically boring modernistically formulated question. The interviewer made a rambling inquiry: was Clinton's perspective "actually" liberal (left) but being covered up by a moderate political presentation, or was it "really" a moderate (more right) position hidden behind a liberal political presentation? The Democratic Party advisor, obviously at once amused and annoyed by the interviewer's naiveté and verbosity, interrupted to say something like, "None of the above. Clinton's position is exactly one-eighth of an inch to the left of Bob Dole's, the Republican Party candidate. Period."

We quite agree. Clinton is America's first self-consciously postmodern, anti-centrist president. Don't be fooled by the use of the term "left" here. The subtext of the enlightened (or, at least, enlightening) advisor's comment is a total rejection of the left-center-right (centrist) political paradigm, for it turns left and right (back) into purely relative terms which, of course, these designations are in their original use as spatial markers; it thereby eliminates any meaningful notion of a reified center. Indeed, the modifier "one-eighth of an inch" implied that Clinton's positioning self-consciously left no room at all between himself and Dole for anyone else or any other point of view ("No room for Ross" [Perot], as some American pundits tagged the utterly disingenuous and bipartisan strategic effort to defuse the pro-independent, anti-two-party fervor of millions of ordinary Americans). There was to be no center. Period.

During the 1996 convention period, C-SPAN, the US cable network of political record, covered a talk on global democracy delivered at the Aspen Institute by political scientist Kenneth Jowitt, who characterized this moment in American history as more than likely embodying (or, at least, requiring) a qualitative transformation in politics. Not simply new parties or new ideas or new programs, but new *kinds* of parties, ideas, and programs, he said, were needed. Jowitt spoke, as well, of new definitions, although—not surprisingly—he did not speak of how definitions transform or are transformed (even the old ones in the old days, not to mention new ones in our days). Like so many in this postmodern moment, Jowitt's analysis rests fully on the modern epistemological assumption (more accurately, the assumption of epistemology) that to *know* x is, at a minimum, to increase the likelihood that x will be done or, as it is sometimes put, nothing will change (nothing will be done) unless there is some kind of antecedent knowing.

Harvard professor Michael Sandel's recent and valuable writings about the need for a new "public philosophy" rest on the same epistemological subtext. Neither in his book, *Democracy's Discontent* (1996a), nor in his conversation (Sandel, 1996b) does he pay attention to *how* a new public philosophy might come into being, no less whether a new philosophy (coming into being) might require a thoroughgoing re-examination and restructuring of the way(s) philosophies (public and otherwise, new and old) come (came) into being.

Might the epistemologically biased method which has dominated Western civilization's understanding (if not practice) of developmental social--historical transformation itself have to go through a qualitative transformation? Might we somehow have to transform what transformation *is* in order to move forward politically and otherwise? Might we not have to find a way to move beyond the tired pseudo-academic language of "offering new definitions" to a qualitatively new "definition" of what definition is? Might we not have to consider the possibility that a new "definition" might not be a definition at all? Indeed, is it not possible that an examination of "definition" from within our postmodern historical moment might reveal that in the past the language of definitions has had much more to do with *justifying* change (epistemologically)[1] than with *making* it—that theories of knowledge have been much more dominant than theories of activity? Arguably, the hegemony of knowing—from the Greeks through modern science to contemporary philosophy—is inextricably connected with the scientific/technological/industrial/political-economic dominance of the West/North. But is it not, perhaps, the very point of postmodernism (or, at least, shouldn't it be) that such epistemological overdetermination is inconsistent with further species and personal development—that such dominance is not only immoral, it is no longer productive, that is, developmental? Isn't this what "the center fails to hold" really suggests?

A MOMENT OF TRUTH?

But what happened? *Why* is the center "suddenly" (historically speaking) failing to hold? And can we, in good postmodern faith, ask such an epistemologically overdetermined question? Marxism, in some of its variations (but in a self-consciously "descienced" form), serves, in our opinion, as the best modern modality for "explaining" the folding (an abbreviation for "the failure to hold") of the center. For the failure of the so-called free market during this century, and the ensuing socio-political efforts to repair and/or reform economic capitalism without endangering the power relations of capitalism as a social system, are best understood by a materialist political economic analysis. And everyone, most especially the rulers of the capitalist countries and their advisors—from John Maynard Keynes to Clinton's Secretary of Labor, Robert Reich—has relied on Marxian insights about the nature of capital to reconstruct their post–free market societies.

Rosa Luxemburg, the early twentieth-century Polish political economist, insisted that free market capitalism's eventual demise (and the internal contradiction which will produce it) is best understood not (as orthodox Marxists do) in terms of "over-production" but rather in terms of "realization" (Luxemburg, 1958, 1972). She argued that the continued expansion of capital (she agreed with traditional Marxists and most other economists that non-expanding capital is not capital at all) required the continued existence of pre-capitalist economies. Why? According to Luxemburg, the realization of the value of the product of a given business (production) cycle in an investment form necessary to move to the next cycle of production ultimately demands pre-capitalist economies. Why? For one thing, the value created in a business-production cycle must hold the promise (and must fulfill the promise at least some of the time) of an expanded value. Capitalists will not continue to invest if they get only the same or less value in return. But whence comes the added value?

According to Luxemburg, nothing occurs *within* the capitalist production cycle to account for it. For while the expanded value itself may well be a unique feature of (exploited) labor—it creates value outputs above and beyond its input— there is nothing internal to the capitalist production cycle which can *realize* this added value. "Economic imperialism" is what makes it all work. Capitalism's overall superiority to pre-capitalist economies causes (coerces) feudal societies to pay much more than a product is worth, thereby yielding the realization of surplus value. In effect, the pre-capitalist societies not only buy particular products, they buy (are forced to buy) capitalism, that is, to buy on capitalist terms. The problem (the contradiction), as Luxemburg saw it, is that in buying capitalism these pre-capitalist societies eventually *become* capitalist (albeit poor capitalist) societies themselves. Ultimately, the whole world becomes capitalist; one day there are no pre-capitalist societies left. The center—the economic gap between capitalist and pre-capitalist economies—collapses and disappears. The consequence is a giant realization crisis, and less and less stimulation for capitalists to continue on to the next business-production cycle unless something is done about it to "guarantee" profits.

There are those who would identify the early twentieth-century completion of German expansionism and World War I as marking the historical moment when pre-capitalist societies disappeared from the face of the Earth, and the international depression of the late 1920s and 1930s as the resulting crisis or crises of realization.[2] Fascism and regulated welfare statism were, broadly speaking, the two competing "solutions" to this monumental capitalist crisis. Welfare statism, combined with Communism, won World War II (fortunately); the last fifty years of political economic history can be viewed as an effort by the US in particular to *recover* from that victory!

The famous (or infamous) "safety net" spoken of so often and with such passion in contemporary American politics has always been, it seems to us, a safety net not exclusively for the poor, but for capitalism as a whole. For whatever the complex motives of varying politicians and political parties might have been (or still might be), the shared concern of Democrats and Republicans alike (as well as their monied and powerful patrons) is, and always has been, the preservation of capitalism as an economic and social system. When free market capitalism crumbled in the late 1920s and 1930s, *regulatory-ism* emerged as the most favored solution. Again, the welfare state is not simply a means by which money and services are administered to the poor; it is the total transformation of the state and all its governmental arms from a loose domestic *coordinating* agency to a highly centralized *regulatory* agency. Everything—banking, the market, business, science, education, labor, the poor (and anything in between)—has become increasingly regulated this past half century to control against future collapse(s), and, meanwhile, turn a pretty profit for the "special interests."

The regulated society has, in turn, changed the very nature of US economics and politics and the relationship between them. For in a highly regulated market system (as opposed to a largely unregulated free market system), profitability (the realization, not to mention the creation, of surplus value) is increasingly determined by who controls and best manipulates the regulations. In *Tales of a New America* (1987), Robert Reich, a key economic advisor to Clinton, speaks of the dramatic transformation in the composition of corporate boards over the past fifty years; having been made up primarily of production or manufacturing related people, they are now more and more populated by lawyers (who know how to manipulate the regulations). The manufacturing sector of the US economy, profoundly (although temporarily) stimulated by World War II and the ensuing rebuilding of Europe and Japan (on the highly favorable economic terms articulated, for example, in the Bretton Woods agreement), failed to restructure itself adequately (as Germany and Japan did) for peacetime production. (Armaments production remained, of course, highly profitable, since it was largely controlled directly by government regulations and policy, the government being the principal purchaser of arms.) With the erosion of the US manufacturing base, the "manipulation of paper" (money, stocks, bonds) became the preferred area of economic growth; the regulated economy became a credit economy and, lawfully, a debt economy; the higher paid workforce became smaller and more middle class (white collar). The US went from being the world's leading creditor nation to the world's largest debtor nation (in recent years Japan, in particular, taking advantage of America's regulatory-ism). Meanwhile, the stock market apparently knows no bounds. Capitalism has been secured, and Communism defeated. But as with Muhammad Ali's highly publicized victory over Joe Frazier in the "thrilla in Manilla," we must ask—at what price?

The radical transformation from a free market economy to a regulatory one did not, in our view, entirely determine the political evolution of America. It did, however, have a significant impact on the very nature of US politics in the second half of the twentieth century. Highly regulated capitalism and the ever-increasing capacity to derive greater and greater profits from the legal manipulation of regulations (at all levels of government, especially the federal level) profoundly transformed the complex historical relationship between the political and the economic in US society. In the most general terms, the political came to determine the economic rather than the other way around—the more typical "causal" connection during America's first 150 years. Not surprisingly, therefore, the major political parties (the Democratic Party and the Republican Party) took shape together as a monopolistic corporate entity: a highly centralized, Washington, DC–controlled, lobby-friendly (and, correspondingly, grass-roots-unfriendly), legalistic professional body of armed (mostly with legal degrees) men who legislatively, executively, and judicially overdetermined the nature of the hardly-free market during their time in office (or working for those in office) and, when they left office, quickly turned around and sold themselves to the highest bidders (still retaining their party connections). While in office, the bipartisan politicians radically altered the election laws so as to exclude alternative parties and candidates from the political process (see Winger, 1995).

Global capitalization—the total elimination of pre-capitalist societies and the ensuing collapse—required a radical restructuring of the American free market economy into a regulatory economy which made government itself (and control thereof) the single most important economic commodity. Increasingly, the two dominant political parties became commodity traders "representing" special interests (including themselves) and not the American people. Politicians became professional (a political class or caste), shifting effortlessly (and, for the most part, unnoticed) back and forth between the "public" and "private" sectors. These matters have been documented by Reich (1987), Choate (1990), and others, but they remain largely hidden from the American public as a consequence of who (the political class) controls and how it controls (the infamous thirty-second sound byte at election time) what the American public actually comes to know.

A BRIEF HISTORY OF LIBERTY[3]

The method of liberal compromise and the search for the programmatic center which typified the first hundred or so years of American political life have gone through a profound change as well in this past half century, even though the rhetoric of the left-center-right paradigm is still officially and opportunistically retained. In fact, the meaning of liberty itself has been transformed. At the very beginning of the American republic (confederation), liberty was identified primarily with the dominance of local (grassroots) institutions in which Americans participated directly, and with political and economic power that was correspondingly dispersed. The Constitution of 1787 laid the foundation for a major consolidation of political power in a centralized federal government; the Bill of Rights was regarded by its supporters as a necessary check on this new power.

However, for a long time the Bill of Rights had surprisingly little practical impact on American liberty. (It was not until after World War I that the Supreme Court declared a law unconstitutional for infringing on the freedom of speech protected by the First Amendment.) For the first century of the Republic, political discourse about liberty did not focus on individual rights so much as on how government could best nurture "republican virtue" and support the development of a nation of self-governing citizens. The fight for liberty during this largely free market period was played out primarily in the political (as opposed to the judicial) arena, in an ongoing effort to give republican shape to the growth and consolidation of economic power.

It is only in the twentieth century (especially since the end of World War II, which brought an intensification of regulatory capitalism) that American liberty has come to mean a primary emphasis on the rights of individuals as defined in the Bill of Rights and subsequent amendments to the Constitution. In this evolution, judicial review by the federal courts and the Supreme Court (and, therefore, lawyering) has come to play an increasingly prominent role in defining American liberty in terms of constraints on the power of government (the regulators) and of political majorities in a bipartisan regulatory arrangement to impose their particular views on individuals and constituencies.

From the contemporary liberal perspective, this evolution of the "neutral state" promised to open up a whole new era in which individual citizens would experience unprecedented freedom to define themselves, their purposes and commitments, and their own associations, and to reject obligations they had not themselves chosen. From this point of view, the evolution of American liberty seemed to be fulfilling the promise of the American Revolution. Yet the changing character of liberty was essentially a reaction formation to the takeover by the professional political caste of regulatory capitalism. Ultimately, there was no room for compromise.

In practice, many Americans felt a growing ambivalence (at least) about the quality of life brought about by the new freedom. The transformed paradigm of liberty, emphasizing the primacy of individual rights, superseded the older republican paradigm in which liberty was understood not primarily as legal constraints on government, but as the participation of citizens in a self-governing nation. But who was "taking care" of the country now?

During the first 100 years of the American republic, there existed a developmental creative tension between the growth of the economy and the growth of liberty. The ongoing effort to give republican shape to the titanic economic power that was evolving ensured (or, at least, gave cause for hope) that economic growth would benefit not a privileged few, but the entire nation (albeit in varying degrees). Conversely, confidence in American liberty enlisted the enthusiastic participation of millions of people from all over the world in America's economic growth.

The new paradigm of individuated liberty, however, reflected the dissolution of this creative tension, and the consolidation of economic and political power (otherwise known as the rise of "special interests") to the exclusion of the republican majority. The proliferation of individual rights and the accompanying "identity politics," despite the many things that can be invoked to justify them, came about in part as an *alternative* to the creative tension between liberty and economic growth. Individual liberty appeared wonderful to many, but the environment in which it was to be practiced came to seem increasingly regulated. There was, once again, no apparent synthesis possible (no compromise, no center ground) between the political/corporate takeover of highly regulated American capitalism and the endless varieties of demands (in most cases legitimate) for rights, liberty, and a greater share of the economic pie on the part of conflicting identity-based groups. They have always been on a collision course. Now, as the twenty-first century nears, they have collided. Most importantly, the developmental tension between old-style republican liberty and economic expansion (arguably, the bedrock of Americanism) has been destroyed. The political-economic center has collapsed. Although there is much profit, there is no real growth. There is structural antagonism, an irreconcilable contradiction, no room for compromise. The center fails to hold.

THE COLLAPSE OF CONTEMPORARY LIBERALISM (IDENTITY POLITICS)

Postmodernism in general and social constructionism in particular, it would seem, have some applicability to the transformation of politics. Indeed, we have seen in earlier chapters that two of the leading Anglo-American voices, Gergen and Shotter, are concerned to restructure political life and dialogue. Here we will explore the (possible) transformation of identity politics via social constructionism through a careful reading of Gergen's thoughts on the matter. We will examine both a paper he delivered at a 1995 symposium hosted by the New School for Social Research and the response to it.

In "Social construction and the transformation of identity politics," Gergen (1995) characterizes identity politics as "initiated by groups excluded from traditional mainstream politics" who "generate a self-designated identity (group consciousness) that is instantiated by the individual identities of its constituents" (pp. 1–2). The major point of Gergen's presentation was that the generation-long "love affair" between liberal identity politics and social constructionism that was rooted in constructionist critiques of "mainstream" objectivity ("truth beyond cultural standpoint") is at an end. The passion of this love affair originally made good sense:

> Not only did constructionism . . . help to incite the political impulse, but it has also generated a powerful set of implements for societal critique. Constructionist inquiry demonstrated how claims to the true and the good were born of historical traditions, fortified by social networks, sewn together by literary tropes, legitimated through rhetorical devices, and operated in the service of particular ideologies to fashion structures of power and privilege. For the sophisticated constructionist, there are no invulnerable or unassailable positions, no foundational warrants, no transcendent rationalities, or obdurate facts in themselves. Most important for the present, many of these modes of deconstructing the opposition are "street ready;" they can be (and are) paraphrased easily in the daily argots of political activism.
>
> (Gergen, 1995, pp. 3–4)

But according to Gergen, the virtue and value of identity politics as the contemporary expression of political liberalism has "unraveled." For one thing, "identity politics has depended on a rhetoric of blame" (p. 4). Responses to it, not surprisingly, are hostile, defensive, and filled with counter-charges. Furthermore, Gergen notes:

> antagonistic replies are additionally invited by virtue of the differing discourse worlds of the critic as opposed to target. What are viewed as "exploitative wages" on the one side are branded as "just earnings" on the other; "prejudicial decisions" on the one side are excoriated as "decisions by merit" on the other; attempts to combat "exclusionary prejudices" are seen as disruptions of "orderly and friendly community"; "rigid parochialism" for the critic is understood as "love of enduring traditions" by the target. Under such conditions those targeted by the critiques are least likely to take heed, and most likely to become galvanized in opposition. As Mary Ann Glendon argues in *Rights Talk*, the rhetoric of rights "polarizes" debate; it tends to suppress moral discussion and consensus building. Once an agenda is introduced as "right," sensible discussion and moderate positions tend to disappear.
>
> (Gergen, 1995, p. 5)

But the blaming *modus operandi* of liberal identity politics has also turned on itself:

> With the rhetoric of blame a favored option for dealing with others, it also becomes a hammer for fixing what is wrong within the political movements. Any movement which finds its voice oppressed within the culture more generally, will soon find that within its own ranks some voices are more equal than others. In the thrust toward economic equality, women turn on men for their patriarchal disposition; in the drive toward gender equality, white women are found guilty of silencing the black voice, the educationally privileged guilty of elitist and exclusionary language, the straight for politics inimical to the lesbian, and so on.
>
> (Gergen, 1995, p. 5)

Over time a growing number of identity groups (left, center, and right) sprang into existence, claiming more and more rights. With the "remedy" for injustice, however, came a host of new problems. For one thing, the proliferation of new rights "devalued" their moral claims (Etzioni, 1993); for another, it produced disaffection: "Strong resentment among many who are implicated in the movements (for example, African and Asian Americans), but who do not share the revolutionary political sentiments and are embarrassed by the ways in which they are incessantly singled out to represent 'their people' " and also outside the movements, where the "disaffiliation within is also paralleled by backlash effects in the society more generally (consider the present Congress)" (Gergen, 1995, p. 7).

But while liberal identity politics (most of it fully justified by the long history of exploitation and oppression, racism, sexism, homophobia, class-ism, and so on) reels from the backlash of "conservative" ideological reactions and political action, a still deeper—if you will, "structural"—problem of identity politics is increasingly recognized by its advocates; there is a distinct tendency for identity politics to take on a realistic, objectivistic, indeed, authoritarian, epistemic, and moral posture towards its own decon-structionist findings. In response, "traditional" constructionism plays more the role of "critical enemy" than friend to identity politics. As Gergen puts it, "constructionism offers strong arguments *against* the realism, essentialism, and ethical foundationalism endemic to much of the discourse of identity politics" (1995, p. 8, emphasis added). He continues:

> In characterizing the barriers of class, the glass ceiling, homophobia, the effects of pornography on rape, and the embryonic fetus as a human being, for example, claims are being [made] about the state of nature independent of our interpretive proclivities. For the constructionist, of course, such claims are not so much reflections of nature as the outcome of social process. The descriptions are inherently positioned both histori-cally and culturally, and myriad alternatives are both possible and creditable from other societal locations. The realist posture is all the more ironic, the constructionist reasons, because such critiques are often coupled with a deconstruction of the opposition's objectivity. The constructed character of the dominant discourse is used by the identity politician to pave the way for the marginalized alternative, with the latter position then treated as if transparent.
>
> (Gergen, 1995, p. 8)

Should social constructionism and identity politics therefore now agree to divorce, with each party recognizing the "failings" of the other? Gergen does not think so. Instead he offers a reconstructionist plan for social construc-tionism and a way forward for identity politics—a move from the primarily deconstructionist posture of social constructionism in the 1970s and 1980s to a reconstructionist posture and, simultaneously, a change from 1970s-style identity politics to what he calls *relational politics*.

In shifting to a reconstructionist posture for social constructionism, Gergen urges that we (re)visit the age-old question of how we "comprehend others' meanings (or fail to do so)" (1995, p. 11). He summarizes the past history of relational theory as follows:

> Since the 17th century virtually all attempts at answering [the above ques-tion] have been cast in terms of resonating mentalities. That is, to understand another requires that their thoughts (intentions, meanings, construals, conceptual worlds) are reproduced in some form within one's own thinking. If you understand me your subjectivity is in some way resonant with my own. From John Locke, through centuries of hermeneutic theory, and into contemporary cognitive theory, however, no

one has been able to give a satisfactory account of how such resonances can occur.

(Gergen, 1995, pp. 11–12)

Constructionism, he says, takes up the challenge, making no reference to mental events:

By focusing solely on the means by which an individual's actions invite or suggest a range of supplements, and the way in which the respondent's supplements function to determine the implication of the initial action, we arrive at a view of meaning as embedded within relational scenarios. . . . I do not convey meaning, save through your graces as an interlocutor; however, your potential meaning[s] as an interlocutor are largely constituted by my actions. As dialogue unfolds, so is meaning formed and transformed within the interstice.

On this view, language (as a vehicle for making meaning) is shaped neither by nature nor mind, but by relationship. All that we take to be true of nature and of mind, of self and others, thus finds its origins within relationship. Or, in Martin Buber's terms, "In the beginning is the relationship."

(Gergen, 1995, pp. 12–13)

To Gergen, this constructionist view has important and positive implications for liberal identity politics; it contains:

the seeds for both revitalization and transformation of the most profound variety. Let me cast such a transformation in terms of *relational politics*— a politics in which neither self nor other, we nor them, take precedence, but in which relational process serves as the generative source of change. I am not speaking here of a mere fantasy, another grand but unworkable design hatched in the ivory tower. Rather, I believe that relational politics are already in evidence—not yet self-conscious, but struggling in multiple sites toward common intelligibility.

(Gregen, 1995, p. 13)

Central (in our view, far too central) to Gergen's reconstructionist stance is rhetoric. He says:

From the standpoint of relational politics, it is essential to develop alternative rhetorics. This is not because we need prettier, sharper, or more sophisticated words in which to wrap the case. I am not speaking here of a "better spin." Rather, rhetoric is important because it is itself a speech-act, a constituent feature of relationship. Because it is a form of action, rhetoric serves to form, sustain, and possibly change patterns of relationship. We have glimpsed some of the major shortcomings of traditional rhetorics—their capacities to alienate, antagonize, and escalate. Required, then, are a new range of poetics, and more specifically, poetics

that invite broader fields of coordination. Let me touch on two significant openings:

Rhetorics of Unity. As we saw, many black intellectuals are now
moving away from rhetorics of antagonism and separation to articulate
visions of unity. This is a move highly congenial with a relational
constructionism and should become a cause for all concerned with identity politics. The move from *me* vs. *you* to *we* has enormous consequences
for relating to the polity.

(Gergen, 1995, pp. 17–18)

Of course, Gergen recognizes that more than rhetoric is required:

A transformation in theoretical resources and rhetorical practices is
scarcely sufficient. Most acutely needed are innovative forms of political
action. In my view, one of the most significant innovations derived from
the identity politics movement was to broaden extensively the arena of
the political. In particular, political practice ceased to be reserved for the
arena of politics formally considered—campaigning, voting, office
holding—and it ceased to be centrist—that is moving from the top down.
Rather, politics moved into the arena of the local and the immediate—
into the streets, the classrooms, business, and so on.

(Gergen, 1995, p. 20)

Gergen concludes his paper by citing examples of already existing forms of
relational political organizing, what he calls "relational politics in action"
(1995, p. 21). He cites "collaborative education," "family therapy," "community focused institutes" (where he generously includes the practical work we
at the East Side Institute and our network of associates have carried out),
"appreciative inquiry" and others.

To us, Gergen never truly moves beyond the rhetorical and, thereby, the
(social) epistemological. At the New School conference at which he originally presented his paper, Gergen was "confronted" by Richard Bernstein,
the chair of the New School's Philosophy Department. Bernstein polemicized against a political view (presumably he was referring to Gergen's)
which draws no distinction between himself (an old-guard left liberal) and
Newt Gingrich (the conservative Republican Speaker of the US House of
Representatives). Now Gergen had not said, or even implied, that "no such
distinction could be drawn." What he *was* saying was that the orthodox way
of "drawing distinctions" was developmentally troublesome. Bernstein's
verbal bullying was reminiscent in style and speciousness of G. E. Moore's
waving his hand in people's faces as a "refutation" of idealism. The
problem? Well, the idealists do not (and never did) question that there is "a
hand waving in your face." Rather, they seek to understand what is meant
(what realists mean) by making such a claim (or having such an experience).
Similarly, Gergen does not deny distinctions or differences. Rather he seeks a
new and more developmental way of understanding such differences. Yet

Gergen's effort to *reconstruct* constructionism, identity politics, and their relationship (in order to create or support relational politics) is highly vulnerable to "Bernstein-ian revisionism" because, we believe, it is ultimately a theory of knowing and not a theory of action (or, more importantly, activity).

Bernstein insists (as do most in our culture, especially academics, the paid knowers) on knowing who is better—himself or Gingrich. Gergen urges that we must find a way of "getting on with it" *without* knowing who is better. But so long as our understanding of "getting on with it" is more an *understanding expressed in language* (rhetorical) than a *getting on with it* (activity), the epistemic bias which, to us, is what ultimately makes it practically impossible these days to get on with anything—personal, political, or otherwise— is reinforced. In our opinion, Gergen has—passionately, politely, and properly—polemicized against the reliance by proponents of liberal identity politics on traditional *individualistic, realistic, objectivistic* mainstream categories in articulating their own "points of view."

Still, in our opinion, he has failed to consider fully the "evil" of "point of viewism" altogether and/or in itself. Instead he calls for a new and more unified and unifying relational "point of view" (a social epistemology), a more serious recognition of *other(s)* even as we demand what we believe is rightfully *ours*. Because, as Gergen argues, persuasively and morally (to our political taste and sensibility), there is no meaningful sense of self or identity (either group or individual) and other that is *not* relational. (We all live by taking in each other's wash!) But from the "vantage point" of knowing, in its current institutionalized form, there is. If the organized cultural environment requires that we *know* who is right, better, closer to the truth—that is, if the organized environment is fundamentally a *knowing* one (as was surely the case with the liberal academic New School forum)—then the rhetorical and the epistemic will dominate, even if "rhetoric . . . is itself a speech act, a constituent feature of relationship" (Gergen, 1995, p. 17).

For while speaking (speech acts) is an activity, not all activity is speaking. More importantly, speaking is a particular (and peculiar, although commonplace) form of human activity, subject in our epistemically and individualistically biased culture to being "related to" more as pronouncement of truth and/or expression of inner happenings (opinions, beliefs, feelings) than activistic, continuously developmental conversation. So long as "knowing" who each of us is and the "truth" of what each one says dominates (which it does in Bernstein's institution, no less at Gingrich's), then what is obscured is the facticity of the activity of social (relational) life. The screaming, judgment-making husband and wife in a modern bad marriage are, after all, relationally joined. But they are each far too involved in the *truth* and *rightness* of what "I" am saying to notice the relational activity in which they are in fact (however destructively) engaging. Yet talk of "we" rather than "you" and "I" will, in our opinion, have little or no impact so long as "we" means "you and I," so long as we do not activistically change the meaning of "you and I." Changed rhetoric will not change meaning so long as the epistemological institution (the knowing way of life) dominates.

What is needed, in our opinion, is not merely a new rhetoric, or even a new (social) epistemology, but a theory/method of *activity* (practical-critical activity, revolutionary activity). The recognition of other in ourselves can be neither religious nor rhetorical if it is to make a developmental difference; it cannot be the arbitrary imposition of new meanings and new rhetoric on unchanged, or even somewhat different, actions, but must be manifest in revolutionary meaning-making, that is, it must be the result of a shared, non-epistemologized activity which creates new meaning.

In a word, the transformation of politics (the search for a new public philosophy or new political definitions) *and* the deconstruction of episte-mology—a tool-and-result connection (unity) if ever there was one—cannot, it seems to us, be a search for a new Truth (or even truth), but a search for a new non-epistemological method (a practice of method) which does not involve truth at all. Such a position "entails" extremism only if we subtextually (subconsciously) retain a centrist, horizontal, left-center-right paradigm. For extremism itself only has meaning (is defined) in terms of such a paradigm. The new politics must be an activity which is anti-programmatic, not in the sense that new ways of doing things are no longer considered and/or enacted and/or carried out, but in the sense that program-matics (and their extension or presupposition, ideology) are not a substitute for shared, collective, democratic human (citizen) *activity*.

A WORD ON MARXISM—NEO- AND OTHERWISE

Karl Marx would have done well to pay much more attention to the activity of how people spoke to each other and much less to what they said. While his early writings can reasonably be taken as the very source of activity theory, his so-called more mature writings, post-1848 (primarily *Kapital* and *Theories of Surplus Value*), largely abandon dialectical, methodological, philosophical, revolutionary method and insights in favor of a more rationalistic, scientific approach. His depth study of capital has been of great value to capitalist soci-eties the world over. These days everyone is a Marxist in quite the way that everyone is a Darwinian or a Newtonian. But Marx's failure to further his studies of dialectics as applied to social transformation, crisis, psychology, and revolutionary activity, among other things, has left future revolutionaries with no real guidance on the critical "subjective" issues. *What Is To Be Done* came to dominate, completely, *what is to be doing*. Little wonder then that *Marxism* (as opposed to Marx) was revisionist virtually from the moment of its birth. The later Marx (not to mention his principal collaborator and intel-lectual proselytizer, Engels, and his most well-known follower, Lenin), like almost all other modernists, bought in on the objective hegemony of the scientific. As such, they continued within the Greek/modern scientific tradi-tion of epistemology, the knowing tradition of Western culture.

The Luxemburgist accounting for capitalism's profound transformation which we discussed earlier in this chapter is, in our view, best related to as nothing more and nothing less than poetry or, perhaps, yet another grand narrative, not science. But calling it poetic or narrative neither diminishes its value nor implies that more traditional empirical, descriptive macro/micro-economic accounts possess greater accuracy. Orthodox economics, much like orthodox psychology, is largely a scam (Newman, 1991a; Newman and Holzman, 1996) which serves those who use it well (if it serves them at all) only insofar as those same people (and/or their institutionally organized friends) have the power to manipulate economic conditions and the sociology of knowing. Thus economics (again, like traditional psychology) is more a self-fulfilling prophecy than a genuine predictive (hard) science. Shockingly, but not surprisingly, traditional Marxists (ever metaphysicians, and thus all but impervious to the collapse of Communism and the abject failure of Marxism that pre-dated it by decades) seek to revive Marxism (now called neo-Marxism) by making it *even more* scientific. In this light, it is worth examining in more detail the neo-Marxist critique of social constructionism as we continue to consider the transformation of politics. And so, we return to Jost's critique (Jost, 1996; Jost and Hardin, 1996) discussed in Chapter 2.

That Jost's agenda is a more scientific Marxism is clear from the following:

> At the end of the day, I think that the greatness of Marx's theory is that he is proposing an empirical theory about how social relations actually are and how they might be better. This is not a rejection of knowing. It's an affirmation of knowledge that we all could/should have and a commitment to acting *on behalf of that knowledge.*
>
> (Jost, 1996, personal correspondence, emphasis added)

Apparently more concerned with "acting on behalf of knowledge" than, for example, with activity "on behalf of" people, classes of people, their desires, needs, and wantings, Jost seeks to preserve knowing (reified and deified)—and its contemporary mythic form, social science. In an article on false consciousness, he defends so-called scientific psychology: "To give up the possibility of locating beliefs on dimensions of evaluations such as accuracy, self-interestedness, adaptiveness, and so on is to relinquish the claim of psychology to be a science" (Jost, 1995, p. 415).

But what if a theory (or pseudoscience) which purports to tell us, as he says, "how social relations actually are," is antithetical (by design) to the *revolutionary activity* which was of central importance to Marx as revolutionary theorist and practitioner? Jost rather cavalierly rewrites (reinterprets) Marx on these matters. In his correspondence with us, he construes Marx's remark about interpretation and revolution ("The philosophers have only *interpreted* the world, in various ways; the point is to *change* it") as follows: "Marx wasn't *against* interpretation; he was against not going beyond *mere* interpretation" (Jost, 1996, personal communication). But if Marx is not polemicizing against interpretation altogether, then presumably he would have said something other than what he said, perhaps something like: *The point is not to interpret the world but to come up with the right interpretation.* To us, Marx's early critique is a thoroughgoing attack on philosophy and its interpretive method in favor of the method of practice, that is, the revolutionary activity of changing the world. To Jost, Marx holds on to the interpretive method and "goes beyond" it. Jost justifies such a theory of "beyondness" (activism as beyond interpretation) with a two-valued "scientific logic." He asks us, "But how do we decide to commit to a particular *action*? Surely you're not advocating action for the sake of action, but action *on behalf of* clear, accurate, moral visions" (personal communication, italics added). In another instance, he comments: "I don't even know what it means to be 'pro-truth.' Does 'anti-truth' mean in favor of lies?" (1996, personal communication). Yet (even on a logical/scientific understanding of *implication*), offering a critique of truth does not imply support for lying. But in Jost's arguments things are either black or white (not even black or not black). We think that putting socialism on a "scientific" basis did much more for capitalism than for revolution, and precious little for socialist societies. To accept Psychology-as-a-(finished)-Science is to alter (by direct or indirect coercion) the subject matter of psychology, which is subjective life.

Jost's interpretation of Marx is much closer to the accepted view of Marx (including, perhaps, even Marx's) than ours. It is Jost's *interpretation of interpretation* that we find to be very far from the tradition of the early Marx and most troublesome. His objection to our critique of reality (Reality) and/or truth (Truth) is a case in point. Calling it an "old-fashioned idealist position that Marx critiqued in the 1840's" (1996, personal correspondence) seems to us to be using the language of interpretation to obscure a commitment to truth. Even in ordinary language, interpretation has more to do with *different* ways of looking at the *same* thing than with correctness. Jost's appeal to interpretation, whether Marx's or his own, appears somewhat disingenuous to us since he calls it interpretation and "uses" it as truth.

"How do we decide to commit to a particular action?" Jost asks. Well, *do* we decide to commit to a particular action? What does *action* (particularized or not) have to do with *activity*? Does speaking of *particular actions* imply or require a theory of identity for adjudging an action α the same as or other than an action α^1? And, if so, what is that theory of action identification? It will no longer do to dismiss these (kinds of) questions (and myriad others) on the grounds that they are too philosophical. Postmodernism in psychology is the asking of such questions as a challenge to the calcified "scientific" institution that psychology has become in this half century of permanent, self-perpetuating institutions, identity politics, and a regulatory economy.

Luxemburg's poetic grand narrative is inextricably (and dialectically) connected with her methodological aversion to Marx's use of ultra-rational (and pseudoscientific) *models* in Volume I of *Kapital* to account for the capitalist business/production cycles. She argues (convincingly, we think) that the models actually obscure the *historicality* (the existential *this-ness*) of capitalist production (as models, in general, are wont to do). Both economics and psychology (Marxist and non-Marxist) are in themselves models in this problematic sense. They are curious maps which purport to tell us how to get from A to B. But there is no reality here other than the map (or the model)—only labels, names, and descriptions without referents. And so we have the illusion that we have gotten, or gone, somewhere. The real task is to make the map (the problem) vanish, in Wittgenstein's sense. To do this we need, it seems to us, not a map or a model but an activity which is not definable (directly or indirectly) in terms of the map or the model. It is neither truth (Truth) nor lie (Lie). It is a practical-critical *study of what we do* even as it is (or, more accurately, is an intrinsic part of) *what we do*.

THE POLITICS OF ACTIVITY

Jost's appeal to a more scientific neo-Marxism as the savior in a collapsing political and economic world, a psychotically psychologized world, seems most odd to us. Our conversation with him (in writing) is, we feel, extremely useful. We shall attempt to articulate our activity-theoretic, postmodern, revolutionary approach in the final section of this chapter largely by attempting to answer the questions we have come up with in response to his formulations.

Our four philosophical questions based on Jost's "common sense" inquiry, "How do we decide to commit to a particular action?" are these:

1 Do we decide to commit to a particular action?
2 What does action (particularized or not) have to do with activity?
3 Does speaking of *particular actions* imply or require a theory of identity for adjudging an action α as the same as or other than α^1? and, if so
4 What is that theory of action identification?

These questions help us to articulate, at least in outline, our understanding of *the politics of activity*. Gergen's relational politics, it seems to us, while of immense value, fall short because ultimately they seek to *reconstruct* (identity politics and) *the failing center* rather than to pursue a new way forward (a way to *reconstruct* the *world*) given the demise of the center. As such, they are analogous (and, we think, somehow connected to) his apparent unwillingness to move beyond epistemology altogether. But highly regulated capitalism, the total commodification of government, the resulting redefinition of liberty (as completely individuated) and identity politics, together with their contradictions and resulting failure, are not, we suggest, reformable. What is required is a new kind of revolution. Furthermore, these deep fissures in modern society (our study is focused, in particular, on the

US) cry out not simply for a "new public philosophy" or "new political definitions" but a movement beyond philosophy and, more specifically, epistemology. There is no room for traditional programmatic compromise. We surely do not support extremism in any of its traditional violent, antidemocratic forms. To move forward we must create new political *activity* which is not rooted in epistemological overdetermined programmatics (Truth and Rightness). Indeed, to us, the new *political activity* must have as one *raison d'être* the elimination of knowing as the dominant mode of human understanding. For, to our understanding, further development and growth, of all kinds—at the personal and species level—demand such a thoroughgoing restructuring. Such, it seems to us, is the postmodern political mission.

Do we decide to commit to a particular action?

On the face of it, given our highly individuated and behavioristic societal frame of reference ("common sense"), the answer to the question would appear to be "yes." We can, so the argument would no doubt go, *do a particular action* (go to the grocery store, re-read *Moby Dick*, join the Air Force, tour the Everglades); if we do any of these things *self-consciously*, as opposed, for example, out of habit, by mistake, unintentionally, or without giving it any thought, then we could be said to have *committed* ourselves to doing it. Furthermore, if we to some degree deliberated about either our commitment or the action (or both), then we can be said to have "decided to commit to a particular action." Yet even if we agree with this modest piece of ordinary language analysis, we would likely also agree that deciding to commit to a particular action *takes place* in a complex and ever-changing world. In a psychological laboratory study of *deciding to commit to a particular action* we would no doubt expect the environment to be as "clean" as possible, free of other factors which might impinge on our capacity to discern the action at issue.

But studies of ecological invalidity (for example, Cole *et al.*, 1978; Newman and Holzman, 1993) indicate that the sterile psychological laboratory is more a problem than a help in understanding action. For even if someone managed to create one, the studied action is so removed from its natural environment that whatever is discovered about it in the lab has little or no applicability to the action in its actual environment; inevitably, the "results" (and the study) are ecologically invalid. The point here, of course, is that psychological actions are simply too interconnected with their environment to be meaningfully disconnected from it. The study of action(s), either through linguistic analysis or empirically, suffers from this arbitrariness.

What does action (particularized or not) have to do with activity?

The concept of actions, we would suggest, begs the question (actually, many questions). Consider Jost's formulation: "deciding to commit to a particular action." It is, to our ears, epistemologically biased and top-heavy. It presumes, rather than explores, a (kind of) relationship between various kinds of mental activity (deciding, committing, identifying particularities) and a physical (behavioral) doing. Moreover, the relationship (its presuppositions) is essentially dualistic, causal, and expressionistic, with physical doings (including, most especially, speakings) understood as expressions of inner (mental) acts or, at least, goings-on; the implied separation between them requires bridging, which is necessarily understood causally (Davidson, 1980).

Vygotsky (and many others) challenged these philosophical assumptions. Unlike action or actions, activity is not over-epistemologized. Indeed, on our account (and Vygotsky's, we think), it is a highly suitable alternative to epistemology—to knowing. Activity is not to be instrumentally understood (it is not a tool for result) but dialectically understood (it is a tool-and-result), to employ Vygotsky's critical methodological distinction. Activity is a dialectical unity which does not require (indeed, it denies) the separation of the world into dualistic components and the ensuing pseudo-theories of instrumentalist mediations necessary to get a bifurcated world "back together again." Activity-language (talk, conversation) is simply a way of speaking socio-culturally of the complex, dialectically intertwined phenomenon that is human life which does not demand the dualistic epistemic distortion characteristic of Western culture. Actions and activity, thus understood, are not simply different; they are antithetical.

Does speaking of particular actions imply or require a theory of identity for adjudging an action α the same as or other than an action α^1?

To reply as simply as possible: of course it does. And (to answer question 4 even before we get to it) there isn't any. The identification of actions presumes substantival particularity (in something of a Kantian and Piagetian sense). But *substantival particularity* has not even fared so well in contemporary hard science; witness the extraordinary revolution in physics of the twentieth century. At the core of the quantum revolution is the methodological recognition that limiting our understanding of the most basic physical elements and their activity to a particle-ized, particularized ontology seriously and systematically distorts our understanding of the physical world. It is not simply that there are various *ways of looking* at (interpretations of) physical elements—for example, as particles or as quantum processes—but that physical phenomena are such that they *must* be construed in both ways simultaneously or we risk misrepresenting how the physical world actually is. An understanding of human social-cultural intercourse which reduces, explicitly or implicitly, subjective life to an infinitude of discrete and identifiable particularized actions fundamentally distorts human life in much the same way that Newtonian-style particle physics does physical phenomena (DeBerry, 1991). Human life, like the complex physical material of which it is *physically* composed, is vastly more complex than that. Simple particularized reductionism as the methodological accompaniment of an over-epistemologized culture has failed; it has reached its limits, it has folded. Moreover, an identity-based theory of understanding (classical modern knowing) has also folded, failed. The folding (the failure of the center to hold) is, it seems to us, indistinguishable from the whole family of foundational failures of modernism which, in turn, are inseparable from the social-economic-political failures of modern liberal capitalist society.

What is that theory of action identification?

Again, there is none. Nor need there be. Activity "on behalf" of (not knowledge or vision but) social change is the new non-epistemic politics for a postmodern, twenty-first century world. Is that action (or activity) for its own sake? No. It is neither for its own sake nor for the sake of (on behalf of) knowledge or visions. It has nothing to do with "sakes" at all. The problem we must make vanish, in Wittgenstein's sense, is the problem of *sakes*. Then why do we do *this* rather than *that*? With the *activity* of the mass performing as the organized political tool-and-result there is no possible answer to this (ultimately religious) why question. While action must be epistemologically justified (as Jost insists), activity does not (and cannot be).

The transformation of politics entails the democratic *organization of mass activity*, not the *compromising of actions defined programmatically and ideologically* by relative handfuls of highly individuated people. Non-epistemic politics is the organized collective activity of (in the case of the US) all Americans as producers taking responsibility (not legalistically, but humanistically) for all the complex social-cultural processes that constitute "America," rather than as individuated consumers seeking in their actions to justify by their particularized identity a larger share of a shrinking (albeit enormously profitable pie) owned (and thoroughly regulated) by a small (spendthrift) permanent commodified government. Non-epistemic politics is conducted with the recognition that it is the *activity* of politics itself (organized democratically for mass participation) that will serve as a tool-and-result (and, thereby, make problems vanish), and that it is not the undemocratically organized *actions* of a select professional few who putatively solve (by their instrumental actions) the problems facing the US and/or the world.

For it is we, the people, who are, at once, the problem and the solution. It is the organized *activity* of the people, by the people, and for the people, not the *actions* of anyone, which is the necessary new anti-epistemological, pro-activity politics urgently needed in this historical moment. This is neither "capitalism" nor "socialism," nor, for that matter, any other "-ism" economically and ideologically defined. Indeed, it is not defined at all but is, rather, the *activity of the people* organized to determine both the tools and the results of our activity. For even beyond the populist rhetorical (however accurate) recognition that "the people own the country" is the understanding that the people, by our activity, "own owning."

Relational rhetoric (and social constructionism) are not enough

Gergen's social epistemology and relational politics; Jost's, Parker's (and others') neo-Marxism; Sandel's call for a "new public philosophy" (without a new understanding of philosophy), Jowitt's demand for "new kinds of political definitions" (without a new kind of "definition" of definition). All, we think, are most insightful and valuable responses to the "folding (collapsing) center" that *is* the postmodern epoch. Yet to us, none of them goes nearly far enough, qualitatively speaking. They are, ultimately, reforms when what is demanded (required, whatever) is a peaceful, democratic revolution (revolutionary activity) against epistemology (the domination of the *knowing* mode of understanding and action), and a reconstructed society (and world) based on democratically organized activity as a tool-and-result.

Social constructionism is more a product of the postmodern collapse than a solution to it. Hence, social constructionist products such as social epistemology, relational politics, politicized discourse analyses, discursive psychology, and narrative therapy, while great advances, embody far too much of what they seek to correct. The reconstruction of social constructionism (from a mainly deconstructionist dynamic to a reconstructionist one), so honestly and insightfully called for by Gergen, requires, as we see it, the abandonment of the social constructionist project precisely as a new politics must abandon the epistemological presuppositions of *relationality* and a new therapy must give up the *self* upon which narrative approaches still subtextually (and, perhaps, subconsciously) rest. Here the early Marx, Vygotsky, and the later Wittgenstein (as activity theorists) will be of great help. Their work suggests that it is neither rhetoric nor reality that must be reinterpreted; it is human activity itself which must be democratically reorganized. Gergen's well-intended effort to transform rhetoric will not, in our opinion, suffice, for it does not fully recognize the *activity that is language* but is overdetermined by a use analysis of language. Hence, Gergen himself ends up articulating a politics of persuasion. But persuasion (even of the most ethically decent variety) will not, as we see it, succeed.

Gergen's brilliant critique of identity politics brings to mind the psychoanalytically grounded analyses of Fanon (1963, 1967) concerning the way in which oppressed peoples (when slightly freer) so typically take on the characteristics of their (former) oppressors. So are we all *persuaders*, appealing in varied ways, employing varied rhetoric, to convince whoever will listen that we speak the Truth (or even the truth). But this is precisely the problem. The *democratic reorganization of activity* (not based on ideology, programmatics, labels, or truths) is the long and arduous independent road toward the creation of a new politics (a new political activity) that will eliminate episte-mology—the ending that, as we see it, is required for further human growth and development. Ever-changing, democratically determined, inclusionary "rules" for the people's activity must replace the exclusionary Robert's *Rules of Order*. The point here is not to favor disorder but to reject any kind of order (including Mr. Robert's) which diminishes the participatory activity of the people. In this "activity-theoretic" approach, *performance* and *conversation* (the activity thereof)—indeed, the *performance of conversation*—will be, we think (and we have found), invaluable. Accordingly, in our final chapter we examine "a *community* of conversations."

5   A community of conversations

THE PERFORMANCE OF CONVERSATION: A THEORETICAL COMMENT

In the preceding chapters we have been building our case for the non-epistemological approach to human life-and-its-study that we have called the practice of method for almost two decades now. Whether or not we have been persuasive concerning the necessity of such an approach at this post-modern moment, we hope we have at least partially succeeded in conveying (non-epistemologically) a sense of what it is. We have used a variety of metaphors from varying discourses in discussing what it is we do (perform, have built): the practice of method; the developing (development) community; walls without a university; practical-critical, revolutionary activity; a zone of proletarian development; unscientific psychology; tool-and-result methodology; and the performance of conversation. We have examined a number of radical attempts to reform modern epistemology and found them wanting, revolutionarily speaking; in every case, at some point the deep-rooted epistemological bias of Western philosophy, educational and research institutions, and science takes hold. With some, such as Gergen and Shotter, that point is a fair distance down the road toward practical-critical, revolutionary (non-knowing) activity.

The problem we have with the "new psychological sciences" we have reviewed—interpretive, narrative, socially constructed and social constructionist, relational, and discursive—is just that: they hold to the fundamental epistemological tenets of science, including the one which insists that there must be something it is *about*. A proper science requires (so the story goes) the existence of some "naturally occurring" phenomenon which is the subject matter of theoretical statements about it. (The point still holds even if we consider theoretical statements to be narratives.)

This epistemic posture (aboutness) is played out, for example, in the various approaches which take conversation (discourse, narrative, text) as their unit of study, for the kind of unit it is (and must be in order to be studied scientifically) is a naturally occurring and naively recognizable phenomenon. Discourse analysis, as we understand it, depends upon the presupposition that discourse is a "natural" (albeit social-cultural-historical) category, just as Chomsky's syntactic analysis of language (often criticized for being overly rational and idealist) depends on the presupposition that well-formed sentences are a natural category recognizable by so-called "native speakers" of a given "natural language," and just as the perception of moving physical objects and growing living objects by "native perceivers" was a presuppositional condition of modern physics and biology. In this way, the efforts to reform modern epistemology (however radical) are pragmatically (subtextually) analogous to the objectivist scientific paradigm they are seeking to overthrow (even those efforts to apply the Marxian method of practice).

Psychology's naive unit of study (human subjective-social life) is of a qualitatively different sort from the motion of the stars and atoms and cells. Human subjective-social activity in general, and conversation and discourse in particular, are not naturally occurring studiable phenomena; conversation is not a naively "real" natural category. We are confronted with a very old, yet still fascinating, paradox. Because human beings invoke and evoke assumed agreed-upon categorization all the time as we live our lives (we even hear what we say most of the time!)—we seem to do things that fall naturally into categories (work, play, sleep, thinking, talking, singing, and so on) whether or not we call attention to them—we are led to believe that the things we do (including understanding and experiencing the things we do) are natural categories (again, even if socially-culturally-historically constructed and thus different for different peoples). But precisely the opposite is the case. If stars and people "did things with each other" like we do with our neighbors, modern science would almost certainly have had a different history, if it evolved at all.

The philosophically and politically revolutionary claim we are making is that there are no naively reasonable and recognizable natural phenomena in the realm of human social life-as-lived; there is nothing that can reasonably be agreed upon as indubitably real (G. E. Moore's waving hand notwithstanding). But, you may ask, if there are no "natural" human-social objects of study to study, can we ever learn more about human life? Our answer? Not by using epistemologically biased scientific method. The new kind of learning (and understanding) we are suggesting must look more like the learning children do—that is, it must not involve knowing.

As we see it, there is no scientific way to study human-social phenomena without distorting them—because such phenomena do not exist apart from their being studied. We are, among other things, a self-consciously studying species. Unlike our relationship to the stars, there is no "natural" (conceptual or even physical) distance between human beings and our own activity. That is very different from our relationship to the stars; it is the distance between the stars in the sky and human beings that makes the scientific study of stars possible. In other words, the distance is what makes it possible for human beings to have something to say *about* stars. And while twentieth-century science has come to recognize significant and profound interactional effects of studying stars (witness, for example, relativity theory in all its variations), it is still the case that we do not—cannot—interact with them the way we do with each other. We—at least some of us who are called poets or mad—may talk to the stars, but they appear not to hear us. Scientific study (logically and historically) requires that there be a conceptual distance (and, as such, an aboutness) between what is being studied and those who study. Perhaps the great distance (physical and conceptual) between human beings and the stars (some of the first objects of modern scientific investigation, some 500 years ago) was necessary for the emergence of science, indisputably one of humankind's greatest inventions. However, the self-conscious human condition (we are a studying species) is such that the distance required for our activity to be an object of scientific study *about which something can be said* does not exist.

However, it does not follow that, because human life-as-lived is not studyable in the way that physical phenomena are, we cannot gain more and more understanding about it. That there is no "natural" object of study is problematic only if we insist—as scientific psychology in all its modern and postmodern forms does—on distancing ourselves so that we can do "aboutness." If we abandon this modern epistemological requirement, we are liberated from the constraints that force us to distort human activity so pervasively as to make it impossible to learn anything at all about human-social life. The myth of psychology—100 years of research that (as some critics, including ourselves, believe) have taught us little or nothing about human beings—is that there is a natural object of study (behavior, consciousness, actions, conversations, discourse, and so on) at the requisite distance which, therefore, makes psychology scientific.

If we abandon aboutness, what can we do? Without it, are we doing anything other than what we are doing? If there are no human-social things which a study of subjective-social human life could be about, is there anything to study? If gaining understanding of ourselves as a species is not epistemological, what is it? It seems to us that these questions are reasonably asked of our own work—of the practice of method. Is there an object of study for such a thoroughly non-epistemological (practical-critical, revolutionary) activity? If there is, and it is not a "naturally occurring" phenomenon, then what is it?

The practice of method is, among other things, the radical acceptance of there being nothing social (-cultural-historical) independent of our creating it; there is nothing "natural" about how we participate with each other, nothing at a sufficient distance from us to "study." There is only what we create. It is the nature of a radically non-epistemological environment (our developing development community) that there is no way of distancing ourselves sufficiently from our activity to study it scientifically. The phenomena that are the objects of study in/with/by/as the practice of method are wholly "unnatural" and "artificial." Activity-theoretic (tool-and-result) methodology—in which, for example, language is not representational, expressive, relational, or rhetorical but creative revolutionary activity—has as its practical unit of study not conversation, but the *performance of conversation*. Again, we are not idealistically saying that there are no such things as conversations; it is likely that there are, but that is not our concern. We are saying that there is no such *study-able* thing as conversation. With what authority (other than its own) does science insist that anything and everything can be studied? As we saw in Chapter 1, hard scientists themselves are now questioning this scientific premise (even if their practical and political position is different from ours). Those inquiring about the human-social realm, it seems to us, have even more reason to be openly (and, for us, optimistically) skeptical. Instead, the approach of many (including radical) critics of modern science and epistemology is to hold on to the scientific premise of *aboutness* and search for some relational-cultural-social entity that has a sufficiently "natural" recognition as an object of study.

Modernism has been, among other things, an extended period of transformation in the making and use of tools, both technological and conceptual. Modern science (its historical catalyst), borne in the ontological shift from stillness to motion as the fundamental ("natural") state of the physical world, required a qualitative transformation in all kinds of tools, as the early scientists faced the great challenge of devising ways to study the things of the physical world. These objects of study—distanced from us—required new tools of analysis and technology. To study the motion of the stars, for example, required the invention of physical tools (such as the telescope) and conceptual tools (such as areas of mathematics) by which they could be seen and studied.

Postmodernism, we are repeatedly told, is a qualitatively different historical period—one marked by the fragmentation of subjectivity, the breakdown of grand narratives, the destruction not of appearances, as during the modern era, but the destruction of meaning. If we take these analyses seriously (and we do), it seems to us that we would need to question what the analogous postmodern (or post-postmodern) activity might be. How can we move ahead (as Vygotsky put it, "solve the tasks raised by history") in a meaningless world? In our view, the activity analogous to the modern transformation of scientific *tools of study* is the postmodern revolutionary transformation of the *objects of study*. If postmodernism is to be something other than an extended period of paralysis, it must transform its object of study of human life from a pseudoscientific "natural" phenomenon into a post-postmodern, distinctly unscientific, "unnatural" one. *Unscientific study*, we are urging, is not a reversion to feudal, prescientific methodology, but an advance over modern science. It is, we now see, the answer to the question we repeatedly posed in *Lev Vygotsky: Revolutionary Scientist*: "What are revolutionary psychologists to do?" We are convinced that it is the creating of unnatural objects—performances—which is required for ongoing human development (developing).

Interestingly, we already live in a world filled with unnatural (alienated, fetishized, god-like) objects, although they are of a very different, anti-developmental sort. As Marx showed, economically and culturally commodified capitalism turns continuous social process into products. Economic commodities are anything but "natural" phenomena; they are artificially created objects produced for the purpose of sale (and exchange value) and, thereby, the maintaining of certain relations of power. Practical-critical, revolutionary activity (developing the development community, performing social interaction, organizing activity) is the creation of artifi-cial, "unnatural" objects for the purpose of human growth.

The unnatural objects suitable for activity-theoretic study are perfor-mances. As language has become one of the dominant forms of human-social interaction, many modern and postmodern human beings seem to be highly skilled at *performing conversation*. The practice of method does not entail an analysis of conversation (as we have said, it cannot, because there is no conversation as a separate "object of study" which can be analyzed). It is, rather, the study of the performance of conversation indistinguishable from the performance of conversation itself. In the remainder of this chapter we will try to illustrate the performance of conver-sation and its study in our developing (development) community.

But first, a word or two about performance, revolutionary activity, and revolution. Our post-postmodern, activity-theoretic, radical claim that the human activity of developing does not produce development depends on it. What we mean by revolutionary activity is human activity that is fully self-reflexive, transformative of the totality, tool-and-result-ish, relative to nothing other than (outside) itself. The existentialists called it a predica-ment. We are liberated by it. It is "all process," creatively and constantly emergent. It is, following Marx, "the practical overthrow of the actual social relations" (Marx and Engels, 1973, p. 58). Marx, of course, was speaking of "making the Revolution." We are not. Instead, we speak of revolutionary activity.

Vygotsky helps to clarify the distinction between revolutionary activity and the activity of making the Revolution. As we read him, Vygotsky's understanding of human development—the social-cultural-historical activity of creating environments for development (zpds)—is the everyday, mundane, practical overthrow of existing social relations. People jointly (collectively, socially) transform totalities ("existing social relations"). Revolutionary activity "abolishes the present state of things" (Marx and Engels, 1973, p. 57) by the continuous transformation of mundane, specific life activities into qualitatively new forms of life (à la Wittgenstein). The activity of making the Revolution is a quite specific (and failed) revolu-tionary activity. But while not all revolutionary activity is making the Revolution, all activity is potentially *revolutionary activity*.

When we say that children become speakers (members of the human conversational community) by engaging in revolutionary activity (Newman and Holzman, 1993), for example, or that the social therapeutic practice of reinitiating emotional growth entails relating to patients as revolutionaries (engaging in revolutionary activity) (Newman, 1991b), we are not referring to children or patients as makers of Revolution, but as "developers," creators of continuous developmental process—engaging in (performing) revolutionary activity.

Revolutionary activity (developing that does not produce development) is an unnatural act. It is performatory, more theatrical and therapeutic than rational and epistemic. Human beings become who we "are" by continuously "being who we are not." Vygotsky's zone of proximal development, in our opinion, is more accurately an historical performance space or stage than a societal scaffold. In the zpd, children perform "a head taller than they are" (Vygotsky, 1978, p. 102). While most of his investigation of the zpd concerns learning and instruction in schools, it is his analysis of the zpd of the language-learning young child that is most suggestive of the unique non-epistemological, revolutionary character of all human development. Here is a description from a lecture originally published in 1935:

> We have a child who has only just begun to speak and he pronounces single words, as children who are just mastering the art of speech tend to do. But is fully developed speech, which the child is only able to master at the end of this period of development, *already present* [italics added] in the child's environment? It is, indeed. The child speaks in one word phrases, but his mother talks to him in language which is already grammatically and syntactically formed and which has a large vocabulary, even though it is being toned down for the child's benefit. All the same, she speaks using the fully perfected form of speech. Let us agree to call this developed form, which is supposed to make its appearance at the end of the child's development, the final or ideal form (as it is called in contemporary paedology)—ideal in the sense that it acts as a model for that which should be achieved at the end of the developmental period; and final in the sense that it represents what the child is supposed to attain at the end of his development. And let us call the child's form of speech the primary or rudimentary form. The greatest characteristic feature of child development is that this development is achieved under particular conditions of interaction with the environment, where this ideal and final form (that form which is going to appear only at the end of the process of development) is not only already there in the environment and from the very start in contact with the child, but actually interacts and exerts a real influence on the primary form, on the first steps of the child's development. *Something which is only supposed to take shape at the very end of development, somehow influences the very first steps in this development.*
>
> (Vygotsky, 1994, p. 348)

What point is Vygotsky making here? In speaking of beginning and end points and developed and rudimentary forms, is he merely repeating a causal explanation of language development? We think not. Shaped by the scientific and philosophical paradigms of modernism, of both the bourgeois and Marxist varieties, his language and conceptions were, lawfully, modernist and his formulations not consistently dialectical and activity-theoretic. This passage is particularly interesting and instructive for our purposes: if read in a particularistic and literal manner it is, at best, obvious and banal; if read from the perspective of the totality of his work and "our completion" of it, it is remarkably insightful.

What does Vygotsky mean by insisting that the developed form "is already there?" Is "already there" another way of saying "natural?" What "there" is he talking about? It clearly is not there "in" the child and it clearly is there "in" the mother, so "already there in the mother" is a trivial point. It would, we think, be silly to read him in such a causally particularistic and dualistic manner. The only way to make sense of Vygotsky's description of the coming-to-be-a-speaker child is to abandon the notion of particularity, in this case, the particular point of origin (the mother), to define what was "already there." For to retain it would be to insist that developed language has a starting point, a beginning, a location (from which it follows that it is dualistically divided from "what follows"), thereby rendering Vygotsky's argument meaningless. It would also be to insist that developed language ("the developed form") is a given, a "natural" phenomenon, a product.

An activity-theoretic reading, in contrast, sees the practice of the ever-changing totality individual-and-society or total environment (that is, the-"existing"-environment-and-the-environment-being-created). Both developed language and rudimentary language are present in the total environment (which has no beginning and no end), but not as already existing phenomena or products. The total environment includes both child and mother—not as particulars that make up the whole or that exist within the so-called bounds of the environment, but as inseparable from and as creators of it. The point is that people *and* language are no more "in" environments in the sense of being included in them, than noodles are "in" noodle soup. (It would be strange indeed to declare that "noodles are included in noodle soup.") The total environment is not a place but an activity.

We think Vygotsky is pointing the way to the paradoxical nature and dialectical practice of human revolutionary activity-and-its-object-of-study. In the zpd (the performance space, the developing development community) where learning leads development, it is development that "comes first" (in the societal sense of being temporally prior). As we have speculated elsewhere, "We must challenge the direction (the flow) of time itself to understand understanding activistically. What we know is what we had to know (had to have known) in order to have had the developmental relational experience of constructive discovery" (Newman and Holzman, 1996, p. 35).

The continuous shaping and reshaping of the "rudimentary" and "developed" forms of speech through joint activity simultaneously is and creates the zpd. It is in the performance of conversations (the language-games that very young children and their caregivers create) that we can first see the revolutionary activity of learning leading development. Here is a typical example of a zpd-creating language-game played by a twenty-one-month-old boy and an adult:

CHILD   (opening cover of tape recorder) open/open/open
ADULT   did you open it?
CHILD   (watching tape recorder) open it
ADULT   did you open the tape recorder?
CHILD   (watching tape recorder) tape recorder

(Bloom, Hood and Lightbown, 1974, p. 380)

In this performance of conversation, the babbling baby's rudimentary speech is a *creative imitation* of the more developed speaker's speech. It is not, Vygotsky warns us, to be understood as the mimicry that some parrots and monkeys do. It is creative, revolutionary activity. It is what makes it possible for the child to do what she or he is not yet capable of or, in Vygotsky's words, "to be a head taller than [she or] he is" (Vygotsky, 1978, p. 102). In imitating in the linguistic zpd, the child is *performing* (beyond her/himself) as a speaker.

Performance is, however, not a "solo act." The more developed speaker *completes* the child in Vygotsky's sense that speaking completes (rather than expresses) thinking. Mothers, fathers, grandparents, siblings, and others immediately accept infants into the community of speakers (on to the performance stage). As Vygotsky made clear in the description just given, and as the above example illustrates, more experienced speakers neither tell infants that they are too young, give them a grammar book and dictionary to study, correct them, nor remain silent around them. Rather, they relate to infants and babies as capable of far more than they could possibly do "naturally;" they relate to them as speakers, feelers, thinkers, and makers of meaning.

Creative imitation and *completion* are the dominant activities in the zpd (the developing-conversational community)—they are the building activities that create the performance of conversation, the relational activities that *simultaneously* produce the environment in which learning leads development (create the stage) *and* the learning that leads development (performance) simultaneously. Their "product" is nothing less than a new total environment of speakers—a developing development community (not development). The significance of the zpd, as we see it, is that the capacity to speak and to make meaning is inextricably connected to transforming the total environment of speakers in the revolutionary activity of performing an ordinary "unnatural" act.

The lesson we might take from Vygotsky is this. A total environment in which very young children are related to by themselves and others as communicative social beings (in which they perform conversation) is how they get to be so. They say things—they babble, utter sounds, use words, make meaning—as an inseparable part of participating in social life. And they participate fully—before they know the rules governing participation. Indeed, it is only by playing the game (performing) that they eventually learn the rules. Vygotsky is identifying perhaps the most important of all human activities—that we can relate to ourselves and others as *other than and in advance of our development*. Or, in our words, that we engage in revolutionary activity—developing that does not produce development. Development "is already present in the child's environment" not as a "natural" object of study, but only as artificially created revolutionary activity.

We are aware that our reading of Vygotsky here is speculative and, perhaps, risky. Certainly, "our Vygotsky" is at odds with the views of most (if not all) contemporary Vygotskians and neo-Vygotskians who typically either embrace him as a more social-cultural stage theorist than Piaget or criticize his tendency toward teleology. Again, we do not defend our position as the correct one; we have no interest in who is "right," for we do not share (we try not to) the epistemic posture. Our revolutionary stance in reading Vygotsky is, at least as we see and do it, *therapeutically developmental* rather than epistemic. We are seeking to complete and be completed (much like performers of conversation), not to understand and be understood cognitively, not to get it right.

In this non-epistemological, therapeutic sense, our reading of Vygotsky is Wittgensteinian. The *activity of philosophizing*, for him, was distinctly therapeutic—it can help to prevent us from institutionalizing our words. Wittgenstein practiced philosophy as method (to do away with philosophy); many have remarked that his approach (in his later writings) was more clinical and therapeutic than analytic (see, for example, Baker, 1992; Baker and Hacker, 1980; Monk, 1990; Newman and Holzman, 1996; Shotter and Newman, 1995; Peterman, 1992; Shotter, 1993a, 1993b). Our "illness," or "presenting problem," is the way we speak and think about speaking, thinking and other so-called mental processes. It obscures, Wittgenstein says, the activity of language:

> I shall in the future again and again draw your attention to what I shall call language-games. These are ways of using signs simpler than those in which we use the signs of our highly complicated everyday language. Language-games are the forms of language with which a child begins to make use of words. The study of language-games is the study of primitive forms of language or primitive languages. If we want to study the problems of truth or falsehood, of the agreement or disagreement of propositions with reality, of the nature of assertion, assumption and question, we shall with great advantage look at primitive forms of

language in which these forms of thinking appear without the confusing background of highly complicated processes of thought. When we look at such simple forms of language the mental mist which seems to enshroud our ordinary use of language disappears. We see activities, reactions, which are clear-cut and transparent.

(Wittgenstein, 1965, *BBB*, p. 17)

Playing language-games "bring[s] into prominence the fact that the *speaking* of language is part of an activity, or of a form of life" (Wittgenstein, 1953, *PI*, p. 23).

Wittgenstein had no love for the scientific method (modern epistemology), especially as it is applied to human-social phenomena. Explanation is reductionism. The practice of seeking the smallest possible number of primitive laws as accountings for phenomena is "the real source of metaphysics" (Wittgenstein, 1955, *BBB*, p. 18). Psychologists, especially prone to metaphysics, could find Wittgenstein of enormous value, and many are now discovering his work. In one recent discussion of Wittgenstein's challenge to psychology, van der Merwe and Voestermans (1995) say that his message to psychologists is " 'to move around about things,' that is to say, to come to grips with the role forms of life actually play" rather than "trying to delineate essential features" (pp. 38–9). It seems to us that forms of life can "play a role" if and only if they are performed in the activity of "getting from here to there," or as revolutionary activity.

HOW TO MAKE A PERFORMED CONVERSATION

Our developing development community—the tens of thousands of primarily Black and Latino inner city youngsters who participate in the All Stars Talent Show Network shows held on weekends in a number of cities up and down the East Coast; the hundreds of people in multiracial social therapy groups which meet weekly at centers in Atlanta, Boston, New York City, Philadelphia, San Francisco, and Washington, DC; the thousands we have trained who are employed in community-based social service programs; the tens of thousands who perform in and attend theatre at the Castillo Cultural Center and the Performance of a Lifetime Performance Space; the hundreds who take part in the classes and programs run by the East Side Institute for Short Term Psychotherapy and its Center for Developmental Learning or the Barbara Taylor School; and the hundreds of thousands who regularly receive phone calls from (have conversations with) our volunteer fundraisers and respond by sending in tax-deductible donations to our non-profit Community Literacy Research Project to support our ongoing charitable work—is, as you might expect, filled with (let us guess) millions and millions (perhaps billions and billions) of conversations each year.[1] Some of those conversations are quite ordinary, a few are remarkable and memorable, almost all go unnoted. Yet we are not eager to report to you on these conversations because, as we have said, we think they cannot be usefully studied, ethnographically or otherwise. Rather, we wish to consider a relatively small number of those conversations (in fact, just a few examples) that are self-consciously shaped therapeutically, pedagogically, culturally, creatively, and—by virtue of such intervention—transformed (sometimes) into proper (though unscientific) objects of study, that is, *performed conversations* (unnatural activities).

To be sure, these performed conversations (and their study) increasingly influence all the conversations that make up our developing (development) community by way of the plays, the books, the articles and, most especially, the word-of-mouth (the conversations) that both emerge from and go back into our community. The line between conversations *per se* and performed conversations is indeed a very fuzzy one, precisely as the line between "our community" and the rest of society is fuzzy (or, more accurately, intentionally non-existent); the members of our community come from every walk of life and therefore live very much in the broader society (not to mention history) even as they are (to varying degrees) community members. As such, our *performed conversations* impact on the world (even as the world impacts on them). How much? Who's to say, and who's to measure? But the performed conversation, the reorganized conversation, the revolutionary activity that is the re-shaping of our (typically) societally overdetermined conversation, is of critical importance to the design and development (or developing) of our developing (or development) community.

A very, very few performed conversations in and of our community are fully scripted as performed conversations (see, in this chapter, the learning-leading-development conversation/play *Beyond the Pale*, first performed/delivered at the 1996 meetings of the American Psychological Association). Most performed conversations are more improvisational—interventions (typically therapeutic, pedagogical and/or political) into conversations by "trained" reorganizers of conversation (see, in this chapter, the annotated social therapy session, dialogue from the Barbara Taylor School, and the philosophy class discussion). Sometimes, in some contexts (for example, the Barbara Taylor School, East Side Institute training weekends), community members will self-consciously (improvisationally) create a performed conversation. At other times and in other contexts, for example, in a social therapy session, the therapist will relate to ordinary (mentalistic) conversation as a play to be directed (a conversation "waiting" to be transformed into a philosophical language-game) and will, thereby, succeed in turning ordinary, truth referential, "representationalist" dialogue into a performance. Sometimes the therapist and the group will fail at this transformational effort. Some social therapists will more self-consciously and explicitly introduce "outside games" in order to produce performed conversations. Such is the case with our teachers (or learning directors/facilitators) as well. As the performances grow, quantitatively and qualitatively, more and more conversations in the hallways (so to speak) are more or less successfully performatory.

PERFORMED EMOTIVE CONVERSATIONS

The social therapeutic process, as we have said, is a collective moving about around things and events in the world. It is, more particularly, a moving about around emotional things and events in the world: "depression," "anxiety," "three painful days," "I'm angry at you," and so on. How do we move about around them? Surely not by analytically seeking to discover their essences. Definitely not by determining the truth value of judgments in which they are contained. And not even by cognitively uncovering the complex societal uses of such language. We do it by changing the form of relational life. In a word, we collectively and creatively perform (not act) our lives without the identity-based presuppositions of the existing alienated form(s) of (our) society. For only as we create new forms of relational life can we understand the existing forms of action. Only as we perform our lives together can we understand our lives as performance.

In social therapy, the (first-person, second-person, or third-person) descriptions uttered by clients and therapists, whether in individual or group sessions, are not treated as referential; that is, they are not related to as true or false judgments but as lines in a play (better still, a poem) that we are at once collectively creating and performing. The social therapist, as performer/director, helps to keep the activity performatory by continually reminding the clients that they *are* in a play and not in "real life," where their descriptions and/or judgments *are* true or false.

(Newman and Holzman, 1996, pp. 190–1)

You are about to read an annotated excerpt from the transcript of a social therapy group session. The transcript was made from notes taken by the assistant social therapist during the session. The annotated remarks, prepared by Hugh Polk, our "resident psychiatrist," summarize an extended discussion over several weeks by the collective staffs of the East Side Center for Social Therapy and the East Side Institute for Short Term Psychotherapy. The discussion itself was a semi-performed conversation, led by the authors, in which the members of the collective (therapists, many of whom are traditionally trained, and non-therapists) worked hard to find non–truth referential and non-representational ways of considering the session. What follows, then, shows the social therapy group "working on depression" as it is brought up by Millie[2] (one of the members of the group) and the staff collective "working on" discussing the group.

The key to transforming conversation (in this case emotive conversation) into performed conversation is to support the conversationalists (the group members) to abandon the realist assumption of truth (or object) referentiality in favor of the activity of performance. The social therapy "medicine" under discussion in this particular social therapy group segment is performing differently. Millie (and other group members) says she cannot perform differently (come to group) because she is depressed ("addicted" to depression). But, of course, such an understanding only makes sense (and thus exercises the control that it does) if the description "I am depressed" is true (or taken to be true) or corresponds to something—a state of mind or being.

No such assumption need be made, for example, by or of an actor or actress on a stage who is saying "I am depressed" (or by or of the other actors and actresses or, indeed, the stage hands, lighting people, or even the audience). On the stage we are typically able to follow the activity of the dialogue with no more of an assumption than that the actor or actress is or maybe is pretending to feel or think in a certain way. But if there is no corresponding state of mind (if there is nothing to be known, no object of knowledge) we do not stop understanding (either on stage or off); rather we come increasingly to see the activity of speaking rather than speaking as referent, that is, what it is "about," just as we do in the Wittgensteinian language-game.

In other words, the effort in the social therapy group is to transform (sometimes subtly, sometimes not so subtly) the actual conversation into a language-game (a performed conversation) by stripping the conversation of its truth referentiality, not by changing what is said—having people say different things—but by changing the truth and referential assumption of what is being said.

At the time of the group session, Millie, a forty-two-year-old Italian American woman with a long history of being labeled with chronic and severe depression, has been in social therapy for two years. Millie grew up in an abusive family, and spent extended periods of time in various Catholic institutions during her childhood and early adolescence. At the age of sixteen, she was hospitalized for four weeks. During that time she was given twelve electroshock treatments. After leaving the hospital she lived on the streets in New York City and used drugs, chiefly crack cocaine, for many years. A very bright, creative woman, she eventually made her way to college, and became involved in dance and theatre while studying social work; she married, had a daughter, and held various social service jobs. Meanwhile, throughout these years she had frequently felt suicidal.

In 1989, Millie attended a lecture by Newman on "The Myth of Addiction" in which he argued that while heavy drinking and drug use are all-too-real, painful, and destructive realities for millions of people, the concept of addiction (addiction talk)—the psycho-biological disease entity and explanatory category—is a myth. In the dialogue after the lecture, Millie strenuously disagreed with Newman; she insisted that she and others were, objectively speaking, addicts. After that, Millie read some of Newman's books and articles. Although she disagreed with much of what he had to say, she also felt stimulated intellectually by it; she recalls that "every now and then I'd feel alive."

A year later, Millie attended another lecture in which Newman spoke of the work to create a development community which defines itself rather than accepting the societal definitions of community (or anything else). Millie loved this idea, and joined a new "community therapy group" that was just beginning in which the social therapist was to be the patient/client, and the group the collective therapist.

Soon she began coming to theatre workshops at the Castillo Cultural Center, which is housed in the same space as the East Side Center for Social Therapy and the East Side Institute for Short Term Psychotherapy. Millie joined a "regular" social therapy group in December of 1992. At this time in her life, despite feeling occasionally alive and stimulated Millie was mostly depressed, tired and worn out. She was using crack and drinking periodically, despite having been in a twenty-eight-day alcohol detoxification program at a local hospital, and was convinced that she was "too old" and too tired to dance, sing, or write poetry any more. She believed that her life was over, that her dreams "had pretty much died."

During her two years in the therapy group, of which she is still a member, Millie gradually "came alive." In the group she talked about herself and supported others to talk as well. She says that doing this reinitiated her life and her creativity. She began to sing, dance, and write poetry; she acted in several Castillo productions; she remarried. She says she has now come to see herself as "basically a happy and contented person."

The following group session took place after Millie had been in the group for about four months and was still feeling very depressed.

MILLIE　Well, speaking of depression and moving forward: I've been depressed and not moving forward. I've been absolutely morbid for about two weeks. I missed two groups. I was sick last week, and the week before I just didn't come. If I'd known I was going to be sick the following week, I wouldn't have not come.

JILL　Why did you just miss?

MILLIE　I was depressed and tired. It was cold and raining. It's been raining a lot.

SHARON　I understand the effort it would take to go out when you're depressed and it's raining, etc. But how come this isn't the place you'd come running to cut through being depressed and morbid?

MILLIE　Because that's what I do. I stay inside and withdraw.

Millie is talking about herself (referring to herself) as "a depressed person." She is giving an explanation of why she acts as she does, namely, "that's what I do. I stay inside and withdraw." Her language is of the objective, syllogistic form, "I am a depressed person. Depressed people stay inside and withdraw. Therefore, I stay inside and withdraw." She is talking about herself definitionally, as she might talk about any object in the world: "Chairs are pieces of furniture with four legs and a seat. That piece of furniture has four legs and a seat. Therefore, it is a chair." Millie is using language in its typical alienated form to describe her feeling (depressed), and to explain why she is feeling and acting that way.

SHARON That's what you did for years. But now there are other things in your life.

MILLIE I know that, but I just don't feel it. I make lists of stuff I have in my life. But I don't feel it. It doesn't matter.

PAULA What's your name? I'm new, so I don't know you. What did you mean when you said you're morbid? I don't know you, so I wanted to know more.

MILLIE Well, Ruth, my daughter, just made a good joke the other day. We were talking about what it would be like if she won the lottery. And she was saying all the things she'd do, like move to the Village, get an apartment, etc. I said, "What about your mom?" And she said, "Well, I'd get you an appointment with Dr. Kevorkian, the suicide doctor. You'd like that!" That's some joke, huh? When I'm depressed, I think, "Why bother living? I've done it all before, for forty-two years."

ELLIE What's been done before?

MILLIE Living. Me. I've done forty-two years. It just feels like such a long, long time. I just keep waiting for someone here to stop me—to say that what I'm doing is not appropriate.

JANE Millie, where are we in this? I'm wondering what you're thinking about the work we've been doing with you.

MILLIE I don't know. I'm here and not here. I'm trying to feel people. I had a fight with the group about my cousin. My cousin died, you know. She died. My very recent history with the group is angry. I'm not sure I want to be with you. I'm trying to go further back so I can have you, so it won't feel like forty-two years is such a long time.

JILL I'm thinking of what *[the social therapist]* said last week. So you have a fight with somebody you're in a relationship with, and you negate the whole relationship. It sounds like you're doing that with us.

WALTER What was the fight about?

MILLIE It wasn't so much the *content* of what I was talking about. I presented my upset in not the right way.

JAZMIN You were getting off on your family being in crisis. The group was engaging you about this. The issue is using that. It sounds like you're not using it.

MILLIE I remember I got that, and was gonna use it. But I don't know. Stuff happened. I wasn't able to.

JAZMIN Did that have to do with why you didn't come back?

MILLIE No. Because I came back. Then I was depressed. It was still bothering me. And I wasn't staying away to tell the group to get lost or anything.

KIT You said you were angry after that group, though.

MILLIE   I *was* angry, but at everyone and everything in my life, before I came to the group that day.

LORI   Then how come you stayed angry at us?

MILLIE   I don't know. I was angry. It felt like I didn't have a relationship to the group.

JANE   This may be off, but I'm having a reaction to how you're relating to us. You assume you'll automatically feel connected. But you know that's not how it works. You have to want stuff. The times you've gotten the most help here is when you'd been giving to the group and not necessarily talking about yourself. It's very passive on your part in terms of how you're relating to us. I just don't like what we're doing with you.

JOSIE   I'm thinking about the discussion we had last week about the political meeting in Harlem—and people needing to break out and say, "This is miserable! Let's do something else." Do you think we could do something else? Could we try this again?

MILLIE   Yeah.

LORI   Where do you come off being mad at us for telling you not to act out?

MILLIE   I wasn't necessarily mad. I was off center and out of sync. I used the word "mad"—maybe it's the wrong word. So how come you're locking me into being mad? What can I say? I felt really bad. And I feel really upset now.

ST   What Millie just said makes a lot of sense to me. I think there's a way that the group was insisting that Millie be angry. Ironically, the group was relating to Millie, it seems to me, much the way in which Millie's been relating to the group.

LORI   You mean tonight?

ST   Tonight and the last several weeks. Although I think it's actually helpful, what Millie is saying.

JANE   How?

ST   What I understand Millie to have said just now is "I don't know *how* I am, except I'm in trouble. And I don't want to get picky about what you call it. I just need something." There's this resistance to saying the predictable things again and again. I have it, we all have it.

    [to Millie] But it's worth doing, you with your forty-two years and me with my fifty-one years. You actually either said this explicitly or implied (and maybe I'm taking it personally) that the reason why you didn't come here was that you were depressed. Given that I say—to the point of tedium—that it is far more likely that you're depressed because of what you're *doing*, rather than that you're doing what you're doing because you're depressed, it's shocking that you never even considered this possibility for a moment.

I don't want to pick on you, Millie. Not only did you not say it, no one else did either. And I don't want to take it away from you. I know you're feeling badly and I want to support you. That's why I want you to take seriously what I'm raising. Here's the drug therapy analog: take three pills when you start feeling depressed. Now, presumably you'd remember to take the pills. What I'm saying is our analog to drug therapy—performing differently. Why don't you take our medicine? What stops us from "performing differently?"

In traditional therapy, they try to find out the cause of the depression, what it's about. What we want to find out is how come you're unable to do anything about the depression. This is not pragmatic. If you discover what to do about the depression, you'll have discovered what "caused" it. We only discover what something is—it seems to me—by creating something else "out of it."

Social therapy relates to depression not as an emotional state of mind located within the individual but as a relational form of life, that is, as social activity which people do with one another. In this session, the social therapist attempts to engage the language people use (unself-consciously) to talk about their depression as if it were a feeling state within the individual that's generally caused by something: "I feel depressed because . . . " The social therapist engages this talk not as a reflection or representation of the truth, but rather as an alienated linguistic form of life. The language of depression plays a major role in creating what depression is. In fact, depression talk is, from the social therapeutic vantage point, inseparable from the so-called depression itself.[3]

Accordingly, social therapy does not work on the patient's depression by trying to discover its cause, interpret the reason for it, or provide the patient or other group members with insights into its roots or the deeper secrets underlying it. Nor does social therapy try to solve the patient's problem, make her feel better, empathize with her, or get her to give it up. The social therapist works on the depression by working on the conversation. Wittgenstein noted that people get into emotional "muddles," that we live our lives in a "mental mist," because we use language in an alienated, representational, denotative way, assuming that words (and the conversations we make with them) simply or primarily refer to (are about) things in the world; he sought to show that language (speaking) is instead a social activity, a creative process that people engage in (perform) together. In this way, the social therapist's activity is akin to what a theatre director might do: she relates to the clients' lives (including what they are doing in the therapy group) as an improvisational play (an ongoing conversation) that we as human beings continuously create together; she directs/leads the development of performance of forms of life, forms of depression talk, by playing emotional language-games.

Here the social therapist takes Millie's statement—"I am depressed because . . . " as an opportunity to transform the "natural" conversation into one that is performed. There are an infinite number of ways to play (perform) the depression talk game. The playing of the language-game, the creation of new depression talk, is simultaneously the showing of the structure and the organization of the alienated form of depression talk that is "natural" in our culture. That form of depression talk overdetermines what depression is; as Wittgenstein said, it produces a "picture which holds us captive." Social therapy attempts to show the picture(s), thereby helping the group "to move about around" the elements of it and in doing so to create something new— new depression talk, and an infinitude of other new emotions/ways of talking emotionally.

Note that the social therapist does not say anything for quite a long time. She is waiting (and actively listening) to see what the group's relational activity (its conversation) is on this particular evening; it is their activity to which she responds (similar, to some extent, to other forms of group-dynamic therapy). Mostly she responds to the Millie–group relational activity, not to any one individual apart from others. She relates to the conversation; the different members of the group participate (in varying ways) in the conversation, and (in varying ways) work to transform it into one that is performed.

In one sense, the group is engaged in a philosophical fight over the nature of human beings—what kind of thing human life is; what an identity is; what emotions are. Social therapy is not identity-based and the social therapist challenges not only Millie's and other people's particular identities, but the belief that they have and must have an identity. In relating mainly to their activity, the social-historical process of human beings creating their lives together— including the alienated ways of talking of themselves and others as individuated objects each possessing (defined by) an identity separate from that of other human beings—the social therapist is relating to the members of the group as creators/performers, with other people, of the meaning-making relational activity of their lives.

In challenging (caringly, though provocatively) Millie's explanation that she didn't come to the group "because she was depressed," the social therapist is playing a language-game which can show Millie's more alienated way of talking/doing emotions.

She continues to talk causally and syllogistically: "I am a depressed person—that's why I didn't come to group. We depressed people stay home. We can't do things like come out of the house and come to group"—a definition of herself as a depressed person whose activities are limited by that identity. The social therapist is challenging that whole conceptual scheme by raising the possibility that she could do something different and thereby break out of the identity paradigm; that is, she could change (create) who she is, even her depression. The social therapist is relating to Millie as a participant in the ongoing relational activity of creating her life, along with other people, refusing to "go along with" the alienated language Millie uses—language which separates herself from herself as the active creator of her life, an active agent who can continuously choose, from moment to moment, how she responds to the world, that is, as a potential performer of her life.

Millie's use of language (normal in our society) locks her into an alienated experience of herself as a passive object to whom things happen, rather than the active creator of her responses and actions. The social therapist is attempting to speak in a way which emphasizes this active form of life. In challenging how Millie talks—not by imposing moral judgments, but performatorily—she is trying to show Millie (and others) how the way they talk traps them in a distorting "picture" of themselves as passive objects who don't (won't, can't) reform (transform) their lives. This engaging of the way the group members talk about themselves and their emotionality (including depression) is the ongoing language-game/performed conversation which social therapists play / lead.

Millie's use of language also presents the pervasive cultural bias that our feelings (and mental states in general) determine our actions. In normal conversation, Millie's causal statement would be accepted at face value. In fact, however, Millie can create new emotionality (including a new relationship to depression) by performing her life—by coming out of her house. But her way of characterizing herself in the language she uses makes it difficult (if not impossible) for her to do anything inconsistent with her "definition." Indeed, she is (in her language) "addicted" to definition, locked into a reified, alienated form of meaning which gives her a seeming way of understanding herself and what is going on (her depression) when, in fact, it is a way of keeping her from being able to deal with her depression as a performer of her depression. This is not a matter of Millie's motives or preferences; it is simply the case that she is trapped in what Wittgenstein aptly called the "fly bottle" of alienated language.

Hence the importance of the social therapist's attempt to challenge how she talks, to expose this alienated and disempowering way of speaking/living through playing the depression language-game to try to help her break out of the prison of her own linguistic self-characterizations.

What is Millie doing (including linguistically) which produces her depression? What form of life is she, along with others, creating? The social therapist is attempting to show her and the other group members that the form of life Millie is creating—staying at home and producing depressive activity (and, no doubt, getting reinforced in this by other people, both present and past)—is a particular (and common) form of alienated relational activity which gets people into trouble, in this case depressive trouble.

The social therapist has a long-term relationship with Millie and knows her long history as a "patient" —a "medical patient," an "addict" with a history of detoxifications, and a "mental patient who was institutionalized." This is Millie's definitional language, a way of talking which she is familiar with and "understands." The drug therapy analog highlights the fact that "our medicine" is creating—performing—our own lives, rather than living them according to preset definitions and categories. Rather than accepting things defined as they are, it is in the playing of a language-game that we can begin to talk / live our emotionality self-conscious that we ourselves are the creators of it.

MILLIE   You know, this could be functional. Sometimes when I'm depressed, it's hard just to function, to go to work, etc. And a lot of activity has to go into me doing the things I need to do.

ST   Yes, I want to support you doing a new kind of activity, a new performance to support your further development. I'm less than fully supportive of what you do, although it's fine, since it's all you've got. I want to give you something more. That's why I'm raising the issue of our medicine and how come people won't take it.

Again, the social therapist extends and advances what Millie says as performance, rather than competing with it (reacting to it).

JAZMIN   I agree with Lori . . . . I keep being depressed because I get off on it and get something from this. And this helps me perpetuate the depression.

ST   I agree with Lori, too. When Millie didn't come to group, she was probably getting off on her depression, more so than tonight.

MILLIE   But I was depressed and couldn't function and couldn't come.

ST   No. You *don't* function, and instead you stay home and feel bad.

Millie persists that she couldn't function because she was depressed. She commits herself to her identity as a depressed person, and attributes her staying home to being caused by her illness. She is, in a perfectly normal way (one with a 2,500-year-old tradition behind it), engaging in an explanatory form of life—an activity common to most forms of therapy, and indeed to most forms of discourse in our culture. (Poetic discourse is typically less explanatory.)

Millie is using language in the way one might talk "objectively" about another person: "Joe is depressed. That's the reason he can't function." In that language, Joe is a static object, a representative of the class of "depressed persons" whose functioning is determined by the fixed characteristics of that class. Such language is even more problematic (pathological) when applied to the very person who is speaking—that is, as an object observed from the outside (even when the speaker is referring to "I" and "me"). For we are not outside ourselves, observing ourselves from a distance. Nor, for that matter, are we "inside" ourselves. We simply are ourselves! We are the active agents of our relationally activistic lives—the livers, if you will, of our lives.

Millie's language distorts the fact of human agency; it presupposes that people come to know what they will or won't do in the same way they come to know what others will or won't do. The subtext of what Millie is saying is that the way she knows herself is by appealing to laws of generalization and causality. The social therapist is challenging this bizarre use of language, so common ("natural") in our culture, to describe ourselves, which denies the human capacity to create our own lives.

MILLIE   I'm not being glib when I say I'm depressed and worried I won't be able to function. There's a lot of emotion in all of this.

ST   I don't question that. But that doesn't explain why you don't take the medicine.

MILLIE   It takes extraordinary effort to move to the medicine.

ST   Absolutely. That's what I'm raising. Why won't people take it anyway? Why don't people perform differently? We've had reasonable success with it. What is it about this "medicine" that leads people to keep it on the shelf even when they're in dreadful pain?

The social therapist, asking why people won't take the medicine (do new performances), is inviting others to participate in building the group relational activity, inviting others to become more active in this process. She continues to lead the performance—an exploration of how Millie (and others) use the identity-based, passive, cause–effect language that we all learn in our epistemological culture—through attempting to speak an "activity language," using our current English language (and conversations using it) as the building blocks for the creation of a new language (a new performed conversation) of relational activity.

In an important sense, then, social therapy is a way to help the group members to have their conversation be "about nothing." This is not in any way to deny the complex and painful feelings. It is rather to deny the correspondence between those feelings and what is said. Indeed, it is to deny that there must or should be such a correspondence. We can communicate quite well without one (and often—typically—quite badly when we insist on one, Wittgenstein observes). It is when we are speaking to each other about nothing that, perhaps, we best understand and appreciate what speaking to each other (the socio-cultural activity) is "really all about." It is only then that we can recognize (a "knowing of the third kind," in Shotter's sense) ourselves as meaning makers in the cultural joint activity of creating conversation. It is, then, by performing conversation that we (non-cognitively) understand what conversation is and our capacity to alter forms of life (including especially, emotive forms of life) by reconstructing our ways of talking and listening.

To understand the Wittgensteinian notion of *form of life* as it is practically employed in social therapy in the performatory moving about around the events of the world, it is useful to view it in its paradoxical and dialectical unity with *forms of alienation*. Our "emotional states of mind" in late capitalist culture are thoroughly alienated, individuated, and truth-referential commodifications. The being of them and the understanding of them are, through commodification, inextricably connected, not dialectically, but by fast-drying (calcified) ideological cement. Whereas knowledge of physical truths (also alienated) employs an aboutness that at a minimum captures a scintilla of the "real" relationship between an observer and a distantly observed inanimate star, the crude application of this physicalistic scientific-epistemic model to human-to-human activity fundamentally distorts the particular, self-referential, (paradoxical) relational, activistic dimension of life-as-lived. It is these cemented, truth-referential, alienated, and individuated so-called expressions of so-called inner life (emotional, cognitive, and attitudinal states of mind) that we must move about around in creating a new, socially completed form of emotive relational life.

The *performance of life* is that creatively varied and continuous movement about around the rigid, alienated events (states) of emotional life in our scientifically psychologized culture. Analysis and/or storytelling will not do, because each, in its own way, appeals to a significant other instead of being practically-critically relational. What is needed, instead, is the performatory, relational, activity-based practice of method. In philosophically performing (moving practically-critically about around cemented alienated mental events) we dealienate (to the extent possible, given the overall societal environment) our individuated selves and re-establish our social relationality *in practice*, that is, in *revolutionary, practical-critical, socially completed activity*.

(Newman and Holzman, 1996, p. 194).

THE IMPROVISATIONAL PERFORMANCE OF DEVELOPMENTAL LEARNING

The Barbara Taylor School[4] is a laboratory primary school which has, over eleven years, developed a pedagogical approach that is activity-based (in Vygotsky's and Wittgenstein's sense). A small group of children (no more than twenty) from four to fourteen years of age spend their days creating life scenes that are potentially developmental. They are aided in this task by adults who function more as theatre directors and reorganizers of conversation than teachers in the traditional sense. To the extent that there is a curriculum, it is jointly created each day by the students and adults through improvisational performance. To the extent that developmental learning occurs, it is created simultaneously with performance.

The multiple languages of our (developing) development community are created in and by improvisational developmental learning. Following Vygotsky, children become successful learners through performing as learners (jointly creating, among other things, conversations and language-games). What is needed to perform is a performatory environment—often a stage—where "unnatural acts" (for example, science talk, emotion talk, philosophizing) can be created. If the existing environment is not conducive to performance, then it must be reshaped—not once, but continuously—into one that is performatory.

Traditional schools are structurally anti-performatory. Beyond kindergarten, play (including pretend play, the unself-conscious performance that dominates in early childhood) is discouraged and even disallowed. The dichotomy "work/play" that is operative in the broader culture is not only strongly reinforced within schools ("stop playing around and get down to work"), it is all but replicated in the dichotomy "learning/playing" that schools organizationally and discursively construct. For example, in most schools a specific time is set aside for play (at least in the early grades; instead of play time, junior high and high schools often have study hall and physical education classes). We speak of doing *school work,* not *school play;* we play *house* but we don't play *reading.*

Thus children are socialized very early on to associate playing with free time, fun, and frivolity; learning is associated with work, what is important and what is real. Adults do this as well. (If you are a teacher or parent, listen to yourself over the course of a day and hear how you talk to your students or children about school, work, play, and learning.) Even Barbara Taylor School parents, who have self-consciously chosen a play/performance-oriented educational environment, can be decidedly uncomfortable when their children respond to the perennial question, "What did you do in school today?" with "We played."

To our way of thinking, no small part of what is "wrong" with play in our overly epistemological culture has to do with the modern commitment to reality and the family of conceptions associated with it, including truth, fact, correctness, and rightness. The dominant mode of instruction (knowledge-focused and acquisitional) is designed to help students "get it right" (the liberal pronouncement "There is no right answer; I just want to know what you think" notwithstanding). Learning-centered schools, those committed to an acquisitional conception and model of learning (knowledge and scientific aboutness), are *philosophically* committed to the existence of Truth. Teaching children to get it right is teaching them to "tell the truth" —about numbers, words on a page, the Civil War, or the shooting down the block. When children are very young we encourage their imagination and care little about reality—the three-year-old who draws a Mommy with green hair floating next to a yellow sun that is half her size is applauded for his drawing, but by the time he is ten, the child will get little praise for drawing unrealistically.

We are not arguing against representational art or perspective. Rather, our concern is with the manner in which we adapt children to a culture which places such a high premium on truth-telling, facts, and reality. For the way the truth-telling (language-) game is played, the way school talk is accomplished, belies that it is a game, a way of speaking, a form of life, a performance. On the contrary, it reinforces a belief in the existence of truth. This seriously limits human growth in varying ways, including, paradoxically, the performing of "truth-telling" itself. (The exposure of lies—as, for example, in curricular reforms that deconstruct such truths as "Columbus discovered America"—is only a partial reform, for identifying some proposition as a lie is meaningful only if there is another proposition presumed to be true—thus, the commitment to truth and a truth-referential epistemology remains unexamined.)

Play and performance subvert truth and truth-telling, for the presumed truth value which utterances have in ordinary discourse is suspended in performatory activity. When a five-year-old girl says, "I'm the Daddy and you're the baby" in pretend play with her eight-year-old sister, there is no presumption of truth or falsity. When a character in a play utters the line, "My name is Cinderella" no one questions its truth value. (No audience member gets up and says, "No, you're not! You're my daughter!") Two-year-olds manage quite well without being held accountable for the truth, indeed, without having any awareness of it at all. Their learning and developing happens at a fantastic rate as they participate in creating life activities with their families and caregivers in an environment that is, to a large extent, performatory and, thereby, unconstrained by truth-referentiality.

The (largely theoretical) questioning of modernism's commitment to truth, objective knowledge, and reality is practically-critically challenged in the Barbara Taylor School's non-epistemological learning approach. (See Holzman, 1997 for further discussion of schooling and developmental learning.) What follows is a sampling of conversations from the Barbara Taylor School (emotion talk, science talk, math talk)—self-consciously shaped, to varying degrees, pedagogically, therapeutically, and philosophically and, thereby, also to varying degrees transformed into performances (the proper unscientific object of study).

I

Eleven-year-old Justin[5] was lying still on the rug, surrounded by several children and an adult kneeling beside him peering at his bare stomach (his shirt had been hiked up to his neck). Len, the adult learning director, was holding a cylindrical piece of paper upright above Justin's belly button. Caught by the scene and the children's rapt attention, a staff member asked what was happening. "We're performing an operation," they told her. "The surgical removal of immaturity."

Later that day, Justin and Len performed a commercial break during a circus scene created by eight-year-old Alice and Julia, another learning director. Len and Justin entered the stage walking. Len said, "Justin, you won't be going to your speech therapist today." Justin stopped in his tracks, yelled, cried and fell to the ground in a screaming temper tantrum. Len looked up at the audience for a moment, took some wads of paper out of the manila envelope he was holding and said, while he arched them toward Justin's mouth, "The miracle cure—[6] 'Matchore Partz' [Mature Parts]." Justin "swallowed the pills." He stood up and he and

Len began the scene again. Len: "Justin, you won't be going to your speech therapist today." Justin looked up at him and calmly said, "Oh well, I guess I'll go home then." The audience applauded.

For years, Justin had been having temper tantrums in situations like the one improvised in the commercial for "Matchore Partz." Diagnosed with a variety of specific and general learning disabilities and emotional problems, Justin had been in special ed schools until he entered the Barbara Taylor School a year before the above scene took place. His parents were concerned that he had "reached a plateau," as they had heard often happens with children like Justin, and that he just wasn't developing any more.

Justin is a performer. We all are. It is through performance—that is, doing what is beyond us (if only for that moment)—that when we are very young children we (learn to) do the varied things we don't know how to do. As Vygotsky described so eloquently, babies transform from babblers to speakers of a language through performing conversation—the relational activity of creatively imitating others (who complete them) is simultaneously the performance of themselves as speakers. Performing is a way of taking "who we are" and creating something new—in this case, a new speaker—through incorporating "the other."

Yet as we perform our way into cultural and societal adaptation, we also perform our way out of the continuous activity of developing. What we (have learned to) do becomes commodified, routinized and rigidified into behavior; we become so skilled at acting out roles that we no longer keep performing. We develop an identity as "this kind of person" who does certain things (not others) and feels certain ways (not others). Anything different would not be "true" to "who we are." Justin's emotional development was at a standstill; he repeatedly did what he knew how to do—have a tantrum. Like most of us, Justin was unaware that this emotional response (perhaps to frustration, change, or disappointment) was and is jointly and socially constructed by himself and others. It did not (perhaps would not and could not, for whatever reasons) occur to him that there is an infinity of things one can do or say upon hearing that the plans have changed, all of them decidedly "unnatural."

In order for us (including Justin) to learn anything developmental, we have to create something together. Creating an environment for Justin to perform—both his tantrum and something other than a tantrum—supports him to go beyond himself, and allows him to create other responses (emotional forms of life), to experience being other than who he is, to produce something new, to develop. This challenge to the cardinal rule of psychology's "hidden curriculum"—that our actions follow from how we feel—is distinctly therapeutic and cultural rather than cognitive and instructional. Justin's performance is a "moving about around" his "emotional state" (which has become a form of alienation), a creating of new emotional forms of life. Performative activity creates a changed environment in dialectical unity with himself and others.

II

This next performance of conversation as recounted by a staff member, is philosophical, therapeutic, and pedagogical.

The students and learning directors were having lunch. Charles, a new student just beginning his third week at the school, begins taunting Alice for being stupid. Both children are eight years old, he has just discovered. Charles had been in a gifted program in a public school and prided himself on being very smart. He was constantly getting into fights with other children, was identified as a problem student, and was routinely sent home from school. For these reasons, his mother decided to place him in the Barbara Taylor School; she thought he needed a more therapeutic environment where he would be supported to grow emotionally and socially.

The scene began when Charles loudly and incredulously proclaimed, "You don't know how to spell 'cat'! I don't believe you're in third grade!" Learning director Len said to the group, "I need some help. Charles is playing the Competitive Game and it's turning into the Nasty Game." When I came over, Charles was continuing to "marvel" at the fact that Alice could not spell "cat." He kept asking, "Why can't she spell 'cat'?" Alice was sinking lower in her seat, her head bowed. Len and some of the students attempted to change what was going on. They asked Charles why it mattered so much to him, why he was being nasty, and if he wanted to do something about it. A twelve-year-old boy said matter of factly, "No one taught her to spell; that's why she can't." I told Charles I thought his question was a good one and that I had another good one— "How come you *can* spell 'cat'?" Charles said, "My mother taught me." Several of us pursued this: "How did she do it?" Charles said that his mother told him to watch the game shows on TV and he did; that's how he learned to spell.

During these conversational exchanges, Alice's brother Kevin whispered to her, "C-A-T" and she began to say repeatedly, "Cat—c-a-t." Charles shouted at Kevin, "Don't tell her! That's cheating." One of the students excitedly said, "She's learning it right now!" We asked Alice if she wanted to learn how to spell; she said she did. We asked Charles and the others if they thought Alice might be able to learn by watching game shows; they said yes. During the next ten minutes an animated discussion took place on how to organize game-show spelling performances both at the school and for Alice at home. By the time lunch was over, it was decided that Charles and Len would be the co-producers and directors of the performances and four students had signed up to be the writers. Over the course of the next several days, the game-show spelling performance became an integrated activity of the school. On one day, Charles spent over an hour making a schedule of all the shows he thought Alice should watch. The writers spent time putting together flash cards to be used on the game show. Different students would come along and add a word or two throughout the course of the day.

Will Alice learn to spell? We do not know. And, in an important way, we do not particularly care. Our primary concern is that she (and others) learn that spelling is learnable (that is, that it is a performance). For learning that you are a learner, it seems to us, must be what developmental learning is. While it was long ago pointed out (for example, by Bateson, 1942) that learning how to learn is a component of learning anything, learning how to learn is not the whole (developing) story. In learning something, young children are learning not just two things but three: the particular thing learned; how to learn; and *that they are learners/that learning is something human beings do* (Holzman and Newman, 1987). It is this third "kind" of learning (akin to Shotter's "knowing of the third kind") that acquisitional, knowledge-based learning leaves out. Without it, learning is separated from and often replaces developing. The relational activity at the lunch table just described, to our way of thinking, is the process of creating a zpd that makes it possible (but, of course, not inevitable) for developmental learning to occur, in part through the reintroduction—as a form of life—of this performatory element of the activity of learning.

This vignette is meant to illustrate some of the important characteristics of the improvisational performance of developmental learning as a non-epistemological (therapeutically developmental rather than cognitively controlling) modality. The group activity was improvisational. The process of coming up with the idea for a collective game-show spelling performance was a reshaping of some of the elements (including some societally over-determined mentalistic, truth-referential dialogue) in the existing environment to create possible learning. Charles' nastiness was not related to as either his problem or the adults' problem, but as something the group needed to deal with. No one tried to stop him from making fun of Alice as an end in itself but, taking his question seriously, worked to reshape what he was giving—competitiveness and abuse (and curiosity, perhaps)—into something potentially developmental for the school as a whole. What was created, among other things, was a new language-game (we could call it the Curiosity Game or the How Do You Learn To Spell Game). Asking him how come he could spell and how he learned to do so was, as we see it, a bit of practical philosophizing. It changed the focus from knowing to learning, from product to process, from fixed mental states and identities to relational possibilities. Perhaps it freed Charles, Alice, and others from that Wittgensteinian "picture that holds us captive" (the one way of seeing things determined by our use of language). And, for the moment, no one was playing the Nasty Game.

Creating this environment engaged the students in a performance of their own learning-leading-development. Spelling is one of the infinite performances of which human beings are capable. Alice could perform as a speller (create who she is by being who she is not); Charles could relate to her as a speller rather than as "a dummy." These new possibilities come into being simultaneously with language activity, the making of new meanings, the performance of conversation.

III

The following vignette was written by a learning director at the Barbara Taylor School.

> Kevin [seven years old] and I were sitting on the floor next to each other in the quiet room. I put two of my fingers in the palm of his hand and asked him to guess what number. He said two. I asked him if he knew by looking; he said, "No, I closed my eyes." Then we started talking about how blind people read. I said blind people use their fingers to read and explained the concept of Braille, saying that it was paper that had bumps on it. From there I thought of getting some paper to make a Braille book but things didn't go that way. Instead, Rafael [also seven], who had overheard us, started walking in the corridor with his eyes closed, pretending he was blind. Kevin and some other kids—Kayla [six], Alicia [five], Chancy [six], Joy [four], and Matthew [four]—followed suit.
>
> The conversation between the kids was loud. "I can't see! I'm blind!" "Where are you going? Look out! You're bumping into me!" "I know where I'm going even though I can't see!"
>
> I asked Rafael how he knew where he was going if he couldn't see and he said that he was using his hands to feel where he was going. Then Kevin said he knew which way he was going because he could hear the movie in the next room. The parade of blind kids lasted about thirty seconds. Then they all tumbled into the office and starting fighting "blind" on the couch. I started singing, "Three Blind Mice." Joy got on her knees and started crawling out of the office with her eyes closed. Kayla and Chancy followed, singing along with me. Things got noisy as kids started wrestling with each other. Carl [fourteen] and I decided we would take these kids outside.
>
> Outside, I asked the group what they wanted to play and they started miming baseball. We "pitched," "hit," "ran bases," and "caught the ball" a few times. Then Rafael asked if we could play basketball: "Hey, can we play basketball? I know! Let's play basketball deaf! No talking!"
>
> A rigorous game of deaf basketball ensued. We passed, dribbled, shot baskets and did tricks with imaginary balls while moving around "the

court." Rafael reminded people a few times that we couldn't talk because we were deaf. After the game fizzled out, the kids played "Ocean Tag" (the shark is It) on the slide, making up the game and its rules as they went along.

The learning director did not, at this time, have anything specific she wanted to teach (at other times, she does). She let her activity with Kevin, and then with the group of children, emerge or come to define itself. We can see instances of her building with what the children were doing and saying, rather than insisting that they do what she intended (even if her intention was only seconds old). She introduced Braille and this might have been developed except that another student went somewhere else with being blind (pretending to be blind). Abandoning her idea to make a Braille book, she drew their attention to their other senses as they pretended to be blind (she brought something to what they were doing). Rather than scold them for fighting, she related to them in character and built on their performance with the introduction of "Three Blind Mice."

What were the children learning? This is a reasonable question, but one that we think is unanswerable—not only in this improvisational situation but in traditional, formal lesson situations as well. Do we know what children are learning when, for example, they are in science class and told the definitions of the five senses or, in a more hands-on class, *instructed* to imagine what it is like to be blind or deaf? To our way of thinking, it is the systematic nature of these lessons (including that they are conceived of beforehand and come complete with specific goals and objectives) that leads educators to think we know what children are learning from them. What if, however, learning is unsystematic?

We believe that learning that leads and constantly contributes to developing is, in fact, unsystematic. While we can always find a pattern in life's continuously emerging scenes, while we can always impose a systematic and rule-governed interpretation on them, Wittgenstein asks us to consider whether this is a form of mythology, whether in fact explanations and abstract generalizations distort life. It is our view that learning and developing do not require cognitive understanding. The improvisational performance of developmental learning is unsystematic, best understood in terms of itself—as a form of life—rather than in terms of models of science and reason. As a practice of method that offers possibilities for people to participate in whatever ways and to whatever extent they choose, it is—from our understanding of what is most human in Vygotsky's psychology and Wittgenstein's philosophy—developmental.

IV

The next conversational performance is more recognizably pedagogical than the previous ones. It is taken from a larger discussion of how to create developmental learning environments as an instance of Vygotskian practice (Holzman, 1995a) in which children are related to as readers, writers, physicists, geographers, historians, mathematicians, and so on—that is, they are encouraged to perform these activities whether or not they "know how." This is especially important with children who have a history of failure to learn in previous schools and classrooms, because such children typically have neither learned very well how to learn nor identify themselves very strongly as learners. Furthermore, the failure to develop in this way is inseparable from the failure to create an environment in which they can perform as learners. In the case of mathematics, for example, repeated attempts to teach the mechanisms of multiplication to a child who is "not good in math" or is "math-phobic"—in the absence of creating an environment for the child to perform as a mathematician (to make meaning, to do "math talk")—typically produce failure (Holzman, 1995a).

The characters are a thirteen-year-old boy, another student, and two adults. The initial interaction consisted of a conversation between David and learning director Carol about how he had been taught math before, what he learned, what she knew about math and wanted to learn, and who in the school might help them. Early on, Carol asked David how he thought he might learn math and what they could do together. This framed their performatory activity as learners, rather than as "knower" and "non-knower." Carol is not seeking to find out David's developmental level so she can "teach to it." She invites David to create something with her, not to learn mathematics from her separate from that creating. The second interaction is here repeated in full:

> The next day Carol, David, and Nancy, a ten-year-old girl, are sitting at a table. Carol says she wants to get to know them and is not sure how. Do they have any ideas? They don't. Nancy leaves. Carol and David begin to work on constructing the multiplication tables they began the day before. Nancy returns with a jigsaw puzzle and begins to put it together. The conversation while they are doing these activities is awkward as Carol urges them to tell her something about themselves and David and Nancy are shyly quiet in the face of these "invitations." Nancy asks if she could turn the radio on; Carol says OK, and rap music was added to the environment. David and Nancy begin to talk about the music, lyrics and rap artists. Carol continues to try to "get to know them," telling them some of her reasons and how it isn't easy. She says that she realizes that she does know some things about them—she now knows David likes [name of a rap star]. All the while, the conversation among the three of them includes "multiplication talk" ("What's 7 x 6?" "The 5's are easy." "8's are hard. I never remember them.")
>
> I have been observing this scene for a while and come over as David is saying, somewhat judgmentally, that Nancy isn't doing math. Carol says she is not so sure of that; how does he know she's not? He says, "because

she's just doing a puzzle." A discussion about what math is ensues. Maybe Nancy is doing math, the kind of math that's about shapes and curves and angles. No, math is paper and pencil; it's calculating. No, that's arithmetic; but math is more than that. Nancy may be doing the kind of math that's called geometry. This brief dialogue on the nature of mathematics concludes with agreement that Nancy needs harder puzzles.

At this point I say that I know a trick for multiplying by 9. Carol and David are interested. I write out 9 x 1, 9 x 2, etc., and ask if they can find the trick. "There's a pattern," I say. I have to help them a bit before David and Carol see that the last integers of the product are in descending order from 9 to 0 (9, 18, 27 . . .). Carol is impressed but asks me how I *use* that. She just "knows" that 9 x 5 = 45; don't I? David excitedly interrupts to say that the first numbers go from 0 to 9! We look and then discover yet another pattern—each product adds up to 9 (18 = 1 + 8; 27 = 2 + 7; etc.). There is a bit of wonder and satisfaction on David's face. We ask each other why this happens and what it means, and joke that we have no idea if any of it is helpful in learning to multiply. We ask each other "How much is 9 x _?" and use the patterns to come up with the answers together. David, in particular, verbalizes the patterns.

Carol then tells us she knows a trick for multiplying by 11, that 11s were always hard for her until she learned this trick. David says that 11s are easy. Carol agrees that up to 11 x 9 they are, but when there are two numbers (i.e., double digit multiplication, for example, 11 x 14) it is hard and her trick makes it easy. She writes out 11 x 1, 11 x 2, up to 11 x 19 and challenges us to find the pattern. David quickly discovers that both columns of the product are in ascending order (11 x 1 = 11; 11 x 2 = 22; etc.). But what happens after 11 x 9 when the answer is over a hundred? Carol asks. The pattern continues for the tens and ones columns, but not the hundreds column. Carol tells us there's another pattern in multiplying 11s, and 11 x 11, 11 x 12, 11 x 13 reveal it. Can we see it? David and I are equally excited to learn/realize/discover "the trick"—you place the integer in the tens column of the multiplier in the hundreds column of the product, the integer in the ones column of the multiplier in the ones column of the product, and add the integers of the multiplier to get the number in the tens column of the product (in 11 x 12 = 132, 1 + 2 = 3, in 11 x 13 = 143, 1 + 3 = 4, etc.). But what about 11 x 19 = 209? Carol thinks maybe the pattern no longer holds—where did 209 come from? David shows us that it still works: 1 + 9 = 10, so 1_9 has to become 209! We create operations through 11 x 29 using our new discovery. The next day, David's mother reports that David said to her, "Hey Mom, I'm learning some math."

(Holzman, 1995a, pp. 205–6)

It is essential to create discourse or "babble"—in this case, to "do math talk"—as part of the process of creating a developmental environment (a zpd). If adults attempted to teach children to speak the way we typically attempt to teach children mathematics, the results would be not only ludicrous but a failure. Meaning-making is the developmental activity that must occur for learning to lead development; this is as true for learning to multiply as it is for learning to speak. Children in our culture are deprived rather early in life of opportunities to perform mathematical conversations. Notions of correctness (the right answer) and formulaic ways of speaking come to dominate and stifle the kind of improvisational "babbling" that is critical to learning a mathematical concept. It is illusory to expect that a mathematical concept or operation can be taught directly, that is, in the absence of the learners and teachers creating discourse. Neither David nor the others know how to do math talk very well. They have to create such talk by performing conversation.

V

As we have seen (in the discussions of social therapeutic conversation and conversational performance), social therapeutic discourse is both like and unlike most therapy talk. People talk about similar things in social therapy, but what they talk about is not the focus. The social therapeutic modality is more completive (in Vygotsky's sense) than competitive, more activistic than interpretive or insightful; it is, as we have said, a moving about around emotional things and events. The following (social-) therapeutic conversation—performed by "non-therapists" and "non-clients" in a non-therapeutic environment—illustrates the interplay between specially constructed conversational performances and conversations that go on "in the hallways" of our developing (development) community.

The conversation took place on a ride home from a meeting of students, parents, and staff; the subject was what to do about fighting among students. It was the end of the first week of school and several fights and destructive incidents had taken place in the first few days. During school hours, the staff and students had been talking about what to do; the evening meeting was called so the entire school community could participate in moving ahead. The meeting ended on a high note with short performances the students had created during the week (including "Running from the Lights," directed by six-year-old Alicia). People then mingled and talked informally for about a half hour, during which time Pete, the father of Rafael, was arguing with another father who, he felt, was not supporting the decision that had been collectively reached during the meeting. Afterwards, Pete offered to drive Barbara Taylor and Lois Holzman home. The four settled in the car, Pete and Barbara Taylor in front, Rafael and Lois in the back. Rafael, nine years old, has been a student at the Barbara Taylor School for two years. His father is forty-nine years old.

LOIS   Rafael, how'd you think the meeting went? Do you think we're gonna make it?

RAFAEL   Well, I think we might close the school next week.

LOIS   What do you mean?

RAFAEL   If you be nice to kids, they do whatever they want and if you force them, they learn. Is that true?

BARBARA Is that what you think?

RAFAEL   I don't know. I'm just wondering. Do *you* think it's true?

BARBARA Well, I don't particularly, but I want to know what you think.

LOIS   It's interesting you say that, Rafael, because you're one of the most vocal about how at the Barbara Taylor School you're always learning to do what you don't want to do. You always talk about how you go to meetings even when you don't want to and things like that.

RAFAEL   Oh, yeah. And you don't force me.

LOIS   I also think that "wants" change. You did such a fantastic performance on the stage tonight and you sure looked like you wanted to do it!

RAFAEL   I did!

LOIS   And just a few months ago, you didn't want to perform at all. That was a big change. I think we develop wants. You want different things. Like now you want to be helpful and decent to your father but when you were little you didn't even know you could want something like that—and sometimes you were nice and sometimes you were nasty.

RAFAEL   Yeah.

LOIS   And a few years ago I *really* would have wanted to express my opinion on those video games we were talking about at the meeting. But I don't want to give my opinions so much anymore. Tonight all I wanted was for us to be having the conversation and deciding together what to do.

[The four of them talk about the meeting for about ten minutes.]

LOIS   Rafael, I think your dad's still angry. I see steam coming out of his ears. You think you can help him?

RAFAEL   I don't know . . . he has to want my help.

PETE   I do want your help.

RAFAEL   What kind of help do you want? What do you need, Dad?

PETE   I'm still so angry. I feel like William *[the other father]* thinks it's okay for there to be violence at the school. I feel like if Ray *[William's son]* touches a kid I wanna take my fist and shove it in his face and out the back of his head. It's crazy; it's macho. I'm holding on to being angry. And I guess I'm angry about a bunch of other things.

RAFAEL   What things?

PETE   Like I have to go into another therapy group and it's with Joan, and I always feel a tension with Joan as my therapist. So I'm nervous about the new group and I'm really angry at Joan 'cause I don't know if I want to go into this group. But I know I should. And then she called me up today about my therapy bill. I forgot last month was a five-week month and I paid for only four weeks. I already realized it. But Joan talked to me like I messed up; she didn't even give me a chance to say I knew it already. I didn't like the way she talked to me.

RAFAEL   Well, Dad, you have a choice.

PETE   I have a choice?

RAFAEL   Is Joan giving you a choice about therapy or forcing you?

PETE   She's giving me a choice. You're right. I have a choice. I'm talking like I don't but I do.

RAFAEL   You have a choice, Dad. You can make a decision about what you want to do.

PETE   Thanks, Rafael, that's very helpful!

RAFAEL   I only said one thing.

PETE   Well, it was a great thing! I drive myself crazy—I should go into the group because it's the right thing to do and if I don't I'll be a bad person and Joan treated me just like that on the phone and I feel bad she thinks that of me.

RAFAEL   Dad, do you feel guilty?

PETE   Do I feel guilty? Yeah, I guess so.

RAFAEL   Well, nobody said life was fair. *(There is a long pause.)* I think I helped all I can. I don't know anything else to say. Maybe somebody else can help.

THE PERFORMANCE OF PHILOSOPHY

Philosophizing is the language of our developing development community which most transforms conversation into the performance of conversation. Philosophizing, à la Wittgenstein, draws our attention to *the saying* of what we are saying by creating, in tool-and-result fashion, *the study* of the performance of "the saying" indistinguishable from the performance itself.

We sometimes characterize philosophizing as "asking big questions about little things" (Newman, 1996). Most often, the "little things" are words, for language activity in our culture has been so thoroughly "thingified" (objectified, reified, fetishized, commodified) that we must play games with (perform) it in order to see that it *is* activity. Like all the other societal institutions in our culture, language "presents itself" to us as a ready-made, already existing natural phenomenon. We believe that the consequent miscomprehension of language and the related philosophical-linguistic issues that form so much of the fascinating postmodern dialogue we have discussed at length in the first part of this book are of great practical importance for both the most mundane, everyday sort of problems (Wittgenstein's "muddles") and cultural-political and social policy issues. The performance of philosophical conversation is the "unnatural" act of challenging the unchallengeable, the "taken for granted it goes without saying"—an attempt to discover what we mean in "the obvious." Like Wittgenstein's language-games, it is a way for ordinary people to see (and, hopefully, prevent) the way language use institutionalizes our words, thoughts, and feelings.

In our many years of therapeutic, educational, cultural, and political work, we have supported young people and adults to "babble philosophically." Often they relate to our improvisational interventions into ordinary conversations as quite odd and, at the same time, remarkably therapeutic (helpful in moving about around the things and events in their lives). The illustrations we have chosen to present are from our most explicitly and self-consciously philosophical performance space—a class entitled "The Performance of Philosophy."

The class is offered at the Center for Developmental Learning in New York City. Divided into three ten-week sections that run from September through June to give new people the opportunity to come into it, it has been ongoing for three years. Newman taught it for the first two years; in 1996–7, it was taught by Holzman and their colleague Phyllis Goldberg, a sociologist by training who collaborated with Newman on his books for general audiences (Newman, 1994, 1996). Not surprisingly, the character of the classes—and the conversational performances—differ widely; while all three are "trained" re-organizers of conversation, Newman is a trained philosopher and practicing therapist; Holzman and Goldberg are neither (philosophers or therapists). The following are excerpts from transcripts of two classes that took place in the Spring 1996 series taught by Newman. (They are nearly verbatim, with only obviously unidentifiable speech removed and the names of students changed.)

As the course title suggests, "The Performance of Philosophy" is not designed for the learning of philosophy as an academic subject (that is, which philosopher said what about this or that great issue, for example, Truth, God, Good, Evil, Beauty, Reality), but for the doing of philosophical conversation. The students (the number varies from twenty to sixty) are adults from all walks of life—psychology and social work, education, medicine, advertising and public relations, theatre and entertainment, law, finance and business, politics. Some people have academic backgrounds, some do not; most are employed in professional or administrative positions, some are unemployed, retired, or students. Some are "new" to the developing (development) community; others have been actively participating for years. This diversity itself is an important element of the performance for, as you will see, the question of whether it is possible to have "a postmodern conversation in a modern culture" (to speak and hear without truths, categories, and judgments overdetermining us; to create conversation, rather than conclusions, out of differences) is self-reflexively performed.

I

JILL   I was thinking about the way I think I philosophize . . . Phyllis and I had a discussion the other day about how we were taking out the trash and I thought it was pretty philosophical. My presumption being there is "a way" to take out the trash, there is the most expedient way to take out the trash and get the trash done as soon as you possibly can. We had an extended discussion about a way of life and a way of living and the how of it, the quality of it. That's my main philosophizing activity with friends who will take me on.

　　The other way of philosophizing is sort of like a burning question. I'll read something you have written and I'll have this burning question and then start asking everybody what they think. Like I had that question about performance. I may pursue it over weeks. A lot it feels dead but that's how I see philosophizing.

FRED   What makes it burning?

JILL   It's definitely burning!

FRED   Why is it burning—these questions that come up?

JILL   They're definitely burning.

FRED   I've got that. How is it they burn?

JILL   They're burning because I think it's so new I can't get it and there is not enough there for me to get and I have to work it to even know what we're talking about here. It seems like it's ungraspable.

FRED   You don't know the answer.

JILL   Right. That's the experience.

FRED   Uh huh.

JILL   And if you pursue it, if you go to people who work it and you talk about it, you could get closer to the answer I guess.

FRED   And what would the answer provide you with, do you think? What is the importance, what is the value, in knowing the answer to a burning question?

JILL   That I'd know what you were talking about, like this thing around performance. Then when I was conveying it, it would be veridical with what you were saying. It wouldn't be a distortion of it.

FRED   And what's the value of veridically communicating what I have said?

JILL   I know I'm digging myself into a hole.

FRED   I don't want to do this in the spirit of putting you in a hole.

JILL   You could talk about the kids in the All Stars being plugged into an environment or you could talk about the kids in the All Stars making an environment. They're coming into something that is an environment; they create something with the organizers who are there.

FRED   To state the obvious, why wouldn't *that* be what is important?

JILL   Because it's important to be able to say, "We're not doing this—we're doing that."

FRED   Right. OK. But I'm trying to raise the question of the distinction between it being important to *do* it that way and it being important to *say* it that way. It sounds like you are focusing on how one says it and I'm wondering how come. What's the difference how we say something? Does it make a difference how we say something? What difference does it make how we characterize something? After all . . .

JILL   You're telling other people what the activity is, they may not be directly in contact with it; you have to communicate with them something new . . .

FRED   Are we? Doesn't that assume there is a way of describing it, a way of talking about it, which optimizes or maximizes the likelihood of communicating what is being done? Is that the belief? Is that what you hold to? Why do you think that? Why do you think that there is a certain description, a certain characterization, a certain way of talking, a certain formulation which is, if not uniquely, then more likely, to help someone get the point—whatever point it is you are trying to make. Why do you think that?

JILL   (inaudible)

FRED   OK, let's grant that. So, what does that have to do with there being some particular way of characterizing which uniquely or semi-uniquely maximizes your capacity to communicate it correctly?

HARVEY You're assuming that correctly is who you're saying it to?

FRED   No, relativized to who you are saying it to. I think what Jill is saying—and it's not such a strange assumption, but one that we probably all hold—is that basically there is a correct way of saying, "Here's what's going on, here's how that's done, here's what happens at the All Stars." I'm just trying to explore that assumption.

ALICE   I have difficulty with that assumption all the time. One, I never know whether what I'm really saying is that way.

FRED   Said in that uniquely descriptive ___?

ALICE   Right. I don't even care that much about whether I am doing that correctly and I know that there is a lot of pressure to do that. To get it uniquely correct. Oftentimes I'm communicating not with that assumption in mind but trying to focus more on who it is I'm talking to and how do I want them to hear it. So I think that there are many ways to talk about what the All Stars Talent Show Network is. But if I'm around some organizer or producer of the All Stars Talent Show Network, they make me feel more uncomfortable expressing it in a way other than the way they say it. And so I think I have difficulty with that assumption and I don't think that everybody hears things like that or says things or talks like that.

FRED   Yeah.

ALICE   And it's like people don't talk, don't express themselves, because of this assumption.

FRED   That's helpful. I guess what I'm raising is that—and even beyond that, whether we have gone overboard in our culture in contemporary times around communication. I mean, communication is sort of deified in our culture. Everything is communication. Language is communication. There is a whole structure around clear and proper communication, but maybe, to raise it in the extreme form, what is so good about communication? What is the big deal about communication?

ALICE   I think it's because it's mythologized to the point that it's useful to the powers that be to have because it sets up a whole class structure. People are told that they don't know how to talk. "If you don't know how to talk, you can't come in here. If you don't know how to communicate, you can come in here but just be quiet. You can be here but don't speak because you don't know how to speak." My mother used to take us to church and leave us at Sunday school and she would say, "Don't say anything. Because you don't know what you are talking about." I used to always break that rule by asking a question. Causing trouble. But you know that was like . . . I was just not good enough.

FRED   Right. This particular hierarchy has to do with your capacity to get the message across, or speak the right way, or help someone else to see things the way that you do, to create some kind of mapping, a successful mapping, between what you have on your mind and what they do or should have on their minds. And so if you effectively communicate, you do that. Again, I'm not saying it doesn't have some real value in certain situations but I'm at least raising the question of whether or not, for example, that increases the likelihood of people knowing what it is that you are talking about.

HARVEY   Isn't the premise of communicating well or properly based on there being some faith that the words trying to describe, or express, or portray, correspond . . .

FRED   Yes, the facts of the matter, the propositions—you call it different things in different contexts—there is something which these words or some variation of these words depict. And if you say those words, then, the story goes, the other person will somehow or another achieve a connection to that third thing which is the fact, the proposition, or whatever it is that is depicted by this language, and then you'll be on the same wavelength, you'll have some kind of identity relationship between what's going on for the communicator and what's going on for the communicant. That is the general picture. Yes, I think that is true.

HARVEY   I understand what we have been working on to question that construct.

FRED   Well, it questions that, among other, constructs.

MARIA   When you said that it felt like, gosh! I mean . . . I think I feel like . . . I always experience myself as someone who has no idea . . . I'm not very good at communicating what it is I'm talking about. I never experience any sense of that . . . and I think I always think that communication is about doing it in such a way that you're successful if you don't produce a question roughly like— "what are you talking about?" I feel like I'm very needy of people who can translate for me. It's such a relief when they say, "Oh, this is . . . " and then turn it into a coherent statement and I'll say "oh yeah." Often I don't know that that's what I was talking about but there is a coherency to it that I feel relieved by. I think it drives me crazy to continuously go through life feeling like I don't learn anything. I think that's how I experience it. Being inarticulate even though I'm not a dummy. It's not like I can't see things. When you said that, I thought, "Oh, I didn't think that that was something you could challenge." The whole thing is flawed.

FRED   The whole thing?

MARIA   Communication . . . that somehow . . . you don't have to communicate, or that's not necessarily what we need to be participating in. There are a lot of things I don't say or participate in because I feel like I can't articulate . . . get it all . . . you know . . .

FRED   Again, I think it's fair to say that in our culture theories and metatheories of language understand it to be about something. It's an about-driven culture in a fundamental philosophical sense. For example, to suggest an alternative to an about-driven language: you could have a theory of language that was rooted in the historical evolution of the development of language. By and large, that's not what we have. Our general understanding of language, both theoretical and practical, is in terms of this conception of aboutness. Again, I'm not making a simplistic claim that every sentence is taken to be about something; obviously there are imperatives, there are commands, there are endless forms of language, but it is still the case, I would argue and most linguists would agree, that the paradigmatic linguistic form is the declarative statement which is about something.

In our culture there is currently a move to question the problems that are generated by the hegemony of aboutness. Because more and more, I think, people are beginning to recognize that that totally overdetermines our conception of everything—including, interestingly enough, communication. We tend to hear things, speak things, say things involving language roughly in terms of what it is we think it's about. But what if it's about nothing? What if it's aboutness has nothing to do with it? What if the function of language, properly understood, is totally different from articulating statements, propositions, corresponding in some manner, shape or form with some state of the universe? What if that isn't how language is at all? What if the origins of language suggest, as far as we can tell anthropologically, that that's not where language comes from at all? More and more people are coming to question that quite seriously.

ALICE   When people say, "What's it about?" then I say, "This is what I'm doing." Is that different from when it's "about?" To me, it's different than "what it's about."

FRED   What kind of an answer would you give to "What are you doing?"

ALICE   I'd say what I was doing.

FRED   What kind of answer would that be?

ALICE   I'd say, "What I'm doing is, I'm collecting signatures to get on the ballot because I'd like to run as an independent and I need your assistance."

FRED   What if they say, "Oh, so that's what you're saying it's about?"

ALICE   I'd say, "That's what I'm doing." If I said that, if we had that exchange . . . So what about that exchange? Is that about petitioning or is it an activity?

FRED   Well, I think it comes closer to being about that than what I'm talking about. So some people, for example, would urge that if you want to understand language and communication you'd be better off not so much checking out what it's about but what its social function or social utility is. That would be consistent with what you are saying: "What I'm doing answers the question—this is how I'm using it," and I think that is a perfectly fair and reasonable claim. What I'm trying to raise, I think, goes, as it were, beyond that. It raises the issue of functionalism, the issue of whether we are even to understand language in terms of its function or the use to which we put it. Can we move to begin to understand language more fundamentally as a particularly interesting form of human life? A form of life activity. Something that we do with each other. Sounds that we make. A human life form much like living together communally, touching each other, people rubbing noses. After all, the "we" who are doing it are human beings. Other species, so far as we know, don't investigate language. But human beings investigate language, and I think that some would argue that there is a profound bias in that we frequently see language as other than simply another one of those very complex and interrelated life forms. So there is more and more of a movement to study languages as life forms, as activity. This is not to deny its functionality. It's not even to deny that in some cases language is about something. The issue here is not whether or not it is about something, or if it's functional; it's whether functionality or aboutness are the best models or paradigms to use for understanding language as a totality—that's the issue.

BETSY   Ten years ago, or whatever, there was a movement to make everything into language. . . . Do you think that that trend has been abandoned now?

FRED   We can hope so. It seems to me far more healthy to see language as nose rubbing than nose rubbing as language. We have made a shift, maybe, at least within some circles—social constructionist circles, postmodernist circles. I'm not suggesting that this is anything resembling a homogeneous picture. The academy is all over the place on this question. But I think that following Vygotsky, Wittgenstein, some social constructionists, and forms of postmodernism, there's a concern within intellectual circles with focusing philosophically, linguistically, socio-culturally, on language *qua* activity. It's very easy to take language—it's been done for thousands of years—and treat it as a thing in itself. To strip it, to separate it, to take it out of the context in which it is employed and to think you can see it abstracted from that. Now I'm talking about alienation. Language is probably more alienated than any socio-cultural artifact. I think there is now a minor revolution in opposition to that and a kind of recognition that what we have to study is the speaking activity, the hearing activity, as life activities. What are the origins of language? Where does it come from? How do children really learn it, how is it acquired? How did the species learn it? How does it advance? Does it advance? What does it mean for it to advance? What are the forms of life that interconnect with this particular form of life?

HARVEY   My dog makes noises and I always find myself trying to figure out what it is that the dog is trying to say.

FRED   Think of it this way. The dog is more correctly trying to figure out what *you* are trying to *do*! It is a very deep-rooted part of modern culture to think that the highest level of language you can achieve is to say what something means. To ascribe meaning to something dominates and we tend to extend it beyond language to everything. There is a search for the meaning of things. Now there is more questioning as to whether language even means anything.

[We pick up about 20 minutes later]

FRED   The metaphor of "more deeply," after all, has its own history. It comes to us from many things, including modern science. The modern meaning of "more deeply" is rooted in the modern model of science. To get more deeply into things is, in a Newtonian sense, to get to the inside of motions, to the inside of force, to the inside of mass. And that's kind of how we talk a whole lot about minds in our culture. You look at somebody and you say, "What's going on inside your head right now?" What if the answer is nothing?

MIKE   There is the appearance of something. Again, doing psychotherapy, one of the things about people telling stories is that somehow that is their experience and they experience it as if it has the characteristics of what would be an inner mind.

FRED   At least it is what they have been socially conditioned to characterize as their experience. I think sometimes when one pursues this—this is my experience as a therapist—you come to discover more and more that this is the way in which people talk. But if you start to pursue whether there is anything at the other end of the sign, people are not so clear that there is. In very short order, in what I hope is a less than manipulative or coercive approach, people come to see, yes, this is what they have learned to say, and it is very much relational, although it is thought of as not relational but individualistic. "This is what goes on for me." Why wouldn't they believe that? The culture suggests it and psychology, which is a major part of the institutions of our culture, reinforces that belief. Not just in psychologists' offices, but in life. It teaches us that there's something going on in here.

JESS   But hasn't neuroscience and all shown us all the chemical and neurological stuff that goes on?

FRED   Let's suppose that it *is* all chemistry. What do we do with these other forms of life? With our dialogues that aren't about chemistry? What do we do with them? Where do we put them? Let's for a moment suppose, let's agree, that it's all chemistry. How do we talk to each other? What do we say about our emotional interaction, our relationships, our lives, poetry? Suppose it's all chemistry; how does that impact on our intercourse?

JESS   You're saying it doesn't matter.

FRED   No, no, no. I'm saying, how would we talk to each other? Would we now start using chemical formulas? Suppose, for example, we could successfully reduce some set of intentions, beliefs and desires to a certain interaction of chemicals within the brain. So what? The point is this—and again I think this raises a whole set of issues that we need to talk about at some length—to say that we can reduce *this* to *that* is, after all, not to deny *this*. It's simply to say that there is some successful way within the paradigm of a certain set of scientific theories in which we can make some kind of correlation between the physical and chemical actions and these things over here. But, you see, one does not negate the other. There is no reason to have to deny the physical, chemical analysis of the brain if you want to articulate that there are forms of discourse in life which don't, in fact, make use of the language of the physio-chemistry of the brain. That represents simply an interesting and probably very valuable life form; it's the discourse of *that* environment. It doesn't impact on people in the sense of them never again saying to each other, "I'm feeling rather sad today." You would never say to somebody who said they were feeling sad today, "Oh, you're absolutely not. What is actually going on is . . . " No, no, no. That might be going on but that is not what is meant by, "I'm feeling sad today."

HARVEY   It's hard to break that connection.

FRED   Why?

HARVEY   Because I think that, I guess what we're talking about—that the explanation of something, or the why of something, or where it came from, or its essence—is caught up in its social function, what it is, what it does. And you're denying that. I understand the logic of what you're saying but there is something about me that says, whether it is chemistry or religion . . .

FRED   Well, it does matter. It matters, for example, if you are going to take some tests which will be comprehensible, meaningful, understandable, within that paradigmatic form of life, in that form of language. That could be meaningful. But we don't live our lives in a single form of language. We actually are a species that lives in an infinitude of life forms, including language life forms.

ALICE   I don't think he is being logical about it at all. I just think that if you want to talk about chemistry most of the time the people who have made the deductions are the only people who can talk about them like when you go to the doctor and he gives you a test. They can sit there and say what they did all afternoon. When you go home and they ask what is wrong with you, you're going to say, "I've got a hole in my gut."

FRED   But the point is: more credit to them for having this form of language! I think the problematic here is that what you're calling logical is, from my point of view, an insistence on some form of reductionism—that this kind of language actually accords with how the world is. This other kind of language is quasi-metaphorical, not mathematically transformable. But, in fact, language is much more complex than that. There has been enough work done over the last forty or fifty years in psychology and the philosophy of science foundational work to appreciate this. There is probably no reason to believe there is any language form, language paradigm, that has this uniquely corresponding relationship to reality. Good grief! Gödel (1962) shows that to be true in the foundation of mathematics; he shows it to be unquestionably the case that there is no capacity for reducing so formal a science as mathematics to a language form which precisely conforms to the way numbers operate. That's not what language is.

ALICE   Is this going back to how we started? We're still not accessible to

people. All of the complexity, those paradigms, those formulations, are the domain of the people who own and people who are
not trained to speak that way, don't speak that way. You can say
that to anyone who's not trained in that and . . .

FRED   I agree with that. But someone might take the position, mightn't
they, that so much the worse for ordinary people. I'm not saying
that's true but one might take that position: "Yes, there is a
substantial differentiation between the language spoken by physicists or chemists or doctors or whoever and how ordinary people
speak, but that's a problem and their imprecision is troublesome."
That is a position one could take. All I'm suggesting is that I think
that position is itself troublesome. Because I don't think it's a
problem so much as a misunderstanding of the complexity of
language to think that this particular mode of language, which is
perfectly reasonable and sensible for this domain of discourse, is
somehow *qua* language better than, more accurate than, the way
we speak when shooting the breeze on the street corner. It's not.
That's all I'm suggesting. As a matter of fact, language is unbelievably complex, unbelievably subtle, and unbelievably relative. We
only tend to think of scientific language as being more precise if
we hold on to a model of language that is rooted in the conception
of aboutness. Then we have the positivists who spent thirty years
trying to create languages which were so connected to ontology, to
reality, that they were literally protocol languages that couldn't be
falsified because they had a proximity to reality. And what they
came to discover is that that's not what language is. Language
doesn't have a greater or lesser proximity to reality. That simply is
not what it is. It is a misunderstanding of the socio-cultural institution known as thinking or talking or languaging. There is where
the problem lies. That's the assumption of what you are saying,
that this is a better language, a more accurate language.

MIKE   The choice of metaphor leads to certain behavior or activity that is
different from the others. I think those are the differences . . . It
depends on what you want to do.

FRED   I couldn't agree more. There is no "metatheory" that one could
appeal to in order to find out which of those different languages is
the best.

MIKE   You just do it and you find out.

FRED   We have different socio-cultural forms. Is there a better way of
eating food? Does this culture eat food better than this culture?
What does that mean? But we are deeply imbued in Western
culture with the conception that language is primarily functions, is
primarily a bearer of truth. *The* bearer of truth. And that this
language bears truth better than shooting bullshit on the corner.
Well, that might be true but it doesn't follow that the whole thesis

is true. That requires acceptance of the notion that the primary function of language is to bear truth.

LINDA   This disagreement, argument, whatever, about scientific language being better reminds me of our disagreement with some people who take Wittgenstein to be much more prescriptive than therapeutic.

FRED   Or, indeed, descriptive.

LINDA   Yes ... There's not such a solid line between descriptive and prescriptive.

MELANIE   You were talking before about exploring how the mind works. So, I got stuck on whether you have thoughts in your mind.

FRED   Do you?

MELANIE   I just wanted to push this a little further.

FRED   Push it.

MELANIE   Like you're sitting there and you're having like a dialogue with yourself. I mean, I do. I'm thinking. I have thoughts.

FRED   À la Wittgenstein, think about what those words mean rather than simply saying that it goes without saying. When you say you have a dialogue with yourself, tell me what is really going on that you are characterizing with the words "having a dialogue with yourself." I don't understand it.

MELANIE   I'll literally, like deciding whether to do something or not. So I'll say, "Well, I could ... "

JESS   You hear yourself saying that?

MELANIE   Yeah.

FRED   Really? What is the distinction you're making between the "Well, I could" you just said and the one that goes on inside your head? Are they the same?

MELANIE   One gets articulated by my mouth.

FRED   That, of course, I understand, but is there any other difference? Why do you have to say, "Well, I could?" Do you feel that if you don't say, "Well, I could" the same way that you do when you speak it aloud that you won't hear it?

MELANIE   Well, what else would I do?

FRED   Do you have to say it in order to hear it when you're thinking it? Is that required? If you don't do what you're calling saying something to yourself are you running the risk that you won't be heard? By you? I'm serious.

ALICE   You say that you say it in a dialogue. The question is, if you don't say it, if you don't have a dialogue, can you hear it? If you're thinking to you?

MELANIE   I think the thing I wanted to pursue is that it seemed like there was a language activity that goes on that doesn't get articulated.

FRED   Why do you call it a language activity?

MELANIE   I don't know what else to call it. I experience it so much.

FRED   Why do you have to call it anything? I'm serious. I'm not asking the question rhetorically. It would be good to know what you think about that. It's true that in our culture, certainly over the last several hundred years, we have been very, very prone, all the way from the earliest linguists to the modern computer scientists, to characterize the mental activity of the mind, if you will, in linguistic terms. Of that there is no question. I think there's a whole lot of deep-rooted assumptions out there if we actually begin to consider what goes on in this mind that you're identifying. I don't think that's a trivial philosophical point. I think they are serious points about our understanding of mind.

MELANIE I know that when you ask me that I start getting upset.

FRED   Why?

MELANIE I'm not exactly sure. It started to bother me a lot. Like, so, you know, I guess I'm really invested in there being things in my head and they're important and they're *my* thoughts.

FRED   I don't think you are unique in that regard. We're invested in it in the sense that we've been socialized to think about our minds in those ways. But I think what's valuable to do, from a philosophical as well as a psychological point of view, is to raise some serious questions, not by way of challenging or negating or denying. My experience is that a not insignificant factor in people's emotional pain is the way they have been socialized to characterize the workings of their emotionality and in that sense the workings of their mind. I don't think that is a trivial element of it. I think my experience of twenty-five years is that it is a critical element.

BETSY   I think sometimes it even goes back to the languagification of thinking. From my experience sometimes I . . . you know, I'm walking down the street and I'm thinking that I'm thinking. I characterize it as language and it is far more articulate and interesting than I would ever be able to say. I always think that. Putting it in linguistic terms puts me in this tough position of thinking I can't say what I mean. Raising the question, why characterize it in language terms at all, is helpful.

FRED   One of the things that Vygotsky teaches us, perhaps the one single, most profound observation in all of the writings that I've read, is that it's a serious misunderstanding of both language and thought to think of language as expressive of thought. It does not give expression to thought. Speaking—languaging, if you will— *completes* the thinking process. It's a unified process completed in one activity. The notion of there being a separate mental activity that then requires expression, and language being the vehicle for making the expression, is, on Vygotsky's account, and I think this has an enormously profound impact, distorting of the entire process. This notion is very much part of the model: these things take place inside and language is a vehicle for communicating what went on inside. To see it as an expressing process leads you to endless metaphysical assumptions.

LOUISE Questioning this thing that you think . . .

FRED What if there isn't this thing that you think? You just think! Does the fact that you are thinking demand that there is a thing you are thinking? Who taught you that? Where did you learn that from? You can't ask that question without me challenging the whole formulation.

LOUISE Alright.

FRED You can ask me another question.

MARIA I find thinking incomprehensible if there is not a thing that you think. I don't believe you probably can "just think."

FRED Why do you have to have a thing that you are thinking?

LOUISE As opposed to just a thought?

FRED Not *just* a thought! As opposed to nothing.

LOUISE This is harder. I appreciate what you're asking. If you don't characterize the activity of the mind in linguistic terms, which I was doing, can you say another way of characterizing the activities of the mind?

FRED As the activities of people. What people do with each other.

MIKE For me personally—I use that language, but it sounds . . . to say "my mind . . . "

FRED Minds are individuated in our culture. You bring in not only the mind, you bring in individuation.

LOUISE So the unspoken activity isn't taking place in your mind.

FRED It doesn't have to be "in your mind." It simply is. It's taking place in the world. It's relational activity with people whether you are by yourself or not. It's no less in the world.

MIKE This gets back to . . . discourse . . . there are many "as ifs"—*as if* there was a mind with a certain boundary; outside of that is *not* my mind and inside *is* my mind. But I think that that is very serious . . .

FRED Absolutely.

ALICE To me it's like always you're imprisoned by the language. If you don't say, "Well, I thought about it and this is my decision." If you say, "I saw it in the eyes of a homeless man and this is what I'm going to do," they'd say, "You're going to be homeless because you're crazy." The way the social arrangement is, you are forced to say, "my mind." One time I was watching a dance rehearsal and I wrote a poem. About three different people asked after it was over "How did you write that? Were you thinking about it before you went in?" I said, "No, I didn't know what the dance was going to be." And that was the hardest thing for me to say—that the poem was created by the dance. So there is a whole reluctance to have a discussion without using those words.

FRED   For years when people would open a sentence with "in my opinion" I would feel obliged to say to them, "Whose opinion do you think it might be?" But it's not trivial. What it does is to reify that this is not just someone saying this, but that "it's been considered." We are so caught up in our individuated minds as producers of language which then bears truth. So, indirectly we are producers of truth; what we want to convey a whole lot when we speak to each other is that this is truth.

MIKE   The tendency is to think of one's reporting on objective truth, as opposed to my experience, without "in my opinion."

FRED   Exactly. But the alternative is to socially create an environment where none of those things mean anything . . . This is deep-rooted stuff. Let's stop. I'll see you next week.

II

One week later . . .

FRED   I would like your help to keep exploring whatever it is that we wind up exploring, reminding ourselves that it would be of real value to simultaneously look at the performance of what we are talking about. It is very seductive—you can wind up being seduced by the topic *itself*. It is kind of ironic: no one cares much about the topic, but once you get into it, people get really into it. So, it is important I think and valuable (and I will take greater responsibility for this) to continually, self-reflexively take a look at the process that is going on in our discussion of whatever it is that we are discussing. From my vantage point, this is what I am eager to share about what philosophizing looks like: it is not even, for me at least as I understand it now, a separate topic, it's indistinguishable from what we are talking about although, ironically, easily separated out. I think it is ontologically indistinguishable, but we can fool ourselves into not looking at it. So that's a note as much to me as to you.

So let's continue our exploration of your philosophical performances. We are kind of back to our question of you sharing with us how you have been philosophizing lately, or if you have been philosophizing lately. What is your performance of philosophy looking like these days?

LYNN   I'm going to try to tag on to something that you were saying early on. The phrases like "It seems to me" or "I see it like that" then, would be phrases that, if you were having this postmodern dialogue, would become sort of not referring to anything at all?

FRED   Right.

MIKE   Unless we agree that within certain conversations, that would be the norm.

LYNN   So, the difference between "I see it like that" and "it is like that" would go?

FRED   Yes. Not just the referentiality, but in terms of the social significance of those formulations.

LYNN   So, is it gone? Obviously, I have an agenda, because I'm struggling with, "Well, is it gone already?" That difference when someone says "I see it like that," and you think, well, is it like that, or isn't it like that? Is it gone?

FRED   I don't think that's answerable outside of a deeper study of the activity and the context in which those articulations are made. I don't know how to answer that question in broad sweeping terms. In one sense, the answer is "Obviously not. We are still living in a very conclusionary, judgmental culture." Is it even gone a little bit, in some environments? I don't know. I think there is a need to constantly explore those environments and emerging conventions to see what something means.

LYNN   So you have to "pull on it"—not look at it, but the activity of yanking it.

FRED   Wittgenstein speaks of the activity of moving around about it. When he speaks about a physical response to it, I think he is referencing an attempt to find ways to create forms of life which are moving around and about elements of alienation. I think he is talking about alienates, I think he is talking about the alienation of language, the alienation of conversation, the alienation of dialogue, and he is raising the possibility that we can somehow engage in a deconstructive, reconstructive process of some kind of de-alienation within localized communities, with particular individuals. I think his approach is fundamentally therapeutic in this sense. I think he is saying, "Can I help this particular philosopher who has entrapped himself in a particularly hideous way, with his understanding of language?" Can I help her or him (usually he says him, but we'll say her or him) to escape from that bottle, to create new forms of life, not in capital letters, not in that gigantic sense, but in the most banal, mundane things? Can we find a new way of creating the dialogue with each other which is contextually and conversationally transformative of the overwhelming modernist presuppositions that dictate how we are human beings with each other? Is that possible? I'm inclined to think that we'll never know, which doesn't mean, going back to what Alice was saying, that we can't do it. It means that we might have to give up knowing that we are doing it.
       Can we create dialogue, if you will, without a destination,

without a capital D? If we do that, I don't think it's just pandering to different opinions; I think it's a matter of using the variety of what people are giving, to try at least to make an effort to create a continuous, though varied and complex, pathway to move somewhere or another from where we have gotten ourselves to. The intentionality of the dialogue is not to reach the answer, which is characteristic of a lot of dialogue in our culture.

ALICE   So you never really get to the end.

FRED   You never get to the end. For me, there is no end and, I would argue, there is not an answer. There is no beginning, either. We find ourselves in the middle of an exceedingly complex conversation. We come into this world in the middle of this gigantic conversation, and when we go out, it will still be going on! And we become participants in that conversation. The question becomes, to what extent can we self-consciously create environments in which we can more and more effectively bring that activity-theoretic reality out, to make it increasingly self-conscious, so that we can avoid the pitfalls of modern absolutism. That becomes to me the question. Can we do it, how do we do it, how do we persist in it, what do we do when it breaks down, and it breaks down all the time. Not surprisingly. Why wouldn't it break down? If we are doing this at all, even if we are being unbelievably successful, we're still being successful in a modern environment! Even if this were the most successful community ever created, we're still overdetermined by the modern environment in which we're located. So, the process continues—the process of trying to create environments in which the focus is more on process.

LOUISE   Earlier you were speaking about radical democracy and the issue of including the people who were also being theorized about. And you said not for moral reasons, but because you think that's the only way . . .

FRED   Yes, for methodological reasons. I happen to be committed to that position morally as well, but I think it's important to see not just for moral reasons, but for methodological reasons as well.

LOUISE   Could you just say more about that?

FRED   I think that we can't get on with this project unless everyone is included. Not just because it's the right thing to do, but because we can't get on with it if we maintain the dichotomy between those who are being theorized about and those who are theorizing. I just think that's a methodologically intolerable distinction which can't move forward. I think that the practice of method is critical, and what we mean by the practice of method is not simply methodology as an abstraction, but that we have to constantly practice, and create together, new methodologies.

LOUISE   So even if the inclusion slows down the process?

FRED   Well, it only slows it down relative to getting somewhere! Slowing down is a very relative term! You can only be delayed in a trip to San Francisco if you fix the date by which you will arrive! If you don't do that, you won't slow it down, it will simply be called the trip to San Francisco. Which is, by the way, how I travel, much to people's frustration!

LOUISE   So, the issue of moralism and not being goal-oriented is important in terms of building the Patriot Party? That's like the practice of our method?

FRED   I think it's very complex, because we are working in an environment where many people in independent politics as well as not independent are, understandably, extremely goal-oriented. The effort we've tried to make is to insist upon a very careful examination of the political process which is taking place, and sometimes, if you will, we get away with it. And sometimes, people want to throw us off the roof. So sometimes we win, and sometimes we lose; it's a mixed bag there, because there are few institutional activities in America more goal-oriented than politics.

LOUISE   Even though it doesn't go anywhere?

FRED   Ironically. Even though, as you frequently point out, and I try to point out, and we go around and around on this—even people who recognize that say, "Well, if we just come up with the right answers to all of the questions, somehow we will create something new." To which we frequently say, "I don't think so."

MIKE   That's the demand for humility, I think—when you start asking, in earnest, the implications of some of these questions, and what can we do, we have to just sort of take a step back. In my experience, that stepping back is an incredibly anxious moment which, needless to say, is only resolved by the generating of a community in which one can say, "Hey, is this going on for you, too?"

FRED   I couldn't agree with you more. Twenty-five years ago I left the university and the anxiety was extraordinary, because I had yet to create anything. I had the sort of vague sense that I couldn't teach philosophy in that environment and so I left, with virtually nothing, and then began with many people to build community which transformed, and continues to transform, in ways that make it more possible to be humble. I was much more arrogant thirty years ago than I am now—because I think I now have the kind of support that makes it possible to do some kinds of things without having the kind of arrogance that I once needed to have because I couldn't get through the damned day without it.

MARIA   I was just thinking about truth—this isn't profound—that it is a particular way to try to get people to go down a particular way. I realized that the whole notion of truth feels very connected to (1) thinking that things have to have a conclusion or an end, and (2) that there is some notion that it has to speed up somehow, that you have to direct people towards some certain end. So, then I was thinking about what you were saying about moving about and around something, I take it that truth or truth-referential dialogue is more replacing one alienated form of language with another— it's not going about around anything. Somebody says something, and you're basically saying, "No, I think you should be thinking about it this way." So, I keep going in and out of knowing what moving about and around is. I have some sense of us doing it here, but I don't know that I know what that activity is, and how it's related to getting from here to there. It seems like you would have to relate to all this alienated stuff that comes into play, but you don't have to be overly determined by it . . .

FRED   It might be that you have to use all the alienated stuff that comes into play, but it could still be the case that your focus, as it were, in terms of activity, is the play and not the alienated stuff that comes into play. See, the thing to understand about alienation is that it transforms processes, activities, etc., not simply into temporary objects, but into *permanent* objects of truth. Going back to human beings as perceivers and conceivers, the road of truth is simply getting closer and closer to these now ontologically reified alienates, and what it means to have knowledge is to get so close to them that you now have a direct relationship with them, either perceptually or conceptually.

The conception that Wittgenstein's using is a continuous process of play, of game playing, of transformation of these alienates whose numbers are growing within a modern culture. It's kind of moving from the alienated object to the activity of engagement. That becomes the fundamental characterization of the social activity. It isn't the perceiver or conceiver (which means all of *us* in the modern paradigm) coming closer to truth, with knowledge, with the correct conception, the correct perception. That isn't the picture that Wittgenstein is using. He is using, in my opinion, a distinctly anti-epistemological conception. Why, he says, must we explain? His answer: We mustn't. We don't have to. We actually conduct a not insignificant portion of our lives not doing that at all. For example, what we identify as the period in which children become interesting, as they become societally adapted, is the period at which they begin to ask that kind of question. But they live a not insignificant part of their lives not asking it at all; they don't even know the words. So the question that is being raised, I think, is fundamentally a question of the epistemological paradigm. I don't think that postmodernism has yet to reach a point of realizing the extent to which postmodernism itself has been overdetermined by the existing epistemological paradigm. I think that's still a cutting edge question in this process of social development.

THE LEARNING-LEADING-DEVELOPMENT PLAY

"Beyond the Pale" written by Newman, was first presented in Toronto, Canada on 9 August 1996 at the 104th Annual Convention of the American Psychological Association as part of a symposium entitled "Performative Psychology Redux." (Other presenters at this performatory session were Mary Gergen, Kenneth Gergen and Ilene Serbin, and Kareen Malone.) The short play (about fifteen minutes) was written and directed as a learning-leading-development play somewhat in the tradition of the Brechtian learning play (*lehrstücke*). But for Brecht, the learning play was a political tool designed to teach the audience members (and the players) a new, cognitive way of understanding (a Marxist and/or communist way of understanding) a somewhat traditional moral-social situation.

The learning-leading-development play is not designed to be cognitive at all, and surely not to teach a new way of *looking* at things. Rather, it is used to have people experience a new way of *doing* things. It is a performance of performance. It is intentionally unclear as to whether it is a play about a therapy session or a therapy session about a play or, indeed, whether it is aptly anything about anything at all. What makes this designed confusion happen, we think, is the repeated use of self-reflexivity ("Is what I said when I said what I said what I said when I said . . . "). Such self-reflexivity is, to be sure, a good way of confusing ourselves. It is, however, also a good way of showing how uniquely bizarre we are as a performing (developing) species.

The play makes us think again of Marx's XIth Thesis on Feuerbach quoted earlier: "The philosophers have only *interpreted* the world, in various ways; the point is to *change* it" (Marx, 1973, p. 123). But perhaps we best see the developmental character of Marx and revolutionary activity if we deny that there is a *point* at all, and linguistically formulate Marx's thesis in the performatory-directorial mode: "Don't interpret the world; change it." "Beyond the Pale" has no point. It is pointless, the interesting cognitive trialogue notwithstanding. It is designed only to remind us, through the performance of it, that we are the *performers* of our varied conversations—not truth makers or tellers, or object describers, but revolutionary tool-and-result activity makers.

"BEYOND THE PALE"

A learning-leading-development play by Fred Newman[6]

Characters

BETTE BRAUN, social therapist
LEV VYGOTSKY
LUDWIG WITTGENSTEIN

(As lights come up, BRAUN is seated in chair and LEV VYGOTSKY and LUDWIG WITTGENSTEIN are entering her therapy office. She rises to welcome them and points to two chairs for them to sit in.)

BRAUN   Good afternoon, gentlemen . . . Please, have a seat. *(They nod and sit.)* Well . . . What can I do for you?

(Pause.)

VYGOTSKY   *(Somewhat hesitantly)* Miss Braun . . . is that correct . . . is that how you say your name? Is it "Miss"?

BRAUN   Yes . . . That's fine, Dr. Vygotsky.

VYGOTSKY   *(Hesitatingly)* Well, Miss Braun, Dr. Wittgenstein *(he gestures)*, Dr. Wittgenstein and I have a somewhat unusual . . . "presenting problem."

BRAUN   And what is that, Dr. Vygotsky?

WITTGENSTEIN   *(Clipped and critical)* He is too slow, Dr. Braun . . . too polite. Here's the problem. Vygotsky and I never knew each other when we were alive. He died in the '30s. I died in the '50s. Now . . . forty years later—against our will—we have been brought together—"synthesized"—by a number of people including, I am told, two Americans named Newman and Holzman, whom I understand trained you in this performatory therapeutic method you call social therapy.

VYGOTSKY   *(Calming WITTGENSTEIN down)* Don't be so harsh, Ludwig. Don't be so harsh. *(To Braun.)* You see, Miss Braun, it's not that we don't like each other. Dr. Wittgenstein is a brilliant philosopher and he has written extensively about the philosophical foundations of psychology. We agree on a great deal.

BRAUN   Then what's the problem?

WITTGENSTEIN   *(Harsh)* The problem, Braun, is that we didn't agree to be put together.

VYGOTSKY   You know, Miss Braun, we each have our . . . well . . . our egos . . . and, . . . well . . .

WITTGENSTEIN   Say it already, Lev. This is a short session! Spit it out, Lev.

VYGOTSKY   *(Shakes his head at WITTGENSTEIN)* Quiet, Ludwig. *(Back to*

Braun.) Well . . . we feel we should have been asked before we were synthesized. Do you know what I mean?

BRAUN   I do. Dr. Vygotsky. I certainly do.

VYGOTSKY   *(He smiles and shakes his head somewhat shyly and childishly.)* Call me Lev, Miss Braun. I prefer it.

WITTGENSTEIN   What? Miss Braun, Dr. Vygotsky is one of the great psychologists of our age. I hope you appreciate that. I do not think it appropriate for you to call him Lev!

VYGOTSKY   Ludwig, Ludwig. Still a stuffy Viennese aristocrat on such matters. *(To Braun)* Call me Lev.

WITTGENSTEIN   *(Sighs disgusted)* Oh—you communists! You communists. Braun *(facetiously)*, why don't you call him comrade? *(He turns away.)*

BRAUN   *(With a smile)* I see there are things you don't agree on. Lev . . . I like how that sounds . . . Lev, let me ask you this: how could Newman and Holzman and others have asked you two about how you felt about being "synthesized"? You were both dead long before they got together to write about you.

WITTGENSTEIN   *(Turns back toward Braun confrontationally)* Then, they should have left us alone! Don't you postmodernists . . . that's the right word, isn't it? . . . don't you postmodernists believe in "Rest in Peace"? No one understands what I was saying. No one even understood when I was alive. I want my work left alone. It is not systemizeable. It is not synthesizeable.

VYGOTSKY   I do not feel the same way that Dr. Wittgenstein does. I am eager to see my work continued . . . or "completed" as I sometimes used that term and concept. But I feel concerned that this synthesis with Wittgenstein's work might . . . er, well, shall we say . . . might water down what both he and I have to say.

WITTGENSTEIN   Might! No! Must! Synthesizing and systematizing are inseparable. My work is therapeutic. It is addressed to specific linguistic philosophical pathologies. It is not meant to be generalized upon. With all due respect, Dr. Vygotsky, you were a system builder; a brilliant one, no doubt, but still a systematizer. You are, after all, a Marxist. You were eager to create a systematic psychology. I was convinced there could be no such thing. We cannot be put together. We cannot be synthesized. Newman and Holzman are opportunists; frauds; phrase makers—not real thinkers. They make even more metaphysical mist than already exists. They are— shall we say—mystifiers.

VYGOTSKY   I am sorry, Miss Braun . . .

BRAUN   Please, Lev, call me Bette . . . if you like.

WITTGENSTEIN   *(Disgusted)* This is too friendly for my taste!

VYGOTSKY   *(Motions to WITTGENSTEIN to keep quiet)* I am not interested in insulting Newman and Holzman. I do not even know them . . . Bette. *(He stares at WITTGENSTEIN.)*

BRAUN   Perhaps, Lev, you are more concerned with . . . Dr. Wittgenstein than you are with Newman and Holzman? *(VYGOTSKY nods.)*

WITTGENSTEIN   Is this a therapeutic trick, Dr. Braun? Are you trying to turn Vygotsky and me against each other to protect your mentors Newman and Holzman?

BRAUN   Not at all, Dr. Wittgenstein. You two are no more opposites—antagonists—than you are the same—synthesizeable. Putting you together doesn't make you one. From Newman and Holzman's perspective—as I understand it—you two have always been together. It was only our individuated and institutionalized way of characterizing matters that appeared to separate you. In history, if you will, you are not simply related—you are relational—relational activity. Newman and Holzman didn't "bring you together"; societal, institutional labeling "kept you apart."

WITTGENSTEIN   This is a semantical trick, Braun.

BRAUN   Perhaps, Dr. Wittgenstein, it is a new language-game?

VYGOTSKY   *(Laughs loudly)* That's a good one, Ludwig, don't you think? She . . . Bette . . . is clever. *(Laughs)* A language-game. *(To Braun.)* Did you make that up, Bette? This language-game idea is a concept of yours?

BRAUN   No. No, Lev. It is Dr. Wittgenstein's.

VYGOTSKY   YES! Wittgenstein . . . was this in the *Tractatus*?

WITTGENSTEIN   No, Vygotsky. It was in my *Philosophical Investigations*—published after I died . . . and long after you died.

VYGOTSKY   And what is a language-game, Wittgenstein? How is it played? What kind of play are we talking about here?

WITTGENSTEIN   *(Somewhat begrudgingly)* It is a philosophical game meant to help one see the activistic origins of language. Not so much to clarify the use of language in societal communication and *surely* not to expose the abstract propositional meaning of language—I rejected that stupid earlier idea of mine completely—but to show the . . .

VYGOTSKY   *(Interrupts)* . . . historical activity of language. Yes?

WITTGENSTEIN   You could say that.

VYGOTSKY   So then language . . . and/or the learning of language . . . is rooted in play; the playing of games.

WITTGENSTEIN   You have written a good deal about play, yes?

VYGOTSKY   I have.

WITTGENSTEIN But play is not so systematic, Vygotsky. It is more cultural than scientific.

VYGOTSKY That is certainly true. Many rules of play do not exist antecedent to the game but emerge in the playing of the game.

WITTGENSTEIN Good. Very good, Vygotsky. Then games, including language-games and, therefore, including language itself, are not systematic in the traditional sense of being understood or explainable in terms of pre-existing rules or laws?

VYGOTSKY Play and work are quite alike in this way. They both create something qualitatively new in their process—something that wasn't there before and therefore cannot be understood simply in terms of things that were there before, i.e., reductionistically.

WITTGENSTEIN That sounds a little too Marxist for me, Vygotsky.

VYGOTSKY Use your own language, Ludwig. It makes no difference to me as long as we understand what language is—and what it isn't. Language—more precisely speaking (or writing)—doesn't *express* anything—thoughts, judgments, feelings, intentions, whatever; rather, it *completes* the unified process that is thinking/speaking.

BRAUN This is a very fine performance, you two. I am honored to watch Lev Vygotsky and Ludwig Wittgenstein working—and playing—together.

WITTGENSTEIN A fine performance of what?

BRAUN A fine performance of Lev Vygotsky and Ludwig Wittgenstein speaking to each other and creating a new understanding.

VYGOTSKY Yes, it is, Ludwig. And I rather enjoy it. Moreover, I do not think either of us is "violated" in this process.

WITTGENSTEIN It is clever, Braun, I grant you that. But, of course, it is a hoax. For as you and I both know I am not *really* Wittgenstein and he is not *really* Vygotsky . . . I assume you are really Braun.

BRAUN You are right, Dr. Wittgenstein. But why must you *really* be Wittgenstein and he *really* be Vygotsky for Wittgenstein and Vygotsky to be working and playing together? Performance, after all, is always about being who we are not. And, Lev, isn't that what "learning which leads development" is all about?

VYGOTSKY But that is for discrete individuals.

BRAUN But can't others complete for us in the zone of proximal development—the zpd?

WITTGENSTEIN ZPD? Is this a concept of yours, Braun?

BRAUN No. It isn't, Dr. Wittgenstein. It's Vygotsky's.

VYGOTSKY   What are you saying, Braun; that zpds might . . . might include *dead* people?

BRAUN   And why not? If it can include various people at differing levels of development then why not dead people. Isn't a zpd more historical than societal?

VYGOTSKY   And performing is how we continuously *complete* and create culture?

BRAUN   Yes. Not a synthesis, an activity—a social relational *completion*; a revolutionary activity.

WITTGENSTEIN *(Excited)* A new form of life—as I put it!

BRAUN   Yes, Dr. Wittgenstein, a new form of life.

WITTGENSTEIN In your . . . social therapy . . . people actually create new *forms of life*?

BRAUN   Indeed. By "moving about and around" . . . old forms of life. If you will permit me, Dr. Wittgenstein, by moving about and around alienated forms of life.

WITTGENSTEIN Oh, how you Marxists *fetishize* that word *alienation*. (*BRAUN* and *VYGOTSKY laugh.*)

WITTGENSTEIN So even though I am not *really* Wittgenstein and he is not *really* Vygotsky we can further develop Wittgenstein and Vygotsky?

VYGOTSKY   And if we can why can't Newman and Holzman?

WITTGENSTEIN Who wrote this damned script anyway? Who created this play?

BRAUN   Newman wrote the script. We created the play.

VYGOTSKY   It's clever, Ludwig. It's clever.

WITTGENSTEIN Perhaps, Lev. But, Braun, does it work when it isn't scripted?

BRAUN   I think so. That's my experience with it. Whether scripted or improvised we can always perform.

VYGOTSKY   It is at once a tool *and* a result as I used to say. It is a *practice of method.*

WITTGENSTEIN Practice of method. Did you make that up, too, Vygotsky?

BRAUN   No. That's Newman and Holzman's.

WITTGENSTEIN I like practice of method. This approach is truly beyond psychology—beyond the pale.

VYGOTSKY   I came from beyond the pale, Ludwig. I am a Russian Jew.

WITTGENSTEIN I know, Lev. I know. My family abandoned Judaism. I was raised a Catholic—a wealthy Viennese Catholic.

BRAUN   I'm from Dayton . . . And we're all in Toronto. Labels are funny, aren't they? They can also be dreadfully destructive. Well, gentlemen, have I made the problem vanish? (*VYGOTSKY* and *WITTGENSTEIN laugh loudly.*)

BRAUN   *(She stands; so do they.)* Good, because we are out of time. (*They all turn to audience and bow.*)

THE ENDINGS STOP HERE

And so philosophy, along with its most extraordinary product and instrument, modern science, have reached the end of their centuries-long quest for Truth. They have been successful in this effort almost beyond belief. Along the way they have discovered features of the universe which have enlightened and advanced our species more intensely than the brightest star and more progressively than the lights of the heavens—even as they have sometimes and in some ways contributed to the metaphysical moral mess that is contemporary international society.

In the end Western philosophy and modern science discovered (and to some extent produced) a world and a universe that are utterly meaningless. We should not be surprised. The various Western establishments (secular and religious), from those who silenced Socrates to those who silenced Galileo (and beyond), correctly anticipated that if philosophy and/or science were allowed to pursue their search for Truth to the end (unimpeded by moral considerations), they would discover (produce) meaninglessness. Postmodernism is not, in our view, a rejection of science and modernism. Rather, it is the ultimate achievement of their pursuit—an accurate characterization of the nature of the world. It is success which has put science out of business as a theoretical pursuit for it has at last discovered by its method the *meaninglessness* of our universe and life upon it. Understandably, the scientific and philosophical establishments seek (for purely pragmatic reasons) to deny this discovery of theirs. But postmodernism is the quite distinctly Western child of Western philosophy and science.

Our small efforts are nothing more than an attempt to clean up, "scientifically" and "analytically-philosophically," revisionist postmodern formulations so that we might more fully appreciate the colossal significance of this discovery of meaninglessness.

What now? To move beyond the remarkable success that *is* modernism we must reconstruct our world and our lives, absent the cultural apparatus that *was* modernism. We must find ways to work not for a new theory or a new paradigm but for a new world. In this developing qualitative transformation (so far as we can currently see through the remaining metaphysicality of modernism), performed activity will be key.

First, we must understand (a performed activity) that we have come to the end of our modernist journey and that what we found was meaninglessness. There need be no existential despair here. Then we must reevaluate (another performed activity) from a developing developmental understanding of meaninglessness all that we have created (both wonderful and wasteful) on this extended modernist journey. And then (although no one can even guess how), we must further develop (perhaps, in some ways, as small children do) in a meaningless world (yet another performed activity).

Neither life nor development requires meaning. Indeed, neither the making of meaning nor the activity of developing requires meaning or development. Hence, we have come to the end of meaning and development even as we must (and can) continue making meaning and developing. Such performed activity, so far as we can tell, is what lies beyond modernism and its remarkable postscript, postmodernism.

We would like to thank Lawrence Erlbaum Associates, Inc., Publishers for allowing us to reproduce passages on pp. 128-33, which are similar to those found in Chapter 7 of *Schools for Growth*.

Notes

CHAPTER 1

1 Cole moved his laboratory to the University of California at San Diego in 1978. Since then, what was open-ended, exploratory methodological activity has become, in our opinion, an alternative instrumental method within the scientific psychological paradigm. The varied work of the UCSD laboratory is experimental and done in the name of a *cultural theory of cognition*. (See Cole, 1984, 1995; Holzman, 1986; Newman *et al.*, 1989.)

CHAPTER 2

1 As examples of the debate inspired by Gergen's writings, consider the following:

Jerome Bruner finds *The Saturated Self* to be "A rousing trip through the reaches of post-modernism with a splendid psychological guide who manages to combine irony and passion in contemplating the challenges of contemporary identity" (back cover), while Donald Spence finds it "unconvincing" and "impressionistic," its genre "uncomfortably close to the sound-bite culture that Gergen criticizes at length" (Spence, 1993, p. 8). *Realities and Relationships* (1994) received this accolade on it's back cover, from Arlie Russell Hochschild:

Gergen takes us on a spectacular tour through the many ways we become secure in how we "know" what's true. Clearly written and immensely erudite, the book attunes us to the "discursive dimensions of paradigm shifts," even while we're invited to make just such a shift, from empiricism and rationalism (for those who were believers) to social constructionism. A brilliant, unnerving book.

2 The most prominent neo-Vgotskians are discussed in detail in Newman and Holzman (1993). The neo-Marxist revisionists include the theorists known as the Frankfurt School and others. Most neo-Wittgensteinian philosophers (with the significant exception of Baker and Hacker) and most of the postmodern psychologists are the neo-Wittgensteinian revisionists.

3 It is difficult for us to understand precisely what Gergen, a social constructionist, might mean by a "literal experience."

4 The notion of an epistemological machine was, to the best of my knowledge, first used by Donald Davidson in his Theory of Knowledge class, which I took in the fall of 1960 at Stanford University. I have reworked the Davidson "story" over the

course of the last thirty-five years, so it is difficult for me to tell how close to the original the following piece of philosophical science fiction is.

Imagine someone walking down the street being approached by another person who offers him $100 for about a half hour's worth of work. Mr. A agrees to this arrangement and is taken to a sub-sub-basement laboratory. He is placed on an operating table and attached by a complex set of cables to a computerized mechanism. It is explained to him by the presiding attendant (presumably a physician) that all of his nerve endings can be stimulated by this attachment and that the nature of the experiment in which he has agreed to participate will consist of stimulating the nerve endings in such a way as to produce a variety of "virtual reality"–type experiences. He is further assured that none of these experiences will be painful and that the entire experiment should last no more than a half hour or forty-five minutes.

After the attachments are completed Mr. A is asked to relax. The next experience that Mr. A has is of himself sitting around a campfire in a heavily wooded area eating a hot dog. This experience lasts for a minute or two, whereupon Mr. A is returned to the laboratory and hears the attending physician ask him how that was. He nods, indicating that it was fine. His next felt experience is that of being on a boat sailing down a river under a pleasantly warm sun. This also lasts for a few minutes, whereupon he is asked by the attending physician if that was satisfactory to him. He agrees that it was. Immediately he comes to experience himself in a single-engine airplane gliding peacefully across what appears to be a midwestern sky. After a few more minutes he is once again spoken to by the attending physician, who this time thanks him, takes a few moments to unhook the cables, hands him a crisp $100 bill and leads him to the door. Mr. A opens the door to the sub-basement in order to exit to the street. But his next experience is that of sailing in the basket of a hot air balloon over a deep blue lake; this lasts for a minute or so. Then he sees the attending physician, who apologizes for this additional experience and thanks Mr. A again for his help. Once more the cables are taken off, and Mr. A heads to the door, opens it into the sub-basement from which he expects to exit to the street, but instead experiences himself swimming in a peaceful pool in what seems to be a suburban area of Los Angeles.

Like Davidson did in his Theory class, on many occasions since 1960 I have used this piece of science fiction, "the epistemological machine," to discuss philosophical issues having to do with perception, reality, knowing, etc. Ultimately, I have come to see this science fiction story as a useful metaphor for exposing the serious limitations of epistemology itself. Perhaps what it shows best of all is that once we are locked into epistemology there is no obvious evolutionary way out.

(Fred Newman)

5 The distinction we are making between revolutionary activity and revolution, which will be discussed further in Chapter 5, was first drawn in "Seven theses on revolutionary art," Artists' Committee of the Castillo Gallery (1989). See also Newman and Holzman (1993).
6 See Kuhn, 1962, as well as his earlier *The Copernican Revolution* (1957), in which he points out that and how it took Europe a century to accept Copernicus. Since the 1970s, Bruno Latour has become increasingly well known for works that demythologize science. In his most recent book, *We Have Never Been Modern* (1993) he puts forth "relationism" as descriptive of the scientific activity (Rorty, 1996a).
7 See Lotringer, 1977; Newman, 1991a; Sarbin and Mancuso, 1980.
8 There is a long history within philosophical circles of discussion of the issues we raise in this section. We do not mean to ignore the decades of dialogue on the

theory and nature of description and denotation which, in this century, dates at least back to Russell's groundbreaking essay, "On Denoting" and *Principia Mathematica* and continues beyond Godel. Rather, our purposes here are better served by examining these issues from a psychological rather than a philosophical vantage point. See Monk's recent (1996) book on Russell for an unusually accessible discussion of this philosophical literature.

9 I was first introduced to this formulation (no doubt, used by many) by Davidson.—F. N.

10 The chief defect of all hitherto existing materialism (that of Feuerbach included) is that the thing, reality, sensuousness, is conceived only in the form of the *object* or of *contemplation*, but not as *sensuous human activity*, *practice*, not subjectively. Hence, in contradistinction to materialism, the *active* side was developed abstractly by idealism—which, of course, does not know real, sensuous activity as such. Feuerbach wants sensuous objects, really distinct from the thought objects, but he does not conceive human activity as *objective* activity. Hence, in *Das Wesen des Christenthums*, he regards the theoretical attitude as the only genuinely human attitude, while practice is conceived and fixed only in its dirty-judaical manifestation. Hence he does not grasp the significance of 'revolutionary,' of 'practical-critical,' activity.

(Marx., 1973, p. 121)

CHAPTER 3

1 While the distinction between social and societal is not often made, both we and Holzkamp (see Tolman and Maiers, 1991) reserve societal for adaptation to and assimilation by society.

2 Among the many sources listed by Parker are: Henriques *et al.,* 1984; Parker and Shotter, 1990; Squire, 1989; Walkerdine, 1988, 1991.

3 For example, on Black psychology, see Fulani, 1988; feminist studies, Holzman and Rosen, 1984, Fulani, 1997; theatre, Brenner, 1992, Newman, 1992, Friedman, in press.

CHAPTER 4

1 See Scriven (1959), "Truisms as the grounds for historical explanation."

2 This is a fairly traditional Marxist analysis, even among those who do not follow Luxemburg.

3 Thanks to Lou Hinman for his valuable input on these formulations.

CHAPTER 5

1 Here is a sample of the activities and events of the developing (development) community during 1996.
    The East Side Institute and Center for Developmental Learning. The varied programs, attended by approximately one thousand students (including twenty adults enrolled in one- or two-year therapist or educator training), include: courses—Developing (Discovering) Vygotsky, The Theater of Development, The Performance of Philosophy, Performatory Short Term Therapy, Life Performance Trainings—Stop Abusive Behavior, Creating a New Family Play, On the Job and in the Director's Chair; lectures and discussions—Talk about Health, Illness and

Pain, The Postmodernization of AIDS; weekend institutes in performance; and supervision for clinicians and educators.

Social Therapy Centers. Eight social therapy centers (in the New York City area, and Atlanta, Boston, Philadelphia, San Francisco, and Washington, D.C.) offer group, family, and individual therapy to approximately 500 adults and children.

The Barbara Taylor School. Laboratory elementary school and training center. Twenty children enrolled, ten to twenty interns in training. CHOICE program (Children Having the Opportunity to Invite Community Educators) involves professionals (doctors, artists, architects, actors, anthropologists, writers) as once a week guest teachers.

Pregnant Productions. A community pregnancy prevention program based on improvisational performance involves, at each location, approximately fifty young people and hundreds more who attend their performances.

The All Stars Talent Show Network. Twelve-year-old cultural organization involving over 30,000 young people who produce and perform in approximately fifty talent shows in their communities and build the Network.

Castillo Theatre. Twelve-year-old off-off Broadway theatre produces seven to nine mostly new, mostly American plays per season; regular performances by Castillo's comedy improvisation troupe, The Gayggles; special musical and one-person shows; annual "New Plays for New Days" readings; and an ongoing playwrighting course. Over 5,000 people attend Castillo Theatre events each year.

Performance of a Lifetime. Interactive growth theatre in which an average of thirty people over a four-week period improvise, rehearse, and perform a play based on their lives. Eight four-week cycles per year. The Performance of a Lifetime performance space also offers courses in movement, voice, and acting.

Fundraising. Fifty volunteers do 560 hours of telemarketing per week, raising $24,500 each week to support development projects, including the All Stars Talent Show Network, the Barbara Taylor School, and social worker training scholarships at the East Side Institute.

2   The names of group members have been changed.

3   The language of clinical depression (of almost all therapeutic schools) is filled with talk of "loss." Although this does not come up explicitly in this social therapy group, social therapy discussions of depression often "deconstruct" and "reconstruct" such "loss talk" (see the chapter on crisis normalization and depression in Newman, 1991a).

4   The founding of the Barbara Taylor School in Harlem, New York in 1985 was the coming together of two progressive traditions—that of African American community schools and the (mostly white) free school movement. Two years earlier, Barbara Taylor, the founder and principal of the St. Thomas Community School in Harlem, met the Institute for Social Therapy and Research (the form and name of the [developing] development community during most of the 1980s). At sixty-two, Taylor had already enjoyed a long career as a successful and dedicated educator—she had been an elementary school teacher, reading specialist, assistant principal, principal and founder of a community school. Courageous and energetic, Taylor had been guided in her professional life by her commitment to helping poor children learn and grow. As principal of the St. Thomas School—a Harlem elementary school operated under the auspices of the archdiocese of New York—she led a group of parents in a prolonged fight against the Church bureaucracy when it decided to withdraw regular funding from the school after Taylor had successfully raised supplementary funds. The result was the formation of the independent St. Thomas Community School, with Taylor as principal.

After several years, Taylor felt that St. Thomas was no longer a dynamic community school. She sought educational innovation that would challenge not only children but their families and community. Our developing (development) community—with a similar social vision, experience in community organizing, the practice of social therapy, and a network of progressive people from a variety of class, professional, and ethnic backgrounds—was eager to support Taylor, and our collaboration began.

During its first six years, the Barbara Taylor School concentrated on creating conditions for children to be emotionally supported and challenged in order to be able to learn and utilized a standard curriculum in innovative ways. We were eager to develop the approach further in a Vygotskian direction which, to us, meant creating an activity-centered (not curriculum-centered) school as a continuously emerging environment where learning leads development—not A Zone of Proximal Development, but many zpds. Our reading of Vygotsky led us to believe that many ever-changing and overlapping zpds have to be created (performed) and that it is through this relational, creative activity that people learn developmentally. We felt that the standard practices of grouping students by age (at the time, students were divided into three groups—kindergarten–grade 2, grades 3–5, and grades 6–8) and following a curriculum might constrain the continuous creation of zpds. The transition of the Barbara Taylor School into a Vygotskian performance laboratory began in September, 1991 (Holzman, 1993). The school was housed on one floor of a Harlem brownstone from 1991 until it relocated to a Brooklyn storefront in 1994.

5 In this and subsequent illustrations, the names of the children and staff (except for Barbara Taylor and Lois Holzman) have been changed.

6 © copyright 1996, Fred Newman, reprinted with author's permission.

Bibliography

Adorno, T.W. (1982). *Against Epistemology: A Metacritique*. London: Blackwell.

The Artists' Committee of the Castillo Gallery (1989). "Seven theses on revolutionary art." *Stono, An International Journal of Culture and Politics*, 1, 1, 7.

Austin, J. (1962). *How to Do Things with Words*. Oxford: Oxford University Press.

Baker, G. P. (1992). "Some remarks on 'language' and 'grammar.' " *Grazer Philosophische Studien*, 42, 107–31.

Baker, G. P. and Hacker, P. M. S. (1980). *Wittgenstein: Understanding and Meaning*. Oxford: Blackwell.

Bakhtin, M. M. (1981). *The Dialogic Imagination: Four Essays by M. M. Bakhtin*. Austin, Tx: University of Texas Press.

—— (1986). *Speech Genres and Other Late Essays*. Austin, TX: University of Texas Press.

Bakhurst, D. (1991). *Consciousness and Revolution in Soviet Philosophy*. Cambridge: Cambridge University Press.

Bateson, G. (1942). "Social planning and the concept of deutero-learning." In Conference of Science, Philosophy and Religion (Ed.), *Science, Philosophy and Religion: Second Symposium*, pp. 81–97. Reprinted in G. Bateson (1972), *Steps to an Ecology of Mind*. New York: Ballantine, pp. 159–76.

Baudrillard, J. (1968). *Le Système des Objets*. Paris: Denoel-Gonthier.

—— (1984a). "Game with vestiges," *On the Beach*, 6 (Spring), 19–25.

—— (1984b). "On nihilism." *On the Beach*, 6 (Spring), 38–9.

—— (1987). *Forget Foucault*. New York: Semiotexte.

—— (1988a). *America*. London: Verso.

—— (1988b). *The Ecstasy of Communication*. New York: Semiotexte.

—— (1988c). "The year 2000 has already happened." In A. and M. Kroker (Eds.), *Body Invaders: Panic Sex in America*. Montreal: The New World Perspectives, pp. 35–44.

—— (1989). "The anorexic ruins." In D. Kamper and C. Wulf (Eds.), *Looking Back on the End of the World*. New York: Semiotexte, pp. 29–45.

—— (1990). *Seduction*. New York and London: St. Martin's Press and Macmillan.

—— (1994). *Figures de l'alterité*. Paris: Descartes and Cie.

Bennington, G. (1988). *Lyotard: Writing the Event*. New York: Columbia University Press.

Berger, P.L. and Luckmann, T. (1966) *The Social Construction of Reality*. New York: Doubleday/Anchor.

Best, S. and Kellner, D. (1991). *Postmodern Theory: Critical Interrogations*. New York: The Guilford Press.

Bloom, L., Hood, L., and Lightbown, P. (1974). "Imitation in language development: If, when and why." *Cognitive Psychology*, 6, 380–420.

Bloom, L., Hood, L., and Miller, P. (1975). "Variation and reduction as aspects of competence in language development." In A. Pick (Ed.), *The 1974 Symposium on Child Psychology*. Minneapolis: University of Minnesota Press, pp. 3–56.

Bloom, L., Lightbown, P., and Hood, L. (1975). *Structure and Variation in Child Language*. Monographs of the Society for Research in Child Development, 40 (serial no. 160).

Bloom, L., Rocissano, L., and Hood, L. (1976). "Adult–child discourse: Developmental interaction between information processing and linguistic knowledge." *Cognitive Psychology*, 8, 521–52.

Bradley, B. S. (1989). *Visions of Infancy: A Critical Introduction to Child Psychology*. Cambridge: Polity.

—— (1991). "Infancy as paradise." *Human Development*, 34, 35–54.

Brenner, E. (1992). "Theatre of the unorganized: The radical independence of the Castillo Cultural Center." *The Drama Review*, Fall (T135), 28–60.

Bruner, J. (1993). "Explaining and interpreting: Two ways of using mind." In G. Harman (Ed.), *Conceptions of the Human Mind: Essays in Honor of George Miller*. Hillsdale NJ: Lawrence Erlbaum.

Bunge, M. (1996). "In praise of intolerance to charlatanism in academia." In P. R. Gross, N. Levitt, and M. W. Lewis (Eds.), *The Flight from Science and Reason*. New York: New York Academy of Sciences, pp. 96–115.

Burman, E. (1994). *Deconstructing Developmental Psychology*. London: Routledge.

Butterfield, H. (1962). *Origins of Modern Science*. New York: Collier Books.

Choate, P. (1990). *Agents of Influence*. New York: Alfred A. Knopf.

Cole, M. (1979). "Epilogue: A portrait of Luria." In A. R. Luria, *The Making of Mind: A Personal Account of Soviet Psychology*. Cambridge, MA: Harvard University Press, pp. 189–225.

—— (1984). "A twelve year program of research and training in cultural psychology." (Unpublished manuscript.)

—— (1995). "Culture and cognitive development: From cross-cultural research to creating systems of cultural mediation." *Culture and Psychology*, 1, 25–54.

Cole, M., Hood, L., and McDermott, R. P. (1978). *Ecological Niche-picking: Ecological Invalidity as an Axiom of Experimental Cognitive Psychology*. (Monograph.) New York: Rockefeller University, Laboratory of Comparative Human Cognition. Reprinted in *Practice*, 4, 1, 117–29.

Danziger, K. (1994). *Constructing the Subject: Historical Origins of Psychological Research*. Cambridge: Cambridge University Press.

—— (1997). *Naming the Mind: How Psychology Found Its Language*. London: Sage.

Davidson, D. (1980). "Actions, reasons and causes." In D. Davidson, *Essays on Actions and Events*. Oxford: Oxford University Press, pp. 3–19.

DeBerry, S. T. (1991). *The Externalization of Consciousness and the Psychopathology of Everyday Life*. Westport, CT: Greenwood Press.

Deleuze, G. and Guattari, F. (1977). *Anti-Oedipus: Capitalism and Schizophrenia*. New York: Viking Press.

Derrida, J. (1976). *Of Grammatology*. Baltimore: Johns Hopkins University Press.

—— (1978). *Writing and Difference*. Chicago: University of Chicago Press.

Diamond, I. and Quimby, L. (Eds.), (1988). *Feminism and Foucault*. Boston: Northeastern University Press.

Dray, W. (1957). *Laws and Explanation in History*. Oxford: Oxford University Press.

Drew, P. and Heritage, J. (1992). *Talk at Work: Interaction in Institutional Settings*. Cambridge: Cambridge University Press.

Edwards, D. (1995). "Sacks and psychology. A review of Harvey Sacks, *Lectures on Conversation*." *Theory and Psychology*, 5, 4, 579–96.

Etzioni, A. (1993). *Spirit of Community: Reinvention of America*. New York: Simon and Schuster.

Fanon, F. (1963). *The Wretched of the Earth*. New York: Grove Press.

—— (1967). *Black Skin, White Masks*. New York: Grove Press.

Ferrara, K. W. (1994). *Therapeutic Ways with Words*. New York: Oxford University Press.

Feyerabend, P. (1978). *Against Method: Outline of an Anarchistic Theory of Knowledge*. London: Verso.

Foucault, M. (1965). *Madness and Civilization: A History of Insanity in the Age of Reason*. New York: Pantheon.

—— (1972). *The Archaeology of Knowledge*. London: Tavistock.

—— (1973). *The Order of Things*. New York: Vintage.

—— (1975). *The Birth of the Clinic: An Archaeology of Medical Perception*. New York: Vintage Books.

—— (1979). *Discipline and Punish*. New York: Vintage.

—— (1980). *The History of Sexuality*. New York: Vintage.

Fox, R. (1996). "State of the art/science in anthropology." In P. R. Gross, N. Levitt, and M. W. Lewis (Eds.), *The Flight from Science and Reason*. New York: New York Academy of Sciences, pp. 327–45.

Friedman, D. (in press). "Developmental theatre at Castillo." *The Drama Review*.

Fulani, L. (1988). "Poor women of color do great therapy." In L. Fulani (Ed.), *The Psychopathology of Everyday Racism and Sexism*. New York: Harrington Park Press, pp. 111–20.

—— (1997). "Moving beyond morality and identity: The Gilligan-Kohlberg debate revamped." In E. Burman (Ed.), *Deconstructing Feminist Psychology*. London: Sage.

Garfinkel, H. (1967). *Studies in Ethnomethodology*. Englewood Cliffs, NJ: Prentice Hall.

Geertz, C. (1973). "Thick description: Toward an interpretive theory of culture." In C. Geertz, *The Interpretation of Cultures*. New York: Basic Books.

—— (1988). *Works and Lives: The Anthropologist as Author*. Stanford: Stanford University Press.

Gergen, K. J. (1991). *The Saturated Self: Dilemmas of Identity in Contemporary Life*. New York: Basic Books.

—— (1994). *Realities and Relationships: Soundings in Social Construction*. Cambridge, MA: Harvard University Press.

—— (1995). "Social construction and the transformation of identity politics." Presented at the New School for Social Research, New York City.

Gödel, K. (1962). *On Formally Undecidable Propositions of Principia Mathematica and Related Systems*. London: Oliver and Boyd.

Goffman, E. (1974). *Frame Analysis*. New York: Harper and Row.

Greenberg, H. (1996). "Introductory remarks: Medicine took an earlier flight." In P. R. Gross, N. Levitt, and M. W. Lewis (Eds.), *The Flight from Science and Reason*. New York: New York Academy of Sciences, pp. ix–x.

Gross, P. R. and Levitt, N. (1994). *Higher Superstition: The Academic Left and its Quarrels with Science*. Baltimore: Johns Hopkins University Press.

Gross, P. R., Levitt, N., and Lewis, M. W. (Eds.) (1996). *The Flight from Science and Reason*. New York: New York Academy of Sciences.

Gumperz, J. (1982). *Discourse Strategies*. Cambridge: Cambridge University Press.

Harré, R. (1979). *Social Being: A Theory for Social Psychology*. Oxford: Blackwell.

—— (1983). *Personal Being: A Theory for Individual Psychology*. Oxford: Blackwell.

—— (1986). *Varieties of Realism*. Oxford: Blackwell.

Harré, R., Clarke, D., and DeCarlo, N. (1985). *Motives and Mechanisms: An Introduction to the Psychology of Action*. London: Methuen.

Harré, R. and Gillett, G. (1994). *The Discursive Mind*. Thousand Oaks, CA: Sage.

Harré, R. and Secord, P. F. (1972). *The Explanation of Social Behaviour*. Oxford: Blackwell.

Hempel. C. (1965). *Aspects of Scientific Explanation and other Essays in the Philosophy of Science*. New York: The Free Press.

Henriques, J., Holloway, W., Urwin, C., Venn, C., and Walkerdine, V. (1984). *Changing the Subject: Psychology, Social Regulation and Subjectivity*. London: Methuen.

Henwood, K. L. (1995). "Adult mother–daughter relationships: Subjectivity, power and critical psychology." *Theory and Psychology*, 5, 4, 483–510.

Holzman, L. (1985). "Pragmatism and dialectical materialism in language development." In K. E. Nelson (Ed.), *Children's Language*. Hillsdale, NJ: Lawrence Erlbaum, pp. 345–67. Reprinted in H. Daniels (Ed.) (1996), *An Introduction to Vygotsky*. London: Routledge, pp. 75–98.

——(1986). "Ecological validity revisited." *Practice: The Journal of Politics, Economics, Psychology, Sociology and Culture*, 4, 95–135.

——(1990). "Lev and let Lev: An interview on the life and works of Lev Vygotsky." *Practice: The Magazine of Psychology and Political Economy*, 7, 3, 11–23.

——(1993). "Notes from the laboratory: A work-in-progress report from the Barbara Taylor School." *Practice: The Magazine of Psychology and Political Economy*, 9, 1, 25–37.

——(1995a). "Creating developmental learning environments: A Vygotskian practice." *School Psychology International*, 16, 199–212.

——(1995b). " 'Wrong,' said Fred. A response to Parker." *Changes: An International Journal of Psychology and Psychotherapy*, 13, 1, 23–6.

—— (1996). "Newman's practice of method completes Vygotsky." In I. Parker and R. Spears (Eds.), *Psychology and Society: Radical Theory and Practice*. London: Pluto, pp. 128–38.

—— (1997). *Schools for Growth: Radical Alternatives to Current Educational Models*. Mahwah, NJ: Lawrence Erlbaum.

Holzman, L. and Newman, F. (1979). *The Practice of Method: An Introduction to the Foundations of Social Therapy*. New York: New York Institute for Social Therapy and Research.

—— (1985). "History as an anti-paradigm: Work in progress toward a new developmental and clinical psychology." *Practice: The Journal of Politics, Economics, Psychology, Sociology and Culture*, 3, 60–72. Reprinted in L. Holzman and H. Polk (Eds.) (1988), *History Is the Cure: A Social Therapy Reader*. New York: Practice Press.

—— (1987). "Language and thought about history." In M. Hickmann (Ed.), *Social and Functional Approaches to Language and Thought*. London: Academic Press, pp. 109–21.

Holzman, L. and Rosen, F. (1984). "Left-wing sexism, a masculine disorder." *Practice: The Journal of Politics, Economics, Psychology, Sociology and Culture*, 2, 113–28.

Hood, L. (1977). "A longitudinal study of the development of the expression of causal relations in complex sentences." PhD dissertation, Columbia University.

Hood, L. and Bloom, L. (1979). *What, When, and How About Why: A Longitudinal Study of Early Expressions of Causality*. Monographs of the Society for Research in Child Development, 44 (serial no. 6).

Hood, L. Fiess, K., and Aron, J. (1982). "Growing up explained: Vygotskians look at the language of causality." In C. Brainerd and M. Pressley (Eds.), *Verbal Processes in Children*. New York: Springer-Verlag, pp. 265–86.

Hood, L., McDermott, R. P., and Cole, M. (1980). " 'Let's try to make it a good day'—Some not so simple ways." *Discourse Processes*, 3, 155–68.

Horgan, J. (1996). *The End of Science: Facing the Limits of Knowledge in the Twilight of the Scientific Age*. Reading, MA: Addison-Wesley.

Hymes, D. (1962). "The ethnography of speaking". In T. Gladwin and W. Sturdevant

(Eds.), *Anthropology and Human Behavior*. Washington, DC: Anthropological Society of Washington, pp. 13–53.

Jameson, F. (1983). "Postmodernism and consumer society." In H. Foster (Ed.), *The Anti-aesthetic: Essays on Postmodern Culture*. Port Townsend, WA: Bay Press.

——(1984). "Postmodernism, or the cultural logic of late capitalism." *New Left Review*, 146, 53–93.

Jefferson, G. (1992). *Harvey Sacks: Lectures on Conversation*, Vols. 1 & 2. Oxford: Blackwell.

Joravsky, D. (1989). *Russian Psychology: A Critical History*. Oxford: Blackwell.

Jost, J. T. (1995). "Negative illusions: Conceptual clarification and psychological evidence concerning false consciousness." *Political Psychology*, 16, 2, 397–424.

——(1996). Personal correspondence to Newman and Holzman.

Jost, J. T. and Hardin, C. D. (1996). "The practical turn in psychology: Marx and Wittgenstein as social materialists." *Theory and Psychology*, 6, 3, 385–93.

Kuhn, T. (1957). *The Copernican Revolution: Planetary Astronomy in the Development of Western Thought*. Cambridge, MA: Harvard University Press.

——(1962). *The Structure of Scientific Revolutions*. Chicago: University of Chicago Press.

LaCerva, C. (1992). "Talking about talking about sex: The organization of possibilities." In J. T. Sears (Ed.), *Sexuality and the Curriculum: The Politics and Practice of Sexuality Education*. New York: Teachers College Press, pp. 124–37.

Latour, B. (1993). *We Have Never Been Modern*. Cambridge, MA: Harvard University Press.

Lave, J. and Wenger, E. (1991). *Situated Learning: Legitimate Peripheral Participation*. Cambridge: Cambridge University Press.

Levin, C. (1996). *Jean Baudrillard: A Study in Cultural Metaphysics*. Hertfordshire, UK: Prentice Hall Europe.

Levitan, K. (1982). *One is Not Born a Personality: Profiles of Soviet Education Psychologists*. Moscow: Progress Publishers.

Lewis, M. W. (1996). "Radical environmental philosophy and the assault on reason." In P. R. Gross, N. Levitt, and M. W. Lewis (Eds.), *The Flight from Science and Reason*. New York: New York Academy of Sciences, pp. 209–30.

Lotringer, S. (1977). "Libido unbound. The politics of 'schizophrenia.' " *Semiotexte*, 2, 3, 5–10.

Luxemburg, R. (1958). *The Accumulation of Capital*. New York: Monthly Review Press.

—— (1972). *The Accumulation of Capital: An Anti-critique*. New York: Monthly Review Press.

Lyotard, J-F. (1954). *La Phénoménologie*. Paris: Presses Universitaires de France.

——(1971). *Discours, Figure*. Paris: Klincksieck.

——(1977). *Instructions paiennes*. Paris: Galilée.

——(1984). *The Postmodern Condition: A Report on Knowledge*. Minneapolis: University of Minnesota Press.

——(1988a). *The Differend: Phrases in Dispute*. Minneapolis: University of Minnesota Press.

——(1988b). *Peregrinations: Law, Form, Event*. New York: Columbia University Press.

Marx, K. (1973). "Theses on Feuerbach". In K. Marx and F. Engels, *The German Ideology*. New York: International Publishers, pp. 121–3.

Marx, K. and Engels, F. (1973). *The German Ideology*. New York: International Publishers.

McDermott, R. P., Gospondinoff, K., and Aron, J. (1978). "Criteria for an ethnographically adequate description of concerted activities and their contexts." *Semiotica*, 24, 245–75.

McDermott, R. P. and Hood, L. (1982). "Institutional psychology and the ethnography of schooling." In P. Gilmore and A. Glatthorn (Eds.), *Children in and out of School: Ethnography and Education*. Washington, DC: Center for Applied Linguistics, pp. 232–49.

Menand, L. (1995). "Marketing postmodernism." In R. Orrill (Ed.), *The Condition of American Liberal Education: Pragmatism and a Changing Tradition. An Essay by Bruce A. Kimball with Commentaries by Noted Scholars*. York: College Entrance Examination Board.

Michael, M. (1994). "Discourse and uncertainty: Postmodern variations." *Theory and Psychology*, 4, 3, 383–404.

Moll, L. C. (Ed.) (1990). *Vygotsky and Education: Instructional Implications and Applications of Sociocultural Psychology*. Cambridge: Cambridge University Press.

Monk, R. (1990). *Ludwig Wittgenstein: The Duty of Genius*. New York: Penguin
——(1996). *Bertrand Russell: The Spirit of Solitude*. New York: The Free Press

Morss, J. (1990). *The Biologizing of Childhood: Developmental Psychology and the Darwinian Myth*. East Sussex: Lawrence Erlbaum Associates.

——(1992). "Making waves: Deconstruction and developmental psychology." *Theory and Psychology*, 2, 4, 445–65.

——(1993). "Spirited away: A consideration of the anti-developmental Zeitgeist." *Practice: The Magazine of Psychology and Political Economy*, 9, 2, 22–8.

——(1996). *Growing Critical: Alternatives to Developmental Psychology*. London: Routledge.

Newman, D., Griffin, P., and Cole, M. (1989). *The Construction Zone: Working for Cognitive Change in School*. Cambridge: Cambridge University Press.

Newman, F. (1968). *Explanation by Description: An Essay on Historical Methodology*. The Hague: Mouton.

——(1977). *Practical-critical Activities*. New York: Institute for Social Therapy and Research. Reprinted in *Practice: The Journal of Politics, Economics, Psychology, Sociology and Culture* (1983) 1, 2–3, 52–101.

——(1983). "Witchdoctory: The method of proletarian misleadership." *Practice: The Journal of Politics, Economics, Psychology, Sociology and Culture*, 1, 2–3, 18–51.

——(1991a). *The Myth of Psychology*. New York: Castillo International.

——(1991b). "The patient as revolutionary." In F. Newman, *The Myth of Psychology*. New York: Castillo International, pp. 3–15.

——(1992). "Surely Castillo is left—but is it right or wrong? Nobody knows." *The Drama Review*, Fall (T135), 24–7.

——(1994). *Let's Develop! A Guide to Continuous Personal Growth*. New York: Castillo International.

——(1996). *Performance of a Lifetime: A Practical-philosophical Guide to the Joyous Life*. New York: Castillo International.

Newman, F. and Holzman, L. (1993). *Lev Vygotsky: Revolutionary Scientist*. London: Routledge.

——(1996). *Unscientific Psychology: A Cultural-performatory Approach to Understanding Human Life*. Westport, CT: Praeger.

Parker, I. (1989). *The Crisis in Modern Social Psychology and How to End It*. London: Routledge.

——(1992). *Discourse Dynamics: Critical Analysis for Social and Individual Psychology*. London: Routledge.

——(1996). "Against Wittgenstein: Materialist reflections on language in psychology." *Theory and Psychology*, 6, 3, 363–84.

Parker, I. and Shotter, J. (1990). *Deconstructing Social Psychology*. London: Routledge.

Peterman, J. F. (1992). *Philosophy as Therapy: An Interpretation and Defense of Wittgenstein's Later Philosophical Project*. Albany: SUNY Press.

——(1983). *Practice: The Journal of Politics, Economics, Psychology, Sociology and Culture*, 2, 3.

Quine, W.V.O. (1963). *From a Logical Point of View*. New York: Harper and Row.

Readings, B. (1996). *Introducing Lyotard: Art and Politics*. London: Routledge.

Reich, R. B. (1987). *Tales of a New America*. New York: Times Books.

Rogoff, B. (1990). *Apprenticeship in Thinking: Cognitive Development in Social Context*. Oxford: Oxford University Press.

Rorty, R. (1979). *Philosophy and the Mirror of Nature*. Princeton: Princeton University Press.

——(1982). *Consequences of Pragmatism*. Minneapolis: University of Minnesota Press.

——(1996a). "Blinded with science." *Voice Literary Supplement*, September, 10–12.

——(1996b). "What's wrong with rights." *Harper's Magazine*, June 18.

Sampson, W. (1996). "Antiscience trends in the rise of the 'alternative medicine' movement." In P. R. Gross, N. Levitt, and M. W. Lewis (Eds.), *The Flight from Science and Reason*. New York: New York Academy of Sciences, pp. 188–97.

Sandel, M. (1996a). *Democracy's Discontent*. Cambridge, MA: Harvard University Press.

——(1996b). Interview.

Sarbin, T. R. and Mancuso, J. C. (1980). *Schizophrenia: Medical Diagnosis or Verdict?* Elmsford, NY: Pergamon.

Schegloff, E. A. (1972). "Notes on a conversational practice: formulating place." In D. Sudnow (Ed.), *Studies in Social Interaction*. New York: The Free Press, pp. 75–119.

—— (1992). "On talk and its institutional occasions." In P. Drew and J. Heritage (Eds.), *Talk at Work: Interaction in Institutional Settings*. Cambridge: Cambridge University Press, pp. 101–34.

Scriven, M. (1959). "Truisms as the grounds for historical explanation." In R. Gardiner (Ed.), *Theories of History*. Glencoe, IL: The Free Press.

Shotter, J. (1986). "A sense of place: Vico and the social production of social identities." *British Journal of Social Psychology*, 25, 199–211.

——(1990). *Knowing of the Third Kind: Selected Writings on Psychology, Rhetoric, and the Culture of Everyday Social Life*. Utrecht: ISOR.

——(1992). " 'Getting in touch': The meta-methodology of a postmodern science of mental life." In S. Kvale (Ed.), *Psychology and Postmodernism*. London: Sage, pp. 58–73.

——(1993a). *Conversational Realities: Constructing Life Through Language*. London: Sage.

——(1993b). *Cultural Politics of Everyday Life: Social Constructionism, Rhetoric and Knowing of the Third Kind*. Toronto: University of Toronto Press.

——(1995). "In conversation: Joint action, shared intentionality and ethics." *Theory and Psychology*, 5, 1, 49–73.

——(1996). "Dialogical realities: The construction of (new) 'social worlds' in practice or the social construction of the lifeworld." Presented at the New School for Social Research.

Shotter, J. and Newman, F. (1995). "Understanding practice in practice (rather than in theory)." Presented at the East Side Institute for Short Term Psychotherapy, New York [manuscript available].

Soyland, A. J. (1994). *Psychology as Metaphor*. London: Sage.

Spence, D. P. (1993). "The postmodern self: Romantic or relational?" Review of Kenneth J. Gergen, *The Saturated Self. Contemporary Psychology*, 38, 1, 8–9.

Squire, T. C. (1989). *Significant Differences: Feminism in Psychology*. London: Routledge.

Stent, G. S. (1969). *The Coming of the Golden Age: A View of the End of Progress*. Garden City, NY: Natural History Press.

Strickland, G. and Holzman, L. (1989). "Developing poor and minority children as leaders with the Barbara Taylor School Educational Model." *Journal of Negro Education*, 58, 3, 383–98.

Tolman, C. W. and Maiers, W. (1991). *Critical Psychology: Contributions to an Historical Science of the Subject*. Cambridge: Cambridge University Press.

van der Merwe, W. L. and Voestermans, P. P. (1995). "Wittgenstein's legacy and the challenge to psychology." *Theory & Psychology*, 5, 1, 27–48.

Vygotsky, L. S. (1978). *Mind in Society*. Cambridge, MA: Harvard University Press.

——(1982). "The historical meaning of the crisis in psychology." In A.R. Luria and M.G. Iaroshevski (Eds.), *L. S. Vygotsky: Collected Works*, Vol. 1. Moscow: Pedagogika. [In Russian.]

——(1987). *The Collected Works of L. S. Vygotsky*, Vol. 1. New York: Plenum.

——(1994) "The problem of the environment". In R. van der Veer and I. Valsiner (Eds.), *The Vygotsky Reader*. Oxford: Blackwell, pp. 338–54.

Walkerdine, V. (1984). "Developmental psychology and the child-centered pedagogy: The insertion of Piaget into early education." In J. Henriques, W. Holloway, C. Urwin, C. Venn, and V. Walkerdine (Eds.), *Changing the Subject: Psychology, Social Regulation and Subjectivity*. London: Methuen, pp. 153–202.

——(1988). *The Mastery of Reason*. London: Routledge.

——(1989). *Counting Girls Out*. London: Virago.

——(1991). *Schoolgirl Fictions*. London: Verso.

——(1993). "Beyond developmentalism?" *Theory and Psychology*, 3, 4, 451–69.

Walkerdine, V. and Lucey, H. (1989). *Democracy in the Kitchen*. London: Virago.

Wertsch, J.V. (1991). *Voices of the Mind: A Sociocultural Approach to Mediated Action*. Cambridge, MA: Harvard University Press.

Winger, R. (1995). "How ballot access laws affect the U.S. party system." *American Review of Politics*, Winter, 321–50.

Wittgenstein, L. (1953). *Philosophical Investigations*. Oxford: Blackwell.

—— (1961). *Tractatus Logico-philosophicus*. London: Routledge.

—— (1965). *The Blue and Brown Books*. New York: Harper Torchbooks.

——(1980a). *Culture and Value*. Oxford: Blackwell.

Index

child development 44, 61, 74; examples
of developmental learning from
Barbara Taylor School 126–38;
language 17–18, 110–13, 128
Choate, P. 88
Chomsky, Noam 5, 106
Clinton, President 84
cognitive mapping 12–13
cognitive psychology 57
cognitivism 26, 27, 29–30, 51
Cole, M. 18, 100
communes 15, 17, 79–80
communication studies 50
community-based programs *see*
development community
Community Literacy Research
Project 114
community of conversations 104,
105–63; improvisational performance
of developmental learning 126–38;
learning-leading-development play
156–62; making a performed
conversation 114–15; performance of
philosophy 138–56; performed
emotive conversation 116–26; theory
of performance of conversation
105–14
conversation 45, 104; Shotter and 60–1;
see also community of conversations
conversational analysis 51–3, 54, 57,
58, 61
Conversational Realities (Shotter) 59
Copernicus 165n6
critical developmental psychology 64,
73–6
critical psychology 50, 53–62
critical social science 49, 80–1
critical theory 10, 12, 29, 48
Cultural Politics of Everyday Life
(Shotter) 59
cultural relativism 2
cultural studies 49, 50, 65

Danziger, K. 7, 50
Davidson, D. 16, 101, 164–5n4, 166n8
De Berry, S.T. 102
deconstruction 8, 16, 48, 64, 73;
scientists and 2–3
Deleuze, G. 64, 65
democracy 1, 104, 154
depression, social therapy for 116–26
Derrida, Jacques 10, 64
description 16, 39, 52

developing, development 109, 163; *see
also* child development; development
community; learning-leading-
development
development community 45–6, 47–8,
76–7, 81, 105, 107, 109; creation of
14–20, 79–80, 155; *see also*
community of conversations
developmental learning 17; examples of
improvisational performance of
126–38
developmental psychology 16, 17, 64,
73–6; *see also* Vygotsky
dialectical historical materialism 13, 19,
56, 72
dialectical method 45, 81
Diamond, I. 54
Differend, Le (Lyotard) 70–1
discourse analysis 53–6, 58, 61, 64, 67,
71, 103, 105–6
Discursive Mind, The (Harré and Gillett)
56–8
discursive psychology 56–9, 61, 103
Dole, Bob 84
Dray, W. 16
Drew, P. 51
DSM-IV 15
dualism 8, 30, 49, 61, 71–2; Cartesian 57,
58; in discourse analysis 56;
epistemological 29–30, 31, 32, 35–9,
43–5, 63, 72; theory/practice 13, 19

East Side Center for Social Therapy
116, 117
East Side Institute for Short Term
Psychotherapy 81, 94, 114, 115, 116,
118, 166n1; *see also* Center for
Developmental Learning
ecological movement 2
Ecological Niche-picking (Cole *et al.*) 18
economics 97, 99; and politics 85–8, 89
Edwards, D. 51
empirical reality 2
"End of Science?" symposium 4
End of Science, The (Horgan) 4–6, 8–9
Engels, F. 43, 72, 96, 109
epistemic metanarrative 7
epistemological bias 7–9, 22–46, 105;
charge of relativism against social
constructionism 39–46; Gergen's
29–30, 94–5, 96, 99; getting beyond
knowing 31–5; of Marxism 97;
ontology vs. epistemology 24–6;

184   *Index*

schools 15, 77: *see also* Barbara Taylor
    School
Schools for Growth (Holzman) 21
science 22–3, 24, 25, 30, 32, 33, 37, 44,
    108, 162; end of 1, 4–6; Lyotard on
    68–70; religious-ification of 6, 7;
    social and literary critique 48, 55; *see
    also* philosophy of science
science studies 48
scientific approach of neo-Marxists
    97–8, 99
scientific method 25, 29, 78, 114; not
    applicable to psychology 106–7
scientists, and postmodernism 1–6, 7, 12
Scriven, M. 16
Secord, P.F. 56
self 22, 24, 35, 38, 39, 56–7, 59, 64, 95,
    103; *see also* identity; individual
self-reflexivity 75, 109, 139, 156–7
sense, making, of the world 8, 10–14, 21,
    57; *see also* meaning
Serbin, Ilene 156
sexism 168n4
sexuality 55, 74
Shotter, J. 14, 59–62, 64, 90, 105, 113,
    125, 130
social action/interaction 51–3
social class 73, 74
"Social construction and the
    transformation of identity politics"
    (Gergen) 90–5
social constructionism 8, 21, 23, 24, 28,
    30–1, 48, 55, 60, 61, 73, 144; neo-
    Marxist critique 97–8; and politics
    90–5, 103; and relativism 40–2, 43
social critique 47–9; *see also*
    development community; reform of
    epistemology
social epistemology 11, 30, 95, 96, 103
social inequality 18, 55
social policy 138
social process 80
social psychology 53; *see also* social
    constructionism
social sciences 7, 22, 59, 97; *see also*
    critical social science
social structure 51, 55, 56, 59
social therapy 19, 21, 45–6, 77, 110, 114,
    166n1; example of conversation
    135–8; performed conversations 115,
    116–26
Socialisme ou Barbarie 67
socialization 127, 150

Society for Sociocultural Research 77
sociocultural research 77
sociology: of knowledge 81; of scientific
    knowledge 48; *see also* conversational
    analysis
Soyland, A.J. 50
speaking/thinking 19, 36–7, 43–4, 45,
    112, 150, 160
speech act theory 51, 67
Spence, Donald 164n1
Stent, Gunther 5
Structure of Scientific Revolution, The
    (Kuhn) 26
subjectivity 14, 38, 44, 58, 63, 66, 108
Syracuse University 4
systems therapy 80

Taylor, Barbara 167n4; in example of
    social therapy 136; *see also* Barbara
    Taylor School
Teachers College, Columbia
    University 17
teen pregnancy prevention programs 81,
    167n1
theatre 80; *see also* Castillo
    Theatre/Cultural Center
theory/practice 12–13
therapy collectives 15
tool-and-result methodology 45, 73,
    78–9, 80, 105, 107–8, 109, 138
totalizing theory 12
truth 6, 22, 23, 28, 38, 39, 42, 62, 96,
    125, 155, 162; end of 1; schools and
    127–8

universalism 2
Unscientific Psychology (Newman and
    Holzman) 21

van der Merwe, W.L. 114
Voestermans, P.P. 114
Vygotsky, Lev 18, 23, 25–6, 27, 29, 40,
    41, 42, 50, 58, 59, 61, 62, 108; and
    activity 51, 101, 103; character in
    learning-leading-development play
    157–62; and child development 128,
    134; and practice of method 76, 77,
    78–9, 80, 81; and revolution,
    revolutionary activity 6, 13–14, 26,
    109–13; significance for development
    community 14, 17, 19, 21, 45–6, 126,
    133, 136, 144, 168n4; and